BREACHING FORTRESS EUROPE

BY

SID BERGER

KENDALL/HUNT PUBLISHING COMPANY
4050 Westmark Drive   P.O. Box 1840   Dubuque, Iowa 52004-1840

Dedication

To those at the Ft. Belvoir Engineer Board
and at the Camp Edwards Engineer Amphibian Command
who had the vision to prepare engineer troops
for a decisive role in assault landings on hostile shores.

and

To my wife Mary, who was a Lt. in the US Army Nurse Corps
when I met her in Normandy a few weeks after D-day,
and who has given me marvelous support ever since—
especially during the last two arduous years while writing this book.

QUOTE FROM PRESIDENT REAGAN

---

*"The men of Normandy had faith that what they were doing
was right, faith that they fought for all humanity,
faith that a just God would grant them mercy on this beachhead or
the next. It was the deep knowledge—
and pray God we have not lost it—that there is a profound
moral difference between the use of force for liberation
and the use of force for conquest."*

Normandy, 1984

AUTHOR BIOGRAPHY

An extensive background in the military arts enables Sid Berger to make an accurate and comprehensive account of the engineer's role in the build-up to and the events of D-day. His first military experience was in the pre-war period with horse-drawn artillery. Subsequently he earned a bachelor's degree in engineering and a commission in the Corps of Engineers at The Johns Hopkins University. Shortly afterwards he was at Camp Edwards for the activation of the 1st Engineer Amphibian Brigade. He served in this brigade throughout the war as a Platoon Leader and Company Commander with specialization in mines and demolition. At Utah Beach his assignment included an early landing on D-day as leader of a reconnaissance unit. Post-war he served as a line officer in Armor-Reserve, including a session as instructor at The Armor School. His civilian career covered diverse research and development projects mainly in the defense field. He was involved in naval anti-air guided missiles. Other typical activities included feasibility analysis of VTOL aircraft at the time of a replacement of Army utility helicopters and operational improvements to the Navy helicopter assist system on small combatant vessels.

TABLE OF CONTENTS

ACKNOWLEDGEMENTS

Many people and several firms have made invaluable contributions to the successful achievement of this project, which originated in 1984. At that time Bill Pugh of MMM Design Group and the undersigned had just finished raising several thousand dollars for repair of the 1st Engineer Special Brigade Monument on Utah Beach. The generosity of individual and sustaining members of the Society of American Military Engineers (SAME), especially those in the European Region, enabled us to meet the urgent fund request of the Paris office of the American Battle Monument Commission (ABMC). Our efforts led to a plan to create a trust fund which would provide a permanent solution to the problem of maintaining all engineer monuments in Normandy. And, we decided in 1985 that we would make arrangements to publish a book which would tell the story of US engineers on D-day—and use the revenue from its sale to create the trust fund. This book is the result, and many of the people and firms that made this possible are recognized herein. As the instigator, leader and coordinator of this project over the last ten years I wish to thank particularly those who are named and apologize to those whose names and contributions are omitted, primarily due to space limitations and my faulty memory.

First and foremost I applaud the author, Sid Berger, who became involved in this project about 1986. He enthusiastically gave his time, energy and extraordinary cooperation in my early efforts to get a rather modest brochure written, focused primarily on D-day actions of US engineers. This subsequently led to his agreement to write an expanded book-length version of the engineer story. His thorough and extensive research efforts have produced this splendid account of the story behind the monuments.

Dr. Barry Fowle, office of history of the Army Corps of Engineers at Fort Belvoir, Va., deserves special credit for producing the first draft—which SAME planned to publish in the fall of 1991; however, we then decided to accept advice from potential publishers that we should produce an expanded version of the story, with additional maps, photos and illustrations. Dr. Fowle's manuscript was subsequently enlarged and supplemented through the efforts of Theodore Hamady and Osama Abi-Mershed. These two important contributors became involved because of Tony Stout, then President of The Battle of Normandy Foundation. Tony Stout has for over five years been unstinting in his support of this project—and just recently his generous personal financial commitment has made possible the publication of this book before the 50th Anniversary of D-day.

Support from several engineering firms and individual engineer executives has been crucial to the success of this effort. Mr. Ted Puckorius of the Arlington, Va. office of The Austin Company, allowed his secretary, Ms. Lisa Stone, to type the initial manuscript produced by Dr. Fowle. Mr. John Sporidis of Henningson, Durham and Richardson, Inc., Alexandria, Va., permitted his secretary, Ms. Jennifer Aumack, to type the expanded and completely rewritten manuscript by Mr. Berger. And, in Frankfurt, Germany, Ray Best and Karl Swartz of Buchart Horne, GMBH, were instrumental in giving time and administrative support in the final phases of manuscript preparation. Also in Frankfurt, valuable suggestions and advice were given during several years by Mr. Peter Bennett-Keenan, who also spent five full days with me in editing the manuscript, integrating photos and illustrations and preparing it for the typesetter. And, of all the firms which supported this project, Weidlinger Associates deserves very special credit—and particularly Paul Weidlinger and Matthys Levy. These two partners permitted me to devote almost all my time to managing the many diverse activities of this project during the last few years. Without their generous support, publication of this book by the 50th Anniversary of D-day would have been impossible.

Also to be recognized are individuals such as Mr. Cary Jones, an SES engineer now in the headquarter of the Army Corps of Engineers. Cary became involved in 1985–86 as the VP of the European Region of SAME and has for the last two years chaired a committee in the Washington Post of SAME. This committee has been coordinating many actions with the Frankfurt Post which were essential for publication and marketing of the book. Other individuals who should be recognized are MG Robert Ploger, BG Paul Thompson and Col. William Gara, all USA (ret.). Each of them led a combat engineer unit in assaults on Omaha Beach on D-day. They have given support and encouragement to the author, Sid Berger, himself a combat engineer veteran who landed on Utah Beach early on D-day. And lastly, I wish to thank Lt. Gen. Joe Bratton, US Army (ret.), my friend and former Commander of the Army Corps of Engineers, for his encouragement and support from the very beginning of this effort.

With apologies again to the many important contributors who are unnamed herein, I thank and commend all of them and those who are named for making possible the publication of this important engineer story—and the ultimate maintenance in perpetuity of engineer monuments in Normandy.

Charles L. Wilson
Major General, USAF (ret.)

FOREWORD

If a landing of US forces on hostile shores should ever again be directed by higher authority, the lessons learned in the Normandy landings should be well understood by those who will be responsible for its planning and execution. For this reason alone I urge all military engineers, and especially those whose careers are just beginning, to read and profit from this exceptionally important and vividly presented story. It is the first and only truly comprehensive account of US Army engineer participation in the planning and successful assault on Normandy's beaches. Its authenticity reflects the combat engineering experience of the author, who assaulted two hostile shores—Sicily and Italy—before leading his engineer platoon ashore on Utah Beach early on D-day.

Arthur E. Williams,
Lt. Gen., US Army
Chief of Engineers

PREFACE

A s President of The Society of American Military Engineers, I'm pleased to provide opening comments for this comprehensive analysis of engineer contributions on the beaches of France 50 years ago. Sid Berger has done a superb job explaining the military situation before the Normandy invasion and the planning for the attack under General Eisenhower's leadership. His exciting account of the landing and the assault, with engineers carrying out their mission while under heavy enemy fire, will leave you with a great appreciation for how vital engineers were to the successful invasion of Normandy—it will make any engineer proud.

The book reinforces the importance of planning and realistic training exercises to military success. Engineers began preparing for Normandy seven years earlier when the Army, Navy, and Marine Corps held joint amphibious maneuvers. The many training exercises and rehearsals held in the months leading up to the invasion brought to light weaknesses in the Allied plan in time to correct them before D-day. You'll gain new insights into "Exercise Tiger," the controversial rehearsal five weeks before D-day that came under a sneak attack by German E-boats.

Through drawings and photographs, you'll come to understand the challenge engineers faced as they hit the "Atlantic Wall." Engineers detected and disabled German obstacles and mines, breached and destroyed fortifications, and cleared beach escape routes. You'll find yourself wading through chilly waist-deep water as the invasion unfolds through a multitude of eyewitness accounts. You may be surprised to learn that 50 percent of the first U.S. forces to land on Omaha and Utah Beaches were engineers; this is an amazing statistic when one considers that engineers normally comprised just under 4 percent of an Army division during the World War II era.

Clearly, engineers played a key role in the invasion of Normandy and this book captures their sacrifices and contributions. As heroic and meaningful as their contributions were, the engineers didn't stop on the beaches of France; they continued providing absolutely vital support to the war effort by building roads, bridges, fortifications, and 119 airfields in western France alone. Like the engineers at Normandy, we must always be willing and able to do what's necessary to keep our world free and make it a better place in which to live.

Jim M. C

James E. McCarthy
Major General, USAF
SAME National President
Washington D.C., 8 April 1994

AUTHOR'S NOTE

V ery early in the project leading to the publication of this book the problem of information sources arose. Several distinctly different approaches were considered. A frequently used technique is to interview veterans of the campaign and collect individual recollections. The process of canvassing participants has been worked nearly to the limit by a large number of authors and military historians. A major campaign was mounted by Cornelius Ryan for the preparation of his book *The Longest Day*. The response to his solicitation was quite good, with broad representation from all ranks and arms of the service. However, a careful examination of the Ryan files led to the conclusion that inaccuracies and lesser discrepancies limited the benefits of the interview approach. The primary advantage of the technique is that the dramatic appeal of recounting individual yarns is greater than the alternative, and drier, source of official documents such as After Action Reports and Unit Histories.

The limitations of the interview technique are widely recognized. The historian Stephen Ambrose, in his *Pegasus Bridge*, remarks that discrepancies in transcripts of interviews had been the general rule. He traced the major difficulty to chronology and was able to solve most of the riddles by constant rechecking of sources. On the other hand, Samuel (SLAM) Marshall, in the capacity of Army historian during World War II, attacked the problem by assembling the entire unit as early as possible after the action. He and his assistants persisted in probing the group with penetrating questions until a fairly unified story emerged.

The problems of information gathering have been discussed by Maj. Gen. Bruce Jacobs, US Army (ret.), in *National Guard*, where he is the Publisher. He notes that "oral history is neither the be-all or the end-all in the recording of events and times. It must be put in perspective by all concerned, but especially by the end-users, the readers and the students of military history". He has found memories to be selective and considers this to derive from human frailty.

The resort to official documents although the primary means to collect sufficient data for the production of this account is also not a totally satisfactory solution to the information problem. However, in searching the National Archives it was evident that most units had submitted material to the minimum acceptable standards of the regulations on documentation of combatant actions. There is only one notable exception to this generally prevailing situation—the 37th Engineer Combat Battalion reports which are quite complete, well written, and identify key individuals in an objective way. Nevertheless, it was not possible to pin down exactly the contributions of a number of units at critical locations, primarily the beach exits. Thus at several locations in the text conflicting accounts are identified but not resolved.

Despite the attempt to concentrate on the most valid sources, the total effort behind the text is a combination of all relevant information. The standard works have all been examined intensively. The Army history series contains three useful volumes. There are entries in the Bibliography covering memoirs of participants and works of historians, all of which have been helpful, at least in varying degrees.

A summary of research activity during the preparation of the text shows that all useful avenues of investigation have been covered. Priority has been attached to accuracy in contrast to an attempt at human interest. There are a number of instances where source material is reproduced in the text, in the exact words of an author, even though in condensed form. All such quotations are fully credited. In these circumstances there did not appear to be any benefit to the use of footnotes.

Sid Berger

CHAPTER I

THE ROLE OF ENGINEER UNITS IN AMPHIBIOUS OPERATIONS

Broad scope of engineer contributions to Normandy landings

Pre-war organizational streamlining—the Division and its engineers

Impact of German techniques on U.S. engineer doctrine

Army shakes off amphibious doldrums

Shore party deficiencies require action

Divergence of Army and Navy positions

Creation of Engineer Amphibian Command and its Brigades

Shore-to-Shore operations influence Army developments

The name change of the Engineer Amphibian Brigades

The entire story of U.S. engineers in Normandy on D-day could be one of overwhelming proportions considering the scope of landing operations, the numbers of troops and units involved, the armament and ancillary equipment, and the myriad of events which led up to the landing operations on the beaches of Normandy. So, the focus of these pages will be on the heroic achievements of engineer soldiers, individually and as units in the spectrum from minor to major, on D-day, 6 June 1944. This was the time of greatest losses and maximum suffering which are memorialized by monuments which were built on and near Normandy beaches. Detailed notes on monument descriptions and locations are given at the end of the book.

The story of the engineers cannot be told in isolation. This immense military undertaking in Normandy is a prime example of a combined arms, joint services, multinational operation. The total effort was directed by Gen. Dwight D. Eisenhower, heading the Supreme Headquarters, Allied Expeditionary Force (SHAEF). Therefore, only limited attention can be given in this story to all the non-engineer force elements. In an effort to relate a balanced account of these momentous contributions from all who had noteworthy participation, overstatement of the engineer role has been avoided. Simple, objective descriptions of engineer actions in the assault phase of the landings is more than adequate. Engineer achievements stand on their own merits, without overstated bravado.

Even a blurring of unit missions can occur in these very large amphibious operations. Engineer troops, in numerous actions, fought shoulder to shoulder with their fellow soldiers of the infantry. There are a number of recorded instances where engineer officers and non-coms absorbed leaderless fragments of rifle companies into their own units and proceeded to engage enemy positions which were holding up Allied progress. At the same time, many infantry personnel had acquired a capability to handle explosives and exercised this engineering expertise in attacking fortifications. Additionally, they were not totally lacking in skills to counter enemy mine fields.

Many military historians have described the achievements of the Normandy landing forces in ways which overlook these important complementary combatant actions. This story attempts to avoid such oversights in its presentation of the dimensions of the Normandy campaign, which are of truly epic proportions. Also, it should be recognized that the heroic achievements of the invading armies were so numerous that it is not feasible to explore them all and the re-telling of individual exploits would fill many large volumes. Suffice to say the German-built Atlantic Wall—a fortified coast of unprecedented efficiency—was overwhelmed by a combination of military skills and raw courage.

The Normandy landings were not the start of the war against Germany, already well into its fifth year, but the start of the end. The U.S. Eighth Air Force, along with the Ninth, had already spilled much blood as it pounded the enemy and in effect contributed to the eventual success of ground operations. The Royal Air Force was active beginning in the early phase of the war, and its Bomber Command was inflicting damage by night to supplement American daylight bombing. Also, the prior amphibious operations in the Mediterranean Theater laid a foundation for large scale undertakings of a tri-service nature. Actually, the initial landings on the island of Sicily involved a force even greater than that which landed at Normandy, and the invaders of Sicily came into contact with German forces which were seasoned and resolute troops. The campaign up the boot of Italy was a further contributor to Allied teamwork and amphibious capability.

Meanwhile, the Combined Operations Command of British forces was testing the northwestern European defenses and progressively refining techniques of landing force operations. The assault on the Atlantic Wall was vital to the Allied strategy of driving straight and directly to the German heartland. This planning approach was expected, in the final aggregation, to achieve victory and end the war at least cost of human and material resources.

Target beaches within the Le Havre—Cherbourg district extended over a 50-mile front and contained five discrete sectors, Omaha, Utah, Sword, Juno, and Gold, the first two of which were the operational assignment of U.S. Army forces (see maps of Fig. 1a and 1b for a general orientation). Elements of five seaborne divisions (American, British, and Canadian) achieved the initial penetrations on the Normandy beaches. Operating to secure the flanks of the invading force were elements of three airborne divisions of which more than two-thirds of the total were American. The responsible headquarters for U.S. operations was First Army, commanded by Lt. Gen. Omar N. Bradley, with subordinate commands being V Corps on Omaha and VII Corps on Utah. An overall view of the beach area distribution on the French coast, the embarkation sites, the transit routes across the English Channel and the German dispositions are all conveyed by the maps.

The very nature of landing operations on intensively fortified hostile shores produces a wealth of assignments for engineer troops. Responding to this calling, engineers provided fully twenty percent of the troops assaulting Omaha and Utah on D-day, and suffered a casualty rate more than its proportionate share. Unit citations and individual decorations for valorous performance of duty are legion among the engineers of the Normandy landings.

ENGINEER FUNCTIONS IN GROUND WARFARE

A concise statement by the Corps of Engineers of the mission of engineer units provided to field forces comes readily to hand: "To facilitate and expedite the advance of friendly forces and to impede the advance of enemy forces". Needless to say, this neat and compact statement has a variety of ramifications. Official guidance can be found in the World War II field manual on engineer troops (current guidance, 50 years later, is essentially the same). The engineer duties enumerated in the box

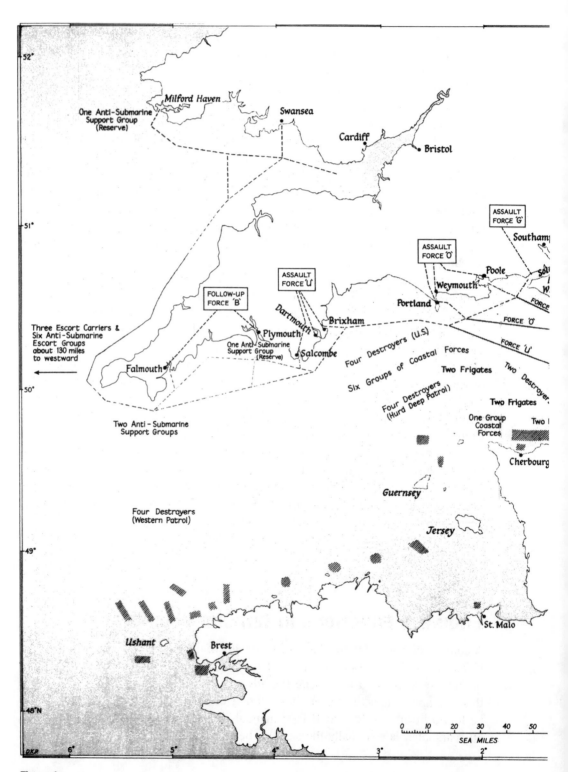

Figure 1a.

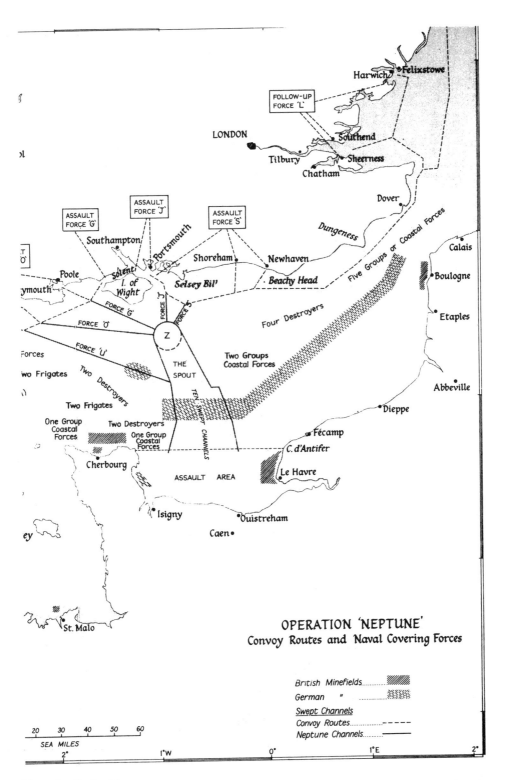

FOLLOW-UP
FORCE 'L'

LONDON

ASSAULT
FORCE 'G'

ASSAULT
FORCE 'J'

ASSAULT
FORCE 'S'

Harwich • Felixstowe

Southend

Tilbury

Sheerness

Chatham

Dover

Dungeness

Calais

Southampton

Portsmouth

Shoreham

Newhaven

Boulogne

Poole

Solent

Beachy Head

Five Groups or Coastal Forces

Etaples

ymouth

I. of
Wight

Selsey Bil'

Four Destroyers

FORCE 'G'

FORCE 'J'

FORCE 'S'

FORCE 'O'

Z

FORCE 'U'

THE
SPOUT

Two Groups
Coastal Forces

Abbeville

Forces

Two Destroyers

TEN SWEPT CHANNELS

wo Frigates

Dieppe

Two Frigates

One Group
Coastal
Forces

Two Destroyers

One Group
Coastal
Forces

Fécamp

C. d'Antifer

Cherbourg

ASSAULT   AREA

Le Havre

Isigny

Ouistreham

Caen

ey

St. Malo

OPERATION 'NEPTUNE'
Convoy Routes and Naval Covering Forces

British Minefields...........
German   "   ....

Swept Channels
Convoy Routes................-------
Neptune Channels........———

20   30   40   50   60
SEA MILES
2°   1°W   0°   1°E   2°

Figure 1a *Continued.*

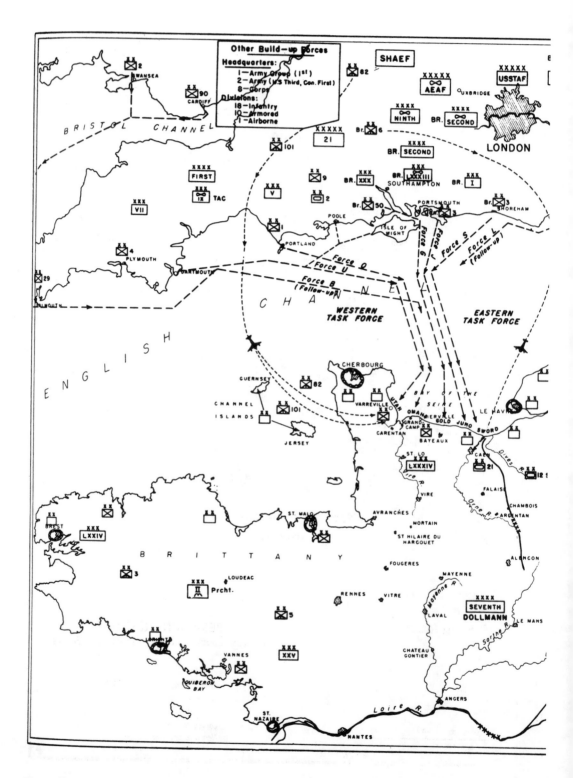

Figure 1b.

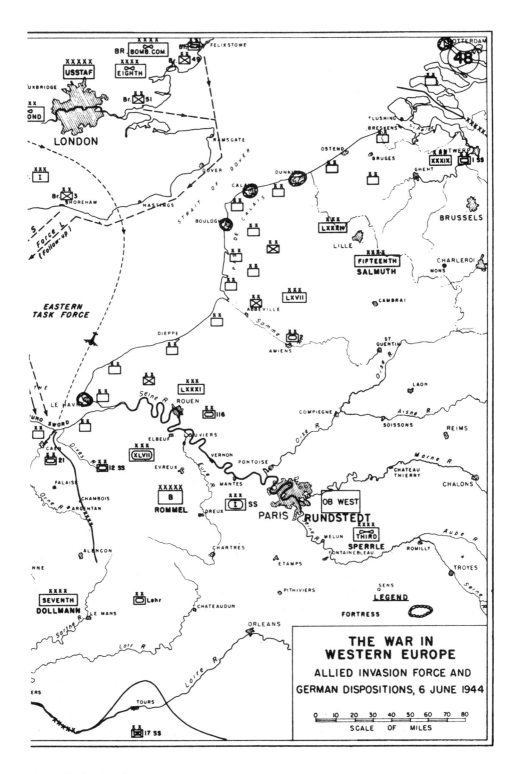

Figure 1b *Continued.*

(Fig. 2) apply to the Engineer Combat Battalion. In specific details, there clearly has been an evolution which becomes obvious as this account proceeds. The unit structure, also shown in Fig. 2, is the one usually found in field armies as an organic element of an infantry division or as a part of corps troops operating under the tactical command of an Engineer Combat Group headquarters.

In the period between the two World Wars there was testing and evolution that ultimately produced the engineer units of the WW II campaigns. Gen. Malin Craig became Chief of Staff in 1935 and promptly directed an examination of the then existing square division structure (i.e. four infantry regiments). In the interest of greater mechanization and consequent mobility improvements, a triangular structure of three infantry regiments was the result. There was a concurrent impact on the engineer component of the division that produced the new battalion organization in the place of the prior existing engineer combat regiment. As it turned out, the apparent cut back in numbers was hardly noticeable. The combat regiment had a strength of just under 900 officers and men while the battalion strength, as first proposed, came to about 520. So, as the division was cut back from 22,000 to 13,500, the engineer unit maintained a 3.8 percent share of total personnel.

There was continual study and testing, by field exercises, of the role of engineers in field force structures. A number of proposals to reduce the size of engineer units and their responsibilities on the battlefield were successfully resisted by analytical and empirical demonstrations. Consequently, among the ranking command and staff engineer officers, there was a degree of satisfaction that the engineer component had emerged relatively whole during the pre-war reorganization planning.

An interesting connection between the events preceding the entry of the U.S. into the war and those concerned with preparations for cross-Channel operations arises in the person of Col. Paul W. Thompson. One of the crucial issues was the extent to which a mobility characteristic would return to modern warfare and how the pre-war rethinking of tactics and materiel design would be implemented. Col. Thompson had been a military observer in Germany shortly before the outbreak of war on the European continent. This experience led to an assignment calling upon his first-hand knowledge of German forces and the techniques which made possible their lightning thrusts through Poland and then in the early summer of 1940 through the Low Countries and France. Col. Thompson then prepared a number of articles which appeared in the *Infantry Journal* and *The Military Engineer*. These papers proved to be widely read and extremely informative, particularly on his coverage of the defeat of Fort Eben-Emael in Belgium. This fortified position was regarded as virtually impregnable by the foremost military analysts. However, it was successfully attacked and conquered in less than 48 hours in an action where an engineer battalion was the key element of the attacking force. The military engineers took positions in dead spaces around the periphery and proceeded to attack the vulnerable parts of the fortification such as port and turret junctions using flamethrowers, prepared ex-

Engineer Field Manual-Engineer Troops
Issue of 11 October 1943 Based on FM5-5;

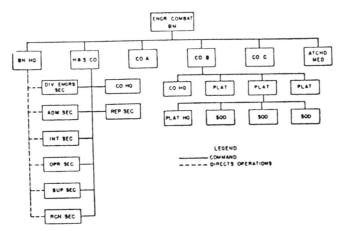

Organization of The Battalion—per Table of Organization 5-15

Most Common Duties (Arranged in priority for amphibious operations):
- Removal and passage of enemy obstacles, including mine fields;
- Engineer reconnaissance;
- Engineer assistance to other troops, including map supply;
- Reinforcement of other engineer units;
- Improvement and maintenance of roads, bridges, and landing fields;
- River crossing operations—use of assault boats, preparation of fords and expedients, construction of ferries and standard portable bridges;
- Providing local security for working parties;
- Construction of or extension of barrier zones.

Less Common but Important Duties:
- Combat as Infantry;
- General layout of positions, marking routes and guiding units;
- Tank hunting;
- Defense of mine fields and obstacles;
- General construction—roads and bridges;
- In stabilized situation—construction of defensive installations;
- Water supply, and engineer material supply.

Figure 2—*Engineer Combat Battalion.*

plosive charges, and grenades. The following box contains remarks of (then) Col. Trudeau and provides an independent view of the events of this period.

The main lessons derived from studies of the successful European actions were that effective coordination was necessary among all the varied elements of a combat team and that the engineers were an elite member of the team. The Engineer School, in late 1941 and in 1942, incorporated the conclusions into its projects and thereafter placed greater emphasis on the combat rather than the technical aspects of military engineering. Of special interest to this account is the inclusion among subjects being studied at the school in that period the matter of attack of fortifications in connection with ship-to-shore operations.

Overall, the new emphasis at the school stimulated thinking and renewed confidence that the streamlining of the Army organization could be achieved without any

Experiences at The Engineer School Assault Course

Extracted from: *Engineer Memoirs: Lt. Gen. Arthur G. Trudeau,* Published February, 1986

Early in the autumn I was assigned to take an assault course at Belvoir. The Assistant Chief of Engineers, Gen. Sturdevant, visited the battalion and he saw some ingenious work that we were doing with ammunition, booby traps, assault of bunkers, and deception. This was intriguing for the officers and men . . . this was fresh thinking . . . we used to try to give at least an extra pass to a soldier who would come up with a new idea for a new device.

In the fall of 1940 . . . you remember France and the Low Countries had been overrun . . . we studied the German tactics carefully. For instance, we found that the British, in their withdrawal, had frequently caused considerable delay to the Germans by stripping the restaurants of dinner plates as they withdrew, leaving them one by one in the middle of the road. A German tank crew would stop and get out at first. Then they'd get careless, and about the tenth one they hit would really be booby-trapped, and up would go the tank or truck. Things of this sort really slow down your movements.

About 30 of my contemporaries were with me in this assault course, which really set the pattern for Engineer doctrine during World War II. The real stimulus was probably the German assault and capture of Fort Eben-Emael in Belgium, using demolitions and flamethrowers, to attack with small forces and special assault techniques.

Program for Qualification of the Engineer Combat Battalion intended for completion in a 13-week period, era: 1940–41

Extracted from: *United States Army in World War II—The Corps of Engineers: Troops and Equipment*

Subject	Hours	Percent
Basic	95	16.6
Technical, combat	82	14.3
Technical, engineer	303	53.0
Field fortifications, camouflage	40	7.0
Tools, equipment, materials	13	2.3
Bridges	80	14.0
Obstacles	50	8.7
Demolitions and mining	40	7.0
Roads, construction and maintenance	24	4.2
General construction	16	2.8
Engineer reconnaissance	20	3.5
Night operations, technical	8	1.4
Battalion field technical training	12	2.1
Tactical	72	12.6
Open time	20	3.5
Total	572	100.0

detriment to the engineer component of the field armies. Some of the recommendations coming out of the school found their way into field manuals and thus reached the level of official doctrine. The emphasis being placed upon the combat function of the engineers was becoming a reality. Above all, the fluctuations in planned strength of the reorganized Engineer Combat Battalion (ECB) were settling down at a reasonably satisfactory level.

The Office of Chief of Engineers submitted a proposed table of organization to the General Staff in July, 1941 at the level of 720 total personnel for an ECB. A fourth company of the proposed structure was disapproved due to the opposition of Brig. Gen. Leslie J. McNair. He feared that pressure from the engineers, along with the other arms, would produce a triangular division as unwieldy as the organization it had replaced. Thus, the strength of the battalion was fixed finally at 18 officers and 616 men.

The capabilities inherent in an Engineer Combat Battalion can be viewed from another aspect. Since organizational, as well as individual, skills derive from training, the training program in the build-up period sheds light on directions being pursued. A standard training program for ECBs was planned for 13 weeks with a distribution of subjects as shown in the accompanying box. The correspondence between engineer duties and the curriculum contents is obvious. Of course, the training plan for a battalion did not comprise the total preparation necessary for units to be qualified for field duty. It was expected that divisional exercises and maneuvers would extend over seven or more months and would integrate all arms and support elements into effective combat teams.

ORIGINS OF THE AMPHIBIOUS CAPABILITY

Engineer contributions to planning and developmental activities related to landing operations on hostile shores began many years before World War II. The popular wisdom had it that military planners were fixed in their thinking by World War I visions of friendly ports with ample means to offload all required cargos and to swiftly move personnel onward to their destinations. This was not strictly true. The Marine Corps based its organization and training on the assumption that requirements for naval advanced bases could lead to assault and capture of enemy positions in many locations around the world, with emphasis on islands of the central Pacific.

There were landing exercises during 1924 and about 10 years later a Fleet Marine Force was established. Army activity in regard to building an amphibious capability was dormant probably due more to budget and funding problems rather than lack of interest, although a reinforced infantry regiment did participate during 1937 in joint Navy-Marine Corps maneuvers.

Amphibious doctrine was evolving in the period between the wars. In the process of putting together a manual for the Fleet Marine Force, the Marine tacticians studied the components of successful landing force operations in totality. They determined needs and techniques for aerial support, including preliminary reconnaissance, spotting of naval bombardment, preparatory air bombing, and air defense over the battlefield. They explored the effectiveness of various combinations of naval bombardment. Of most relevance to this account are the studies of interactions involving the landing force. The obvious importance of debarking troops at correct locations and on schedule received much attention in the studies. The importance of correct loading of troops in landing craft, preserving integrity of troop units, and control of craft during ship-to-shore transit were all factored into the doctrine. It was established that special shore parties should be incorporated into the landing force with such responsibilities as marking beaches, assuring steady flow of personnel and material off the beaches, providing communications between shore and ship, and evacuating casualties back to ships. Shore parties were expected to make emergency repairs to landing craft. Finally, the required characteristics for efficient landing craft began to be formulated in this period.

The Marine Corps continued to pioneer the amphibious art up to 1940. A series of maneuvers was held annually, despite limited availability of funds. Development of specialized equipment was initiated. A landing craft for delivering tanks directly to shore reached the demonstration phase in 1937. One year later the Higgins boat building establishment in New Orleans submitted a prototype landing craft which soon took the lead over its competitors.

The Engineer School initiated efforts which brought the Army out of the amphibious doldrums. In 1939 a school problem was launched to concentrate on engineer functions in landings on hostile shores. A research course followed in early 1941. The findings of these efforts departed radically from existing doctrine by advocating a more basic role for engineers in an amphibious attack. It was propounded that engineer troops would form early waves and, upon landing, immediately commence destruction of fortified positions.

Other important items contained in the study results dealt with Army-Navy coordination and the composition of shore parties. It was felt that naval beach groups had exhibited a minimum of engineering interest and henceforth in joint forces should be limited to assignments strictly dealing with boat traffic. In past maneuvers, the naval beach parties had broad responsibilities including control of shore parties, and this had been laid out clearly in published doctrine, so the new Army thinking was a profound change. Shore party duties included removal of land mines and other obstacles, construction of expedients for moving vehicles off the beaches, and preparation of positions to be available for fighting off counterattacks. The shore party was to be patterned after that found in the Marine division organization, and to be composed primarily of engineer personnel. Finally, the study findings called for infantry divisions in amphibious operations to have three engineer combat battalions instead of only one.

In the period late 1941 through early 1942 joint Army-Navy exercises were held on both coasts. An Atlantic Fleet Amphibious Corps consisted of the 1st Marine Division and the 1st Infantry Division. A Pacific Fleet Amphibious Corps consisted of the 2nd Marine Division and the 3rd Infantry Division. The landing forces were under Navy control. A critique of the exercises tends to confirm that the thinking at The Engineer School was moving in constructive directions. The joint exercises were plagued by the lack of a well-trained shore party with engineer capabilities. Communications between the Army and Navy were unsatisfactory and coordination between beach and shore parties remained poor. Also, during the east coast landings the Army units were put ashore in a disorganized way and well off their target beaches. The exercises were anything but a rousing success.

Establishment of The Engineer Amphibian Command

Two sets of events were converging in a way that positioned Army engineers into a prominent role in the most momentous events of the war. With the entry of the United States into the war against the Axis powers in December 1941, the tempo of military preparations stepped up. First, the Army General Headquarters was dissatisfied with the conduct of joint exercises with the Navy. This indicated a need for independent action to create a large-scale amphibious capability. Second, plans for actual operations against enemy controlled areas and their forces were beginning to take form.

An approach evolving in Washington in early 1942 attempted to resolve Army-Navy antagonisms along both functional and geographic lines. A new division of responsibilities was formulated which separated amphibious operations where shore-to-shore distances were rather short as compared to the traditional amphibious operations over long distances which were the ship-to-shore type, where naval attack transports were a mainstay. This proposed split enabled a more nearly unified Army control over an important group of assault landings of the shore-to-shore type. As part of the original negotiations, the Navy was to furnish landing craft and instructors for training Army boat crews. Craft of sea-going size would be manned and operated by the Navy. In a further display of compromise, within the Atlantic Amphibious Force (a naval organization) the divisions supplied by the Army would be grouped under a corps commander of the Army. As major events unfolded, the results of the bargaining turned out to be not very durable, particularly in the Mediterranean and European Theaters.

Command arrangements for amphibious operations within the Atlantic and Pacific Theaters were expected to be different. Planning in the Atlantic had been initiated for cross-Channel operations from England under the assumption that a shore-to-shore system would be feasible. This would be under total Army control. Of course, in early 1942 the possible engagement of U.S. forces in Mediterranean actions was not foreseen. The situation in the Pacific would be decidedly different. It was agreed that a Pacific Amphibious Force would include corps comprised of both Army and Marine divisions, but that a Marine officer would be in command. It was expected that this force would operate in the central Pacific. In the south Pacific an amphibious corps entirely composed of Marine divisions would conduct island hopping operations. Arrangements for the conduct of Southwest Pacific operations were left to be determined at a later date.

A response to the new Army assignment was promptly placed in the hands of the Corps of Engineers. The anticipated schedule would stagger a normal imagination. A planning group was assembled in Washington during early May, 1942 and faced the prospect that training of infantry divisions should commence in July. Little was known about a possible invasion of continental Europe. The lessons of The Engineer School studies had hardly been disseminated; no training site existed, and no boat-handling training had been undertaken. While the Engineer Combat Battalion of the existing divisional structure was adequate for its purpose, little thought had been applied to formation of shore parties.

Two urgent requirements dominated Army actions at this point. A training facility had to be located and readied for immediate use. The other dominant problem was the acquisition of amphibious craft from the Navy which was even more urgent than assembly of personnel. Camp Edwards, on Cape Cod in Massachusetts, was preferable to several southern locations because it made possible a fast start on training without any new construction and was in close proximity to suitable beach areas. It was recognized that a southward move would be necessary before the next winter set in. Additional space was leased for boat maintenance and practice landings. The activation of the Engineer Amphibian Command (EAC) was formalized on 10 June 1942. Command was placed in the hands of Col. Daniel Noce (later Maj. Gen.) with Lt. Col. Arthur G. Trudeau (later Lt. Gen.) assigned as chief of staff.

A new tactical structure was formulated on the supposition that a cross-Channel operation from England, and indeed other landings involving Army forces, would be of the shore-to-shore category. The result was the Engineer Amphibian Brigade (EAB), with a capability to support an infantry division. The proposal integrated an Engineer Boat Regiment with an Engineer Shore Regiment, and also included essential services such as signals, maintenance, medical, quartermaster, and ordnance. The combined division-brigade force assured that landing operations could be conducted under unified Army command. A request by the Corps of Engineers for activation of eight brigades was approved and led to activation of the 1st Brigade on 15 June and the 2d Brigade on 20 June. It was expected that five brigades could be trained before winter set in, and the Command relocated. Of course, the full scope of the plan never came to fruition.

The boat problem pervaded all the planning at the Engineer Amphibian Command. In early May the plans called for 12 infantry divisions to go through a program of training in landing techniques, along with the associated engineer brigades, at the Amphibious Training Center, an adjunct of the EAC. To accomplish this training mission, a requirement for landing craft came to 1,000 of the 36-foot type and 225 of the 50-foot type. These craft came to be known as LCVP or Landing Craft, Vehicle/Personnel and LCM or Landing Craft, Mechanized respectively (Fig. 3). Initially Navy officials agreed to turn over 300 of the smaller craft so that 1st Brigade training could start on schedule. Then a further small increment would be delivered and with this inventory of craft it would have been possible to put a regimental combat team through combined arms landings. It was obvious that the ambitious plans were in jeopardy. Additionally, the 103-foot type of craft was not included in the program at all, these coming to be known as LCT or Landing Craft, Tank with a capability to land six main battle tanks, depending on sea conditions and other tactical factors (Fig. 4a). Also shown is the much larger LST or Landing Ship Tank (Fig. 4b) which later became an important vessel in amphibious operations.

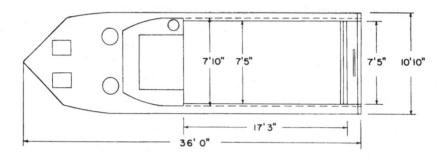

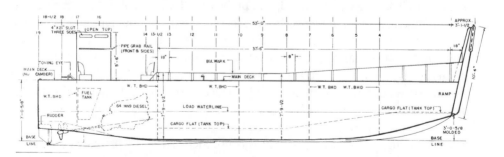

Figure 3—(Top) **Landing Craft, Vehicle/Personnel (LCVP).** *Smallest of the landing craft fleet with a capacity of about 30 troops.*
(Bottom) **Landing Craft, Mechanized (LCM-6).** *The 56-foot version developed when an increase in the main battle tank weight from 30 to 34 tons required greater lift.*

Figure 4a—Landing Craft, Tank (LCT). *Basic vehicle-carrying craft, widely used for main-body engineer forces with dozers, depending on model, capacity could be up to six main battle tanks under favorable operating conditions.*

Figure 4b—Landing Ship, Tank (LST). *Ocean-going vessels capable of beaching with a full load of 20 tanks or various mixes of track and wheel vehicles plus about 200 troops; overall length— 328 feet; full load displacement—2,100 tons.*

The question of whether a cross-Channel operation could be pulled off with only the smallest types of landing craft came under careful scrutiny. The engineer officers at EAC began to doubt that troops could endure the choppy waters of the English Channel and arrive in a condition to fight. The observer and staff personnel at Camp Edwards included representatives of British forces, the U.S. Navy, the Coast Guard, and the Marines and they were in unanimous agreement that a small boat crossing of the Channel would not be feasible. There was a notable exception to this school of thought which makes the subject very interesting. Col. Trudeau was not prepared to yield and maintained an optimistic outlook (see box on following page).

The implications surrounding the feasibility of small craft crossing the Channel were definitely profound. The Engineer Amphibian Brigades were organized for shore-to-shore operations with their organic boat regiments and with control in the hands of the Army. If the concept turned out to be unsound, then a reorganization would be forced on the engineer management at the EAC.

Accomplishments at Camp Edwards were striking. A light ponton company and a heavy ponton battalion were ordered in as cadre. However, processing of personnel from diverse sources was the rule. Boat operators and experienced yachtsmen were recruited from civilian activities. Officers came from reserve status and some from Officer Candidate Schools. The proportion of those newly commissioned was much higher than normally found. Notwithstanding the chaos, the 1st Brigade was manned, outfitted, and trained to a reasonable proficiency and readied for transfer to the European Theater between activation on 10 June, and sailing in early August, 1942. Gen. Eisenhower had made an urgent request for the Brigade to be overseas on the most expedited timetable humanly possible. Otherwise, joint training with infantry divisions could have taken place on Cape Cod as in the original plan. As it actually happened, some landing exercises with infantry battalions did take place at Martha's Vineyard as early as August (Fig. 5).

The anticipated number of brigades for European duty did not materialize. Plans for activation of eight brigades were trimmed to four. A visit to the Southwest Pacific was made to brief Gen. MacArthur and his staff on the new capability evolving at the Engineer Amphibian Command and this effort met with an enthusiastic reception. It so happened that means for mobility in movement along the coast of New Guinea were woefully inadequate, and compounded by strained relations between the Army

Figure 5—*Amphibious Training at Camp Edwards, MA*. *Engineer troops operate landing craft during exercises, summer of 1942.*

On The Seaworthiness of Small Landing Craft

Extract from: *Engineer Memoirs: Lt. Gen. Arthur G. Trudeau*
(Published February, 1986)

. . . The Navy naturally favored the Bureau of Ships tank lighter
(Note: Undoubtedly referring to an early version of an LCM); the Army
favored the Higgins tank lighter . . . 50 feet long. The main difference between the lighters which any layman can understand is that
the deck of the Bureau tank lighter was above the normal water level
when loaded . . . this adversely affected its seaworthiness. The
advantage of the Higgins lighter was that the treads of the tank . . .
were below the water line.

. . . we ran two tests down at Little Creek and at Norfolk. One of
them was the test on the Bureau tank lighter versus the Higgins
tank lighter. The Bureau lighter almost foundered . . . it couldn't
stand the kind of currents we were in, while the Higgins tank lighter
looked beautiful . . . in tough cross-currents and high seas at the
mouth of the Chesapeake Bay.

Shortly after we were activated (Editor's Note: Obviously referring to
the Engineer Amphibian Command) Washington agreed, since the
British said that you cannot cross the Channel in small craft like
that, that tests would be made. I was put in charge of the tests.
There was quite a wind and the seas were rough. The plan was to
take us out past Cape Henry into the open sea and then head to
shore . . . at which time the Navy, the British, and all the people
from Washington were supposed to see that men just couldn't come
ashore in fighting condition.

Most of the men were sicker than hell. These landing craft were . . .
not very seaworthy . . . so we had a lot of green water over the bow.
So I said, "See what you can do to pull yourselves together here."
Some didn't care whether they lived or not; it's easy when you're
seasick. We started toward the shore and I saw this gang—Navy
admirals, British admirals, Joint Chiefs of Staff, Army—on the
skyline along the shore. I said, "You see that line with all the
goddamn admirals and generals there . . . you go up there in a line
of skirmishers and keep moving." And, by God they did.

and Navy. An amphibian brigade under Army command appeared the ideal solution to the problem. Eventually, three such brigades shipped over to the Pacific.

An obstacle to large-scale deployment to the Southwest Pacific was shipment of small landing craft. Conventional practice by the Navy was transport of small boats as deck cargo on merchant liners or naval transports. Deck space on these ships was in demand as aircraft and tanks were also moved this way, the result being that only a dozen or so boats could move per ship. At such a rate it might take several years to get a division afloat. A solution was conceived within the EAC to break the boats into sections, stow the sections as hold cargo on the transport ships, reassemble the sections at a boat yard in the theater, and reach a delivery rate of 300 boats a month. While several others claim credit for the sectioning concept, it was the Army engineer scheme which was implemented and actually put the craft in service in an overseas theater in amazingly short time.

Two methods were used to prepare landing craft for hold stowage. Production arrangements at the Higgins yard were revised so as to deliver sectioned boats to the Army. Concurrently, boats delivered in a fully assembled condition, were cut into 12 segments. A facility for final assembly was prepared in Cairns, Australia and based on a plan approved in December of 1942, shortly afterward went into production. By early April of the following year, the first LCVP was in the hands of troops, and very soon, the peak monthly rate of 300 assembled boats was achieved.

An effective by-product came out of the engineer sectioning process. At the same time that the boats were being cut into pieces for shipment, an upgraded tank model was taking the field with a weight of 34 tons as compared to 30 tons for the model being superseded. The new tank exceeded the cargo carrying capacity of the 50-foot lighter, the LCM-3, a naval design. Obviously, word of the new tank design was slow in reaching the Navy design and procurement agents. It became apparent to those at work on the sectioning job that a *plug* could be inserted into the craft structure during final assembly stretching the length to 56 feet and adding sufficient buoyancy to accommodate the heavier tank. A further serendipitous benefit came along: the lengthened hull produced a gain of two knots in speed for no change in fuel consumption. This design change led to the LCM-6 which remained a Navy standard for many years.

Navy efforts to capture the Army amphibious capability persisted through the early part of 1943. Not long after the 1st Brigade arrived in the European Theater, Adm. Harold Stark cabled back to Washington his feeling that the honor of the Navy was at stake if their seaman did not operate all landing craft. At the headquarters of Gen. MacArthur the case for the Army mission took several new twists. The brigades were to fill a role which was not altogether compatible with Navy concepts. Their short range shore-to-shore movements were regarded as a simple extension of land operations. They even went so far as to suggest removal of *amphibian* from the name of the brigades and a substitution of the word *special*. This change was adopted and applied to all brigades regardless of the theater in which they operated.

CHAPTER II

CROSS-CHANNEL PLANNING

T o follow all the planning convolutions that led up to the Allied invasion of Normandy would be a long and tedious process. But, there are some strong interactions between the backing and filling in the planning process and the fortunes of the engineer units destined for duty with landing forces, particularly the engineer amphibian brigades. Following the name change these were designated as Engineer Special Brigades and ultimately, in the European Theater, became primarily concerned with ship-to-shore operations, although the cross-Channel operation was an amalgam of all amphibious techniques.

An outline of the essentials of the development of plans will illustrate their impact on the engineer units. It immediately becomes obvious that the complexities of conducting affairs through a Grand Alliance are indeed daunting.

EARLY DIVERGENCE IN REACHING AN ALLIED APPROACH

Even before the U.S. was directly involved in the war some of the far-sighted leaders began to anticipate contingencies. When Gen. George C. Marshall was sworn in as Chief of Staff, on the very day that German forces crossed into Poland and initiated hostilities, the U.S. Army numbered fewer than 200,000 officers and men combined total. Prior to his taking the office there had been some moves toward streamlining, as noted earlier in this account. But it remained for Gen. Marshall to put some force into solving the problems of rapid expansion. This became the primary focus at general headquarters at the time.

Shortly following the fall of France, there was intensification of defense activity. The expansion of the Army to 1,500,000 personnel was in process. More to the point, however, was a position stated by then Chief of Naval Operations, Adm. Harold Stark, that in the event of a two-ocean war Germany would be the more dangerous power and an American Expeditionary Force would be required. Joint planning was initiated with the British to plot strategy if and when the U.S. entered the war. Naval observers were dispatched to London. The Army also sent special observer personnel to Britain; this team was directly responsible to Gen. Marshall. Additionally, agreements were reached for a British Joint Staff Mission to be established in Washington. These exchanges established the foundation for coordinated planning—which persisted for the duration of the war.

There was, however, an impediment to smooth progress in joint planning. An uncertainty persisted among the American military leadership as to the British intentions regarding a return to the Continent. Public pronouncements appeared to be convincing, especially those coming from Prime Minister Winston S. Churchill. At the time of the evacuation from Dunkerque, Churchill addressed the House of Commons with the words "Britain will fight on, if necessary for years . . . if necessary alone . . . we shall go back." In October of that same year (1940) British strategists commenced the study of invasion possibilities. In the meantime Combined Operations Command was formed and a 120-man commando team had raided Boulogne across the English Channel.

Nevertheless, many facts mitigated against excessive optimism and firm planning. Britain had experienced numerous further military reverses around the world and her resources, both human and material, were drained.

With the attack on Pearl Harbor and the entry of the U.S. into the war, the outlook for offensive action in the European Theater brightened. A mechanism for coordination of planning between the U.S. and Britain evolved in the form of what were known as historic conferences (see following box). A thumbnail sketch of the major conferences is shown in the box. At these conferences Roosevelt and Churchill, meeting personally and with their key military advisors, reached critical decisions for the conduct of operations in the foreseeable future periods. In the intervals between these conferences planning was to conform with the decisions.

Arcadia, in Washington during December of 1941, was the first conference of the U.S. and Britain as war allies. The Prime Minister crossed on the battleship H.M.S. *Duke of York* and used his time aboard ship to prepare a paper which reviewed the strategic situation and proposed a course of action spanning at least two years ahead. Several items in the paper are pertinent to this account. The full text of the paper is readily available in the Churchill memoirs, Volume III, titled *The Grand Alliance*. Part One deals with a review of the Atlantic front and proposes several lines of action for 1942. There is heavy emphasis on the situation in French North Africa and a conclusion that if diplomacy fails there must be a military campaign to take both Mediterranean and Atlantic coastal regions. There are a number of other topics in Part One, including a proposal to transfer three U.S. divisions to North Ireland, continuation of aerial bombardment of Germany and of the sea blockade. Part Two deals with the Pacific Theaters. Part Three deals with actions for 1943 and contemplates that an invasion of the Continent could be launched, supposing that the more immediate projects come off successfully. There is no mention of cross-Channel operations in 1942 and the feasibility of such action in the year after is laced with caveats. A tone of opportunism permeates the thinking behind the paper, as displayed in various passages. The Russians must be supported with equipment and supplies from the U.S. arsenal even though the quantities shipped would subtract from what might be available to Britain. The German war machine would be squeezed by an ever tightening naval blockade. The subjugated peoples of all conquered nations in continental Europe should be encouraged to rise up, and the like.

Despite the great likelihood that Gen. Marshall would not approve of any undue delay in cross-Channel operations, President Roosevelt was receptive to the British presentation. He seemed to be pleased that a mechanism to get U.S. ground forces into action was available even if the locale would be off in the Mediterranean. The problem of supporting a campaign in that direction when ocean shipping was in such critical short supply and when shipping resources would be doubly productive in sup-

Roster of Historic Conferences

These conferences reached decisions by agreement of the heads of government on major issues of the conduct of the war. The plans and policies as approved were to guide Combined Chiefs in the intervals between conferences:

- **Washington—December 1941 (Arcadia):** Unified Theater commands; priority to defeat of Germany; contemplate control of French North Africa; U.S. field forces to U.K.; cross-Channel operations in 1943.

- **Casablanca—January 1943:** Establish special American-British planning staff for beachhead in 1943, exploitation in 1944; contemplate continued Mediterranean operations.

- **Washington—May 1943 (Trident):** Postpone cross-Channel venture to May 1944; fix details on Sicilian operation; contemplate activity to remove Italy from war.

- **Quebec—August 1943 (Quadrant):** Overlord to be main effort in 1944; confirm target date and approve COSSAC plan subject to augmentation; consider interim use of Mediterranean troops.

- **Cairo (Sextant)/Teheran—November/December 1943:** Set definite date for Overlord at 1 May 1944; agonize over designation of Supreme Commander, then select Gen. Eisenhower; reject expedition to Greek Islands; coordinate Overlord timing with Soviet drive.

- **Quebec—September 1944 (Octagon):** Consideration to Pacific problems; broad survey of post-war problems; contemplate coordination with Soviets on Balkan operations.

- **Malta/Yalta—January/February 1945:** Confirm non-interference with Gen. Eisenhower's tactics against Germany; negotiate terms for Soviet combatant status against Japan, arrange occupation of Korea.

port of European northwest coast operations does not appear to have entered his thinking.

Arcadia seems to have a result where political considerations dominate those based on military principles. Gen. Marshall continued to argue that valuable resources might be squandered on peripheral adventures in North Africa and that the opportunity to strike at the heart of the enemy by early cross-Channel assault could be lost. British fears that a premature attempt to enter the Continent could lead to catastrophic failure and another evacuation on a scale to compare with Dunkerque do not enter his thinking. Nor is he concerned with the way military campaigns would influence the post-war settlement (Fig. 6).

Figure 6—Gen. George C. Marshall. U.S. Army Chief of Staff, architect of Army expansion, advocate of early cross-Channel operation, outstanding judge of leadership potential.

Two lines of planning activity emerge shortly after Arcadia. The War Plans Division at the War Department was then in the hands of Maj. Gen. Dwight Eisenhower, after he took over from Maj. Gen. Leonard Gerow (later to emerge as commander of V Corps, the Omaha Beach landing force). Gen. Eisenhower was the instigator of plans for carrying the war back to the Continent and penetrating directly to the interior of Germany. The Joint Strategic Committee of the Joint Chiefs contributed much detail analysis including the problems of air cover at a multitude of potential landing areas, the necessity for further troop training, the development and procurement of landing craft, and other essentials involved in landing on hostile shores. The search for locations in the Balkans or anywhere in the so-called soft underbelly of the Continent, such as suggested in the Churchill paper, were not rewarding. Suitable landing sites quickly led to difficult terrain which favored the defender. The naval members of the joint body were less than enthusiastic about such an undertaking while they were still reeling from the effects of the losses at Pearl Harbor and would have a new responsibility of safely delivering a large army to Britain through submarine infested waters. Notwithstanding these difficulties the Navy did cooperate, especially by accelerating the program for procurement of landing craft and training of crews. The results of this planning activity and recommendations for cross-Channel attack in 1943 reached the President by late March, and on the first of April 1942 he approved the conclusions and dispatched a team consisting of Gen. Marshall, Col. Albert Wedemeyer, and Mr. Harry Hopkins to convey the findings to the British.

At about the same time a series of planning studies were proceeding in Britain along very similar lines to those in Washington. Commodore, Lord Louis Mountbatten was heading up Combined Operations Command, and together with Gen. Sir Bernard Paget of Home Forces was assigned to study a cross-Channel invasion which carried the code name Roundup. The work was undertaken in appreciation of the inevitable need to close with the enemy and defeat its forces in the field in Europe. The thought process and consequent actions of Mountbatten are shown in the accompanying box which is an extract of his remarks in the Foreword to Warren Tute's book *D-Day*.

Despite the scenario differences in the two separate sets of planning studies the same code name was picked up in Washington. Thus, there were two Roundup versions. The most obvious difference grew from the factors which might trigger the invasion. In the American studies there was an underlying fear that the Russians might not be able to stabilize their situation. The Germans had launched an attack in late June of 1941 with massive forces including 135 divisions on the ground. After two weeks they had captured 150,000 Russian troops and 1,200 tanks. After five months they had occupied 500,000 square miles of Soviet territory. Therefore, the situation was regarded as urgent. Logic had it that with this kind of success many of the German troops could be released from the eastern front and made available to take up defensive positions to thwart an Allied invasion. Evidence that the Russian resistance was stiffening was not yet clearly established.

Early Planning Activity at Combined Ops

Extracts from remarks of Lord Louis Mountbatten contained in his Foreward to *D-Day* by Warren Tute, published by Macmillan Publishing Co., Inc., 1974

In November 1941 I was ordered, in conjunction with General Paget . . . to prepare for a large-scale raid, and two months later we were told to work on a plan for Allied permanent re-entry into Continental Europe. . . . So I insisted we should land in the Baie de la Seine area just to the eastward of Cherbourg. I put my case to Churchill. . . . Space does not permit me to enlarge on the dispute that raged over the target area. Thank God I won through and we landed sucessfully in Normandy. . . .

The British version of Roundup was not so concerned with accelerated scheduling. The thinking in London had it that favorable conditions for returning to the Continent were most likely to prevail when the blockade began to grip and aerial bombing took a progressively heavier toll. They hoped that uprising of the subjugated peoples would also benefit the invasion. With this kind of attitude scheduling was characterized by flexibility.

The U.S. approach presented by the visiting delegation consisted of three parts: Bolero, Roundup and Sledgehammer. Bolero covered the transfer of U.S. resources to the United Kingdom. The transfer of troops and the buildup of supply depots had already commenced on the terms agreed to during the Arcadia conference. Roundup had an objective of penetrating the defenses of the Continent somewhere between Boulogne and Le Havre probably during the summer of 1943 if not sooner. Associated with Roundup would be some actions of a raiding nature during 1942. Sledgehammer was a smaller scale proposal put forward tentatively as a 1942 operation to land on the Cotentin Peninsula (also known as the Cherbourg Peninsula) as necessary to relieve pressure on the Soviet forces of resistance. If Sledgehammer were to be mounted in 1942 it would be expected that the landing force could hold on until the more forceful Roundup could take place later.

THE INTERACTION OF PLANNING WITH ENGINEER EVOLUTIONS

With this brief examination of the planning activity in early 1942, it becomes rather easy to understand the urgency attached to formation of engineer troop units and joint training with infantry divisions on amphibious techniques. Previously we followed the establishment of the Engineer Amphibian Command and the activation of two brigades with their boat and shore regiments, their boat maintenance capability and their other support units. It was noted that the brigades were designed for shore-to-shore operations under unified Army command and that naval participation in these operations would be of a minimum nature. A good start was being achieved to bring Sledgehammer and Roundup to reality.

The U.S. presentation to British Joint Chiefs met with something less than an enthusiastic response. There was give and take as Gen. Marshall addressed the British War Cabinet and the Chiefs of Staff. A major issue was the size of the American contribution to an Allied landing force going into action in 1942. The initial determination by the Imperial General Staff planners was that a force of seven infantry divisions and two armor divisions would be an absolute minimum requirement and Gen. Sir Alan Brooke considered this to be on the risky side. Gen. Marshall made an estimate that after immediate requirements for the Pacific and for Iceland were satisfied there would still be two and one-half infantry divisions, one armor division, associated amphibian support, plus 900 aircraft in position in Britain by September 15th. Thus, the U.S. would be able only to supply less than half the required strength for Sledgehammer. Nevertheless, Gen. Marshall persisted in the reasoning that landing operations in 1942 were essential to the success of the more ambitious plans for 1943.

After the stay in London, the team flew back with the impression that they had agreement in principle to proceed with plans for Sledgehammer and Roundup, and that Allied troops would be crossing the English Channel before the end of the year. It was April 1942 at this point. Shortly afterwards things started to unravel as British fears resurfaced about the possibility of another expulsion from the Continent. Prime Minister Churchill dispatched Adm. Mountbatten to Washington to reopen planning discussions with the intention of substituting the expedition to French North Africa in place of Normandy as means to get American troops into action in 1942 and in the process to satisfy the growing chorus of advocates for a second front. The Prime Minister himself followed up with another trip to America, arriving on 19 June. The British arguments carried the weight of their position as the supplier of the majority of troops in the event that Sledgehammer could be launched. Furthermore, President Roosevelt was warming to the idea of taking northwest Africa and improving the safety of ship transport through the Mediterranean.

It must be emphasized at this point that the President seemed to be taking an ambivalent position on which direction the planning should take. This may explain why a clear decision was so long in coming. While ready to forego a cross-Channel operation in 1942 (Sledgehammer), he was more firm about the possibilities of going ahead with the 1943 crossing (Roundup). The records show that he believed a modest excursion to North Africa in 1942 would not preclude more ambitious plans for later. Above all else he was anxious to get U.S. forces into action on the Atlantic side at the earliest possible date, regardless of exact location.

Another mission to London followed on 19 July 1942, the team this time consisting of Gen. Marshall, Mr. Hopkins, and a new participant, Adm. Ernest King. Adm. King was in an ascendent position since the offices of Fleet Commander and Chief of Naval Operations had been combined in his hands. Adm. Stark had been moved to the European Theater. Adm. King emphasized that the troop transfer to the Mediterranean and the necessary draw down of stocks would deplete American resources and a cross-Channel operation would necessarily be pushed back to 1944. This reinforced the work that had been done in the War Plans Division of the War Department. Also by this time Gen. Eisenhower had moved to London in command of an expeditionary force uncertain about its destination, and the 1st Engineer Amphibian Brigade was under alert to move to the United Kingdom to join the force, after a very hectic few weeks at Camp Edwards.

The die was irrevocably cast at that point. After the protracted discussions and trans-Atlantic meetings of the spring and summer, came the severe losses of the Dieppe raid on 18–19 August. Gen. Sir Alan Brooke, of the British I.G.S. was the one most nearly aligned with the American position that a decisive invasion of Europe was the only possible way to end the war. Also he did not share the Prime Minister's tendency toward endless probing at scattered locations. However, at that point he became a strong supporter of Torch. This was the new code name for operations in northwest Africa. He came to the position that a successful invasion would need more attrition of the German Army on the Russian front, more progress against U-boats in the Atlantic, and higher production rates from American weapons plants.

The effect on engineer troops was immediate. The new North African mission involved a long sea voyage and a naval-type ship-to-shore landing. Within the 1st Brigade the boat regiment was reoriented toward shore party and stevedore duties and the boat maintenance capability was lost. Brigade training continued in the U.K. in preparation for landings of the Torch Center Task Force in the general vicinity of the port of Oran. For duty with the Western Task Force, to land at several locations on the coast of Morocco, a 540th Engineer Shore Regiment was quickly formed with a cadre from the 2d Brigade. Additionally, the 20th Engineers (later to appear in the V Corps organization at Omaha Beach) and the 36th Engineers were to prepare for duty as shore party engineers. This force sailed from continental U.S. ports under command of Gen. George Patton. The Eastern Task Force was destined for the general area of Algiers and sailed under British command. This force contained in the aggregate about one U.S. division but its engineer support, in proportion, was less.

THE COSSAC INTERLUDE

Following the landings in November of 1942 at the key port areas of French North Africa planning began to focus on the next of the historic conferences. This was set for Casablanca in January of 1943. Gen. Marshall, during his preparations for the conference, was as adamant as ever that there be no extensive drain on American resources into the Mediterranean and that planning be directed forthwith to cross-

Channel operations in 1943, to commence certainly not later than August. He considered it unfortunate that the buildup of material in Britain under Bolero arrangements, had been drawn down to the point where a new start would be required.

Another set of difficulties was surfacing. A continuation of Mediterranean operations was, at that point, favored by Gen. Henry "Hap" Arnold, on behalf of Army Air Forces, and by Adm. King. Each felt that bases in North Africa and the Mediterranean area for their operations against Germany would be an asset in the long run.

As was his usual practice, the Prime Minister prepared a memorandum beforehand stating a sort of agenda for the conference: Casablanca was no-exception. This account of how things went deals only with items bearing on the cross-Channel aspect of the deliberations. An abstract of Churchill's memo, further condensed, states these notions:

> . . . . *paramount task . . . conquer the African shore . . . . set up there naval and air installations which are necessary to open an effective passage. . . . for military traffic . . . using the bases . . . strike at the under-belly of the Axis in effective strength and in the shortest time.*

The conclusions of the conference were not favorable to the prospect of an early venture across the Channel. Gen. Marshall had been in a fall-back position standing behind a plan for the establishment of a limited beachhead in 1943 which would hold on till relieved by a landing in greater strength at the earliest feasible time in 1944. This amounted to the Sledgehammer-Roundup concept with a one-year delay. But even this did not carry.

After hard work over ten days the report of the Combined Chiefs was presented. The primary thrust was to be the occupation of Sicily with a three-fold objective: to make the Mediterranean line of communication more secure, to divert pressure from the Russian front, and to intensify the pressure on Italy. Concurrently there would be activity in the U.K. along these lines: maintain the air offensive against German war efforts, limited offensive operations with available amphibious forces, and assembly of a force to re-enter the Continent as German resistance is weakened. Among other items there is a statement that operations in the Pacific will be kept at a level that does not jeopardize opportunities for the decisive defeat of Germany in 1943.

The report was well received by the President and the Prime Minister. A few comments were added for the guidance of planners. Among them one dealt with the need to build up more quickly the U.S. striking force in the U.K. so as to be able to take advantage of favorable August weather for some form of Sledgehammer. The only concession that Gen. Marshall could extract from the assemblage was an agreement to set up a special planning staff with British and American representation to work on those items in the report dealing with cross-Channel activity. This planning staff was to be a sort of proxy for an invasion supreme commander until such time as the position was filled.

The officer to head up the planning was designated Chief of Staff to the Supreme

Allied Commander (Designate). The appointment went to a British Officer, Lt. Gen. Frederick Morgan, on 13 March. He had held command positions at various levels including an Army Corps, was regarded as capable in staff work and as an organizer, and most important of all was popular among the American contingent. He put the acronym COSSAC into use in quick order. He had an American deputy, Brig. Gen. Ray Barker who came over from ETOUSA (European Theater of Operations, U.S. Army). The intention was to operate the planning group with opposite numbers for each function, thereby assuring equality of both British and American influence.

At the time the COSSAC staff was assembled in April 1943 a substantial body of planning data and decision-making analysis had accumulated. Some of the early efforts in both Washington and London have been noted earlier in this account. The most serious work appears to be that directed by Maj. Gen. J.A. Sinclair, chief British planner, and Maj. Gen. Barker, at ETOUSA before moving over to COSSAC. The time period of this work was from November 1942, onward into March 1943. The work is generally referred to as the Combined Commanders planning. They considered all factors relevant to a successful landing in an attempt to select the optimum target beaches. Typical preferred characteristics included, for example:

- ☐ Beach defenses to be as weak as possible;
- ☐ Beach defenses to be vulnerable to naval fire, air bombardment, or airborne troop actions;
- ☐ Beach area to be conducive to rapid buildup of invading force; that is to contain or be nearby one or more ports;
- ☐ Alternatively to or supplementary to preceding item, beach to be suited to over-the-shore deliveries;
- ☐ Beach area to contain exits for expeditious egress of heavy volume vehicle traffic;
- ☐ Beach area to be within range of aircraft providing continuous air cover.

A process of elimination quickly focused on Normandy. The Netherlands coast line is easily eliminated by the fighter cover need and by low floodable conditions behind the beach. The Belgian coast has small beaches, the probability of decent weather was not as high as elsewhere, and the defenses were relatively strong. The Pas-de-Calais sector, having the obvious attraction of proximity to embarkation sites and providing a relatively short distance to the German heartland was very heavily defended, it was lacking in useable beach exits, and the nearby ports were on the small side. Brittany would have provided the ports but could be easily eliminated by its other characteristics. The preferred location turned out to be the coastal region between the Orne and Vire Rivers, also referred to by many military analysts as the Caen sector. Additionally, the east coast of the Cotentin Peninsula was found to have a favorable combination of characteristics. Essentially, the earlier work at the War Plans Division in Washington and the study projects at Fort Leavenworth, along with that of Commodore Mountbatten, were confirmed.

Before leaving the contributions of the Combined Commanders planning group their work on force size will be briefly noted, along with the implications in regard to landing craft. Their finding was that an assault by four divisions would succeed against "determined opposition" and that the total landing force should be composed of 10 divisions, with the six follow-on divisions to be preloaded. The plan called for the total landing force to be ashore on the first four tides, in other words, before the end of D-day plus one. The work was not well received on two counts. First of all, the uncertainties arising from use of the concept of "determined resistance" in any analysis detracts from the validity of the results. Secondly, the fleet of landing craft required by a force of this size could not possibly be available at any time in 1943 and probably 1944 as well.

Procedures for the conduct of planning at COSSAC were being spelled out by Gen. Morgan. He was not inclined to accept any of the earlier planning studies on cross-Channel feasibility, target beaches, force sizing, and the like. He directed his team back to square one.

While COSSAC planning was beginning to make some progress several new problems appeared. The first directive to the new organization (dated 23 April 1943) called for contingency plans to be studied for raids and diversions against German defenses along with plans for an abrupt crossing of the Channel in the event of a collapse of German forces, the latter designated as Operation Rankin. These planning assignments were in addition to the primary task centering on the invasions in 1944, and undoubtedly slowed progress on the main task.

The other troublesome problem area concerned a division of authority, particularly dealings with ETOUSA. One of the policy planks at COSSAC called for the planning team to take a stance as an operating military entity, as opposed to an academic undertaking not involved in the implementation of the plan. But, the planning group had no authority over any tactical units to be assigned to invasion forces. Conversely, ETOUSA had the responsibility to bring U.S. field units to a high state of readiness for landing operations. But, the ETOUSA people had no access to the plans as they were evolving. Recall that Gen. Eisenhower had vacated the command in early 1943 when his headquarters moved to North Africa following the successful Torch landings. His replacement, Lt. Gen. Frank Andrews, was appointed in February but in May had the misfortune to be in a fatal crash when aboard a transport aircraft which impacted a mountain in Iceland. Lt. Gen. Jacob Devers who previously had a key role in the creation and training of armor divisions was assigned to the command. A number of memoirs and histories record the frustrations experienced by Gen. Devers and the ETOUSA staff in this period. Without access to COSSAC deliberations the task of readying a U.S. invasion force was complicated by a large number of unknowns. Furthermore, with the passage of time it became evident that there would be a high degree of incompatibility between COSSAC plans and U.S. doctrine on command arrangements, force composition, logistic matters, and the like.

During this period when COSSAC planning was taking form there were assumptions and conditions laid down which had a profound impact on the outcome. The most crucial matter centered around the landing craft problem. It was noted in this account earlier that some planning studies found that the numbers of required craft exceeded what could be expected to be ready for service, even looking ahead to 1944. The COSSAC approach seems to be predicated on no control over the numbers of craft available and takes as axiomatic the numbers in planning directives.

The consequences of the COSSAC approach show up in the draft outline received at ETOUSA in July of 1943. Determination of the target zones for the landings contained no surprises. The methods conformed closely to those of previous analyses as did the results, with the beaches best suited for attack being the Normandy coast between the Orne and Vire Rivers. There was no plan for landing on the coasts of the Cotentin Peninsula. The nature of the operation as planned can be characterized as compact. Three divisions were to land on a front of approximately 20 miles. The reasoning for keeping the units in close proximity was a fear that they each might be cut off individually and defeated. The plan spent much of its content on duties and responsibilities of commanders at the higher levels with the apparent intent of removing the Supreme Commander from direct control of ground, sea, and air operations. Another controversial feature of the plan was the grouping of assault elements of the landing force under a corps headquarters, obviously not American, and the introduction of U.S. corps and field army commanders into the chain of command only after their troops were substantially all ashore. Otherwise, the plan called for the landing of eight additional divisions early after the successful assault, the capture of Cherbourg within two weeks, and an invasion of southern France concurrent with the Normandy landings.

The question of whether a three-division assault could have succeeded leads to an interesting investigation. The assault forces of the Husky and Torch landings were approximately twice as numerous as that proposed by COSSAC. Furthermore, defenses to be found along the Normandy coast were expected to be much more robust than those encountered by the Mediterranean expeditions. The COSSAC position was that the available landing craft would not have supported a larger force. Some of the more prominent military historians have defended the stance taken by Gen. Morgan on the ground that he did in fact appeal for greater resources and in particular larger numbers of landing craft. To further obscure the conflicting positions, Gen. Morgan has been quoted as favoring the use of additional craft that might be assigned for the purpose of accommodating follow-up units which were originally planned to be aboard converted merchant vessels. Another possibility has it that he was rebuffed by the need to emphasize the production of escort vessels required for trans-Atlantic service, and without which the American build-up in the U.K. could not have happened. Some British observers have even gone so far as to suggest that certain U.S. officials were promoting their preferred interests at the expense of landing craft production.

The COSSAC draft outline plan for Overlord next had to pass through the approval process of an historic conference, that is, be subjected to the scrutiny of the Combined Chiefs and also the heads of government. The month following the delivery of the draft outline (August 1943) was the time for the Quebec conference also known as Quadrant. From the records of the debates it appears that major attention was focused on the command arrangements for the invading forces. Prime Minister Churchill proposed Gen. Brooke, his military chief, for the slot of Supreme Commander but no agreement was reached. However, it was an apparent conclusion that an American would fill the position. The draft plan was approved and the COSSAC team was authorized to proceed on the detail planning. However, the Prime Minister added a qualification to the approval—that the assault elements of the landing force should be increased by 25 percent. He believed that with nine months yet to go the required landing craft could be found.

Dismay continued to prevail at ETOUSA. After some difficulty, a site had been located for a U.S. training facility, designated the Assault Training Center, in the charge of Col. Paul Thompson. He has been introduced earlier in this account for his analysis and publication of pioneer tactics in the assault of major fortifications. But the problem of landing craft shortages had not been solved. An insider at ETOUSA believes a fateful, chance event had much to do with eventual solution (see box).

A major impediment to the completion of the Overlord plan was tackled at the Cairo/Teheran (November/December 1943) historic conference. First, Gen. Brooke announced that the date for the operation would be in May and that the supporting landing on the south coast of France would be included. Otherwise stated, the agreed date of the Quebec conference was still valid. But the crucial problem of a Supreme Commander came up in Tehran under the prodding of Marshal Josef Stalin. The President had been vacillating between Gens. Marshall and Eisenhower over agonizing weeks. He felt that Gen. Marshall had earned the job and that prospects for success would be greatest with him in charge, but the loss of Gen. Marshall in Washington would have been unbearable to world-wide continuity and the needs of the President. Thus, the selection process finally came to an end and Gen. Eisenhower was named.

REWORK OF THE COSSAC PLAN

With the appointment of a Supreme Commander detail planning so necessary for readiness of the invasion force could be assured. During Quadrant COSSAC had been granted approval of their draft outline plan, subject to conditions, and instructed to proceed to fill in the details. Obviously, no changes were made to the essential features of strength of the assault elements and frontage of the attack.

The first move of Gen. Eisenhower, prior to leaving the Mediterranean, was selection of some key personnel. He immediately communicated to Gen. Marshall his preference for commander of the U.S. field army, Gen. Bradley. Additionally he noted that Gen. Bradley should move up to command the U.S. Army Group just as soon as there was a build-up to more than one field army. His preferences for commanders of field armies were Gens. George Patton, Courtney Hodges, and William Simpson. He had a strong desire to retain Maj. Gen. Walter Bedell Smith as Chief of Staff, thereby displacing Gen. Morgan. Further personnel moves included transfer of Gen. Devers

An Insider View of the Landing Craft Problem

Col. Ralph Ingersoll relates his experiences at ETOUSA in his book *Top Secret,* published in 1946.

At Quebec the COSSAC planners had commented that the situation with regard to British landing craft is somewhat confused . . . we found almost 55% missing . . . the missing bottoms were there alright . . . in repair yards from the Thames to Scapa Flow . . . laid up for essential parts, or whole engines, or hulls that required complete rebuilding . . . no stockpiles of parts . . . no maintenance yards . . . no trained men. . . .

How is a war won? This one may have been won because Donald Nelson, the chairman of the War Production Board in America, needed a rest . . . a tourist trip to England, and because when he got to England, a group of young Regular Army officers conspired to give him so many figures and got him so interested in the shortage of landing craft . . . he telephoned back to the United States and played a trick on the production priorities. He ordered the already approved quotas . . . for 1944 put in the shipyards, not in the appropriate quotas of the coming year but immediately. . . .

When Donald Nelson first heard the story . . . he had exploded . . . when he heard the whole story of the futile attempts . . . he made his telephone conversation off the record . . .

. . . I made one trip myself back to Washington. It was October. My mission had nothing to do with high level planning. But it took me to the Pentagon . . . It was amazing how little they knew of what was going on in London.

. . . I could talk to Harry Hopkins as a pre-war acquaintance. . . . I had been an editor and publisher . . . I had no authorization from Devers . . . to see anybody outside the Pentagon . . . Gen. Devers never knew of this conversation . . . He (Hopkins) seemed to be astonished . . . and he asked rhetorically why the problem (landing craft) had not been solved for once and for all? I left him with that one.

to a key position in the Mediterranean and a rearrangement of air commanders which put Gen. Carl Spaatz in the group moving to the U.K.

Of equal importance was the need to get some rework started on the Overlord plan. As it happened Gen. Eisenhower was under orders to be in Washington while Gen. Montgomery was heading directly to London. The two had some discussion about what needed to be done and the rework was promptly initiated. A brief sketch of the attitudes of the key commanders about rework on the plan is contained in the box which covers a critique of COSSAC effort.

The determination of the target date is another essential ingredient in the plan. As the situation developed it became a close race between the need to accumulate the required volume of landing craft and the need to meet the commitment given the Soviets to land in early May. The earliest possible date was desirable to relieve German pressure on the eastern front. It was also expected that a Soviet thrust would be spurred to the mutual benefit of both fronts.

The solution as adopted consisted of two parts. Gen. Eisenhower had been firm in his belief that the attack on the south coast of France, code named Anvil, would produce the maximum benefit if it were coincident with Overlord. But with a one month separation between the two operations a goodly number of ships and craft could do double duty and provide nearly the lift for one of the two added divisions. The balance of the additional lift would be gained by a set back of one month in the schedule for Overlord so as to procure the output from U.S. shipbuilders for the extra period. On this new foundation detail planning proceeded. Primarily this was accomplished at the field army echelon, bypassing Gen. Montgomery's headquarters, in keeping with his desires to place matters of detail in subordinate hands.

ADJUNCTS TO THE OVERLORD PLAN

Two features of the plan have so far not been directly considered, but not because they lack importance. Indeed, in some quarters they are regarded as making contributions of critical importance. But direct treatment of these subjects would have diverted attention from the events of D-day.

The first item has to do with deception. It has previously been noted that the Pas-de-Calais sector has certain attractions as a target for the landings. Thinking among the planners was that if the German defenders thought in that same way, and their construction of defenses did so indicate, they might be induced to distribute their forces in a way favorable to our intentions. The deception was known as Fortitude. It consisted of mock installations, mock equipment including landing craft, armor vehicles and other military impedimenta disposed mainly in the southeastern corner of England. The impression was conveyed to hostile reconnaissance that forces were in readiness to attack through the Pas-de-Calais. The impression was reinforced by the known presence of Gen. Patton and the appearance that he was head of the force. In addition to displays on the ground there was radio traffic to add further realism to the ploy. Additionally, there was a Fortitude-North which conveyed the impression that

Critique of the COSSAC Outline Plan

A few extracts from the memoirs of the central figures of the Overlord operation convey the nature of the planning results produced by COSSAC:

From: *Closing the Ring* by Winston S. Churchill

I had asked Montgomery to visit me on his way home from Italy to take up his new command . . . When he arrived in Marrakesh we had a two-hour drive out to our picnic . . . I had given him early in the morning the plan prepared by . . . the Anglo-American Joint Staff . . . After he read it in summary, he said at once, "This will not do. I must have more in the initial punch!"

From: *Crusade in Europe* by Dwight D. Eisenhower

I was doubtful about the adequacy of the tactical plan because it contemplated an amphibious attack on a relatively narrow, three-division front with a total of only five divisions afloat at the instant of the assault . . . it failed to provide effectively for the quick capture of Cherbourg . . . and for rapid build-up.

From: *The Memoirs of Field-Marshal the Viscount Montgomery*

The more I examined the proposed tactical plan . . . the more I disliked it. The front of assault was too narrow; only one Corps H.Q. was being used to control the whole front and the area of landing would soon become very congested. No landing was being made on the east side of the Cherbourg Peninsula, although the capture of the port of Cherbourg was vital to our needs . . . There did not seem to be any clear idea how operations would be developed once the armies had been put on shore in Normandy.

From: *A Soldier's Story* by Omar N. Bradley

. . . with only three divisions in the D-day assault and two more afloat as a follow-up force, COSSAC had proposed that we embark on a shoestring in the most decisive assault of the war . . . Overlord was now to be gambled on an undersized landing fleet.

a force existed to move against Norway. Both sections of Fortitude were augmented by naval traffic to complete the deception.

Secondly, on the subject of artificial harbors, the planners at COSSAC, and even before that at Combined Operations, were heavily occupied with the problem of bad weather in the English Channel. Therefore, the early capture of a port, in working condition, was a requirement for the support and buildup of a landing force. If on the other hand, the taking of a port was not achieved on schedule, over-the-shore cargo deliveries would be the rule. The concept of an artificial harbor was intended to improve working conditions on beaches during severe weather. The original thinking on this subject dates back to 1917 and to Winston Churchill. He then proposed the construction of flat bottom concrete barges that would be towed to positions offshore Flanders where the sea cocks would be opened and the structures would settle to the bottom. In this position they would provide a harbor with weather-proof and torpedo-proof characteristics. The designs for Overlord were somewhat more impressive. Code named Mulberry, their design capacity was a delivery of 2,500 vehicles per day and 12,000 tons per day of supplies and equipment. The number of structures planned was 200 with the largest weighing in at 6,000 tons. Floating dock-like components were connected to shore by floating driveways so as to operate at all stages of the tide. Systems were planned for both the British beaches and for Omaha Beach for American forces. At Utah the provisions for over-the-shore cargo handling in severe weather consisted only of a breakwater formed by sinking a string of Liberty ships.

CHAPTER III

HOSTILE DEFENSES: STRUCTURES AND TROOPS OF THE ATLANTIC WALL

Battle of Britain alters German outlook

Invasion of Russia forces defensive posture in west

Atlantic Wall concept implemented

Fortification structures standardized; weapons diverse

Command problems in west

Rommel arrives from Italy but von Rundstedt is senior

Rommel emphasizes use of mines and obstacles

Tidal obstacles predicated on high-tide landings

T he evolution of the German defense posture on the western coasts of the European Continent commences at about the same time as the Allied powers were beginning to think about offensive operations. In this brief account, it will be seen that the German commanders and their planning staffs went through a process equally as tortuous as that facing their opposite numbers on the Allied side. While it may seem that some military advantage might follow from a single governmental authority, when the leadership role was filled by the Fuehrer Adolf Hitler, any perceived benefits were quickly wiped out. The decision-making process at the highest level proved to be erratic, subject to personal hunches, and founded on an individual make-up which was slim in qualifications for the highest job.

The disintegration of French forces after the lightning 1940 campaign of the German Army left the victors with no plan for further operations. It was expected that the British would sue for peace terms as the French had done. This, of course, never happened. Instead, the British showed defiance and prepared to defend themselves to the last ditch. An army of nine divisions had been saved at Dunkerque but was totally lacking in weapons. The U.S. was prompt in getting some shipments off . . . mostly rifles and machine guns from leftover World War I stocks. The Royal Navy and Royal Air Force were the primary guardians of Britain's shores.

A response on the German side to the British resolve led to a belated gesture toward invasion. The plan for a northward crossing of the Channel was hurriedly put together under the code name Sea Lion. The time at this point was July 1940.

GERMAN TRANSITION FROM OFFENSE TO DEFENSE

An essential ingredient in any plan to invade Britain was the establishment of air superiority over the potential landing beaches. Once German bases for the air campaign were completed, the Battle of Britain was on. German bombers raided cities up to the limits of their fighter escort. On some days there was a concentration on coastal ports and nearby airfields. German losses were at a severe level as R.A.F. Spitfire and Hurricane fighter planes were getting the best of unarmored Messerschmitts. The British radar capability, along with the manifest superiority of the Spitfire aircraft, provided a decisive edge to the defenders. Altogether in the first 10 days of the action the Germans lost 697 aircraft as against 153 British. In addition, the British were recovering about half their downed pilots.

During the air battle there were several changes in tactics as the Germans tried in vain to stem their losses. There was a switch from cities to a series of attacks on fighter airfields. The loss rate held steady. Then a switch back to the cities but with a major concentration on London and its environs. The next variation was a switch from daylight bombing to night raids. The cost remained high and the attempt at morale breaking and general softening up of the population did not meet objectives. For the Battle of Britain, i.e., extending through October of 1940, the aggregate of German aircraft losses reached a total of about 2,500, with all aircrews lost. By comparison,

British pilot losses reached about 400 with roughly double that number of fighter planes down. It is generally agreed that the R.A.F. pulled off a stunning victory. Through the winter and then the spring there were further air attacks, mostly sporadic night raids against industrial and population centers, with fleets that numbered between 100 and 400 bombers. This level did not nearly match operations during the Battle of Britain. Then the bulk of the German air power transferred to their eastern front for the impending move into the Soviet Union.

Almost on a par with the need for air domination, was the matter of quickly raising a fleet of invasion craft. The German planning staffs had absolutely no background in amphibious tactics and this deficiency quickly became evident. Their first move was to collect barges from the inland waterways of northwest coastal regions. In training exercises in rough waters of the Channel, the concept of towing these barges proved to be distinctly unrealistic. The German high command of naval forces first recommended as early as July of 1940, against an attempt at crossing the Channel. On top of the practical difficulties of using towed barges, it developed that the barges were essential to the economy which supported the war machine. Thus, Sea Lion had an early demise.

Turning to Field Marshal Gerd von Rundstedt, he had commanded an army group in the invasion of Poland, which precipitated World War II. The following spring he was again in command of an army group, this time for the rapid over-run of the Low Countries and France. Following these hostilities, von Rundstedt was Commander in Chief West with a concurrent assignment as commander of Army Group A, the force intended for the invasion of Britain. After the abandonment of Sea Lion, he retained command of the army group and led this force during the invasion of the Soviet Union, commencing in June 1941. His troops took such advanced positions as Kiev, Kharkov, Odessa, and Rostov. His background was steeped in Prussian military tradition. He had practically no interests in common with the Fuehrer and was no admirer of the Nazi regime; he held his position by virtue of his integrity, devotion to duty, and military proficiency.

There is a short gap in the Field Marshal's record, probably attributable to his advancing years. Toward the end of 1941 he was relieved of his command on the eastern front, due to ill health. The following March he reported that his health was improved and that he was ready for duty. He was reassigned to his old post as Commander in Chief West. This was the period during which construction was initiated of the "Atlantic Wall" coastal fortification system. At this time, he was 67 years of age.

The situation facing German forces as the year 1941 unfolded was that the Luftwaffe had been dealt a severe blow by the R.A.F. Because of their inability to dominate the air space over the Channel and further the lack of landing craft, there was no plan for invasion of the British Isles. The attempt to keep the British isolated from their potential allies appeared to be going well at least for the time being. Allied tonnage going to the bottom of the sea, due to U-boat attacks, was astronomical. And on the eastern front, at least initially, the conquests had been achieved at relatively low cost. Therefore, the transition to a defensive posture on the western front was easily justified.

CONSTRUCTION OF FORTIFICATIONS

Priorities in the early phase of construction along the coast went to the submarine pens and the heavy caliber naval guns installed in the Pas-de-Calais sector. The importance of the U-boat campaign has been noted. Installation of guns initially had an offensive orientation as their range was adequate to provide some of the cover fire for Sea Lion maneuvers. When the idea of an offensive across the Channel was dropped, the construction continued since the guns had obvious defensive uses. Some other coastal batteries were added to the construction program. This early work on fortification was under Navy direction with the work performed by Organization Todt, the same construction group that had built the western frontier defenses of Germany in 1938.

Some early planning of integrated fortification construction along the Atlantic coast began in 1941, during the period when von Rundstedt was off to the eastern front and Field Marshal Erwin von Witzleben was in command in the west. During this time primary emphasis was placed on defense of the Channel Islands. Hitler especially prized these small pieces of territory not for any tactical value but rather for the psychological uplift he felt by holding British territory. The islands were occupied by the 319th Division, one of the more able units of German forces, reinforced to a strength of about 40,000 personnel, which saw no action for the rest of the war.

Formalization of defensive preparations took a major step in early 1942. The situation was turning for the worse from the German point of view. The Russian winter had taken a costly toll on the field armies operating in the east, the U.S. had been brought into the war, and the British appeared to be growing stronger as time passed, despite heavy losses of shipping in the Atlantic. The successful raids of the Combined Operations forces along the coast were a bit of an embarrassment. Another important factor was that von Rundstedt had been returned to command in the west, and had sole responsibility for defenses.

Against this backdrop there came Directive No. 40 in March 1942 from Berlin, signed by Adolf Hitler. This paper was probably the most significant single factor in the initiation of the Atlantic Wall. Text topics included such items as the need for unified command, interservice cooperation, the policy of stopping enemy attack before or upon actual landing, disposition of fortifications toward most probable landing sites, stockage of fortified positions to assure their endurance, and the like.

Almost immediately after the issue of the directive, British Combined Operations Command pulled off a daring and successful raid on the German naval base at St.-Nazaire. The objective of the raid was to disable the major dry dock at this base and deny its use to the battleship *Tirpitz*, a sister ship to the already sunk *Bismarck*. This facility was the only one on the Atlantic coast capable of accommodating so large a ship as the super-dreadnought *Tirpitz*. The technique used was a ramming of the locks of the dock by H.M.S. *Campbelltown* (formerly the U.S. destroyer *Buchanan*).

The reaction in Berlin was immediate. The belief persisted in the mind of Hitler that with enough concrete and determination, such a disaster could be prevented. The admirals cautioned that such events were inevitable from time to time without stronger naval and air forces. Such professional advice was rejected and the emphasis on improving fortifications was strengthened even more.

A concept evolved in Berlin to make the Atlantic Wall invulnerable. The plan called for a long series of fortified positions which would produce a continuous belt of interlocking fire. The structures would be capable of resisting aerial and naval bombardment. The apparent intention of the approach was that with adequate structures, the manpower requirements could be minimized. It must be noted that after the winter campaigns on the eastern front there was very little manpower reserve to be applied elsewhere. The total number of positions was to be 15,000. With the length of coastline to be covered being on the order of 2,400 miles, it would appear that the wall would turn out to be quite porous. However, it may be recalled that the original directives noted a density of defensive positions that would vary with the attractiveness of various beach areas as landing sites. Particular emphasis was focused on port defenses.

As a means of expediting construction, standardization was introduced into the design process. Notwithstanding this objective, the number of standard units grew to be on the order of 700. Then, by selecting the most appropriate design for one or more units, each position could be made most effective for its function. The various sites had such functions as housing coastal guns, antiaircraft protection, artillery and antitank weapons, machine gun pillboxes, and observation towers. Designs were also available for such logistic requirements as supply bunkers, communication facilities, and medical service. The accompanying illustrations show several of the different designs available (Fig. 7).

Several of the design features of structures can be seen to enhance the tactical effectiveness of defenses assembled from the standard units. The primary characteristic was resistance to bombardment. Embrasures did not face directly to seaward but rather were aligned to an oblique orientation. In this alignment resistance to naval fire was superior, but the guns were still able to shower enfilade fire on attacking waves. Wingwalls were integrated into many structures to serve a dual purpose: they shielded the muzzle blast of the gun from seaward observation and also provided additional protection to the embrasures. This is especially noticeable on the Utah Beach fortifications. The illustration of the Omaha Beach pillbox near the Vierville draw (see Chapter VI) shows a similar characteristic. Note also that the Vierville unit is in an elevated position with respect to the landing beach and thus better able to deliver aimed fire on attacking forces. This advantage to the defenders is found to a greater degree on Omaha Beach than on Utah. The 210-mm guns housed in fortress-type structures at Crisbecq, just north of Utah Beach (see Chapter VII), show a step-

Figure 7—Heavy Concrete Construction of The Atlantic Wall. *Structures at key locations include gun position in upper view and observation post in lower view.*

type construction in the overhead protection. This was intended to maximize resistance to aerial bombardment.

The strategically important defensive installations covered such prizes as ports and submarine pens, and, of course, the Pas-de-Calais sector and were more ruggedly built than those on open beaches. However, since none of the super design structures appeared on the beaches of Normandy they have not been treated here. The Crisbecq (also known as St.-Marcouf) forts are closer to super design structures than any of the other beach fortifications which are covered in this book.

Following the completion of the campaign in Normandy, a technical survey of the fortifications was made by the Chief Engineer of ETOUSA with support from the Office, Chief of Engineers. The Crisbecq structures were examined carefully. The roofs were measured to have a thickness of 12 feet. The sidewalls were found to be 10.25 feet thick. Operation of the guns in traverse and elevation was by manual means. No mechanization of ammunition handling was provided.

The findings included some test results on the concrete. It was believed that the cement was of German manufacture and of good quality. However, the concrete was usually made with an excess of fine aggregate and the resulting material was not up to the standards prevailing in the U.S. Three samples were tested and the average strength in compression was found to be 3,600 pounds per square inch, not a good value for fully aged concrete. Reinforcing bars were found to be plain, round bars of one-half inch diameter, spaced approximately 10 inches apart, running in three orientations, with hooked ends.

The desired standardization was more applicable to concrete construction than to weapons. The illustrations in Chapters VI and VII show that several of the emplacements have Renault tank turrets, these having been taken over from French stocks. Additionally, in many other defenses there were captured guns of various national forces adapted to the fortification structure. The interior overhead had protection against spalling of concrete in the form of steel plate lining. The plates were held in position by steel I-beams. Examination of the structures in the port defenses at Cherbourg showed that typical wall and overhead thicknesses were even greater than the levels described above.

An overall impression of the scale of the Atlantic Wall construction is impressive by any standards. In the process of creating the 15,000 fortified positions, a reliable estimate is that 20 million cubic yards of concrete were poured and more than a million tons of steel were installed. Over the period of intense activity 250,000 slave laborers summarily deported from the occupied countries worked back-breaking hours on inadequate rations. The work gangs at the high priority U-boat bases reached 15,000 most of the time. Anti-invasion beach sites were covered according to the priorities contained in plans from Berlin, that is to say from Hitler directly, as follows: Pas-de-Calais, the Channel Islands, fortress Cherbourg, east coast of the Cotentin Peninsula (including the future Utah Beach), and the stretch of Normandy beaches which included the future Omaha and British beaches. As work progressed and decision making took the usual swings, the effort placed on Omaha Beach moved up in importance.

GERMAN DEFENSIVE COMMAND ARRANGEMENTS

The machinations in reaching a command structure on the German western front had a decided impact on the tasks assigned to engineer troops of the invasion forces. As noted earlier Field Marshal von Rundstedt, after a spell of poor health, returned to duty and resumed command of the entire western theater. The time of this assignment was March of 1942, about the same time Directive No. 40 from Berlin initiated construction of the Atlantic Wall. The first conflict to arise involved the attitude held by von Rundstedt that coastal fortifications dispersed along the entire coast could not possibly hold off a determined force of invaders. His thinking was that the Wall was not a sensible investment of resources. His approach called for concentration of defensive forces to strike a counterattack once it could be determined where the invasion was taking place and while the invaders were still disorganized and unable to fight off his forces. Furthermore, the target date for completion of the Wall was May of 1943 and von Rundstedt considered this to be impossible to attain no matter how vigorously the project was pushed.

As the months passed there was continuing progress on the Atlantic Wall notwithstanding the lack of enthusiasm on the part of the Commander in Chief West. Apparently he lost patience and following a detailed inspection of the coast he submitted a decidedly negative report to the authorities in Berlin. A summary of his findings was that the coastal fortifications were inadequate for the intended concept of defense and that the troops were spread much too thinly. The report went forward in October of 1943. Within several weeks, there was a response from Hitler in the form of Directive No. 51. This directive emphasizes the threat posed by an invasion from the west noting that whereas the vast spaces in the east allowed a trade-off of territory against time, in the west any penetration of German defenses could be a mortal blow. Minute and precise instructions were provided for such typical matters as distribution of new weapons, reorganization of forces, and training programs.

At roughly this same time, Field Marshal Erwin Rommel was made available for an assignment in the west, as Field Marshal Albert Kesselring was placed in command in Italy. The first post for Rommel was Commander Army Group for Special Employment in which position he also studied defenses and generated plans for fighting off the invading forces. In January of 1944 he was placed in command of Army Group B which included the 15th Army, defending primarily the Pas-de-Calais sector but having boundaries reaching northeastward to just beyond Antwerp and southwestward almost to Caen; and the 7th Army, defending primarily the Normandy coast but having boundaries encompassing also the Brittany shoreline. Fig. 8 shows German Army dispositions at the time of the invasion.

Field Marshal Rommel had a number of limitations to his authority despite the ostensible position of command on the crucial sectors of the Atlantic Wall. He appears to have enjoyed cordial relations with Hitler even though he had to deal with Berlin through higher headquarters, namely Field Marshal von Rundstedt (Fig. 9). It is well established that these two had some conflicts of tactical plans. The extent of

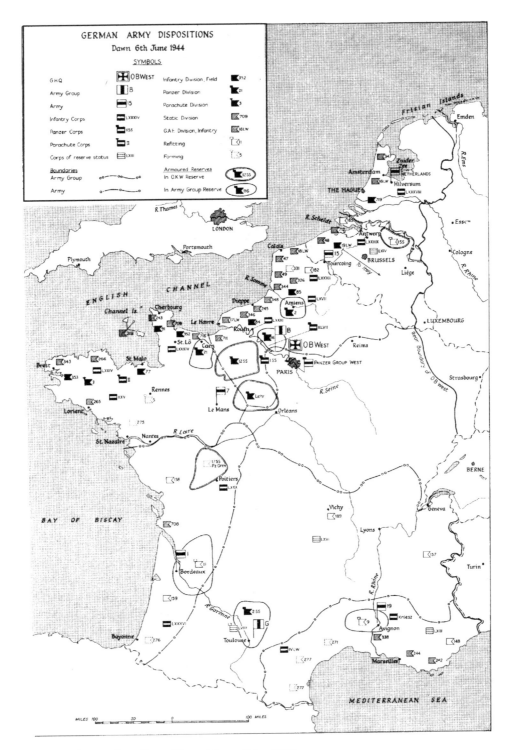

Figure 8—German Army Dispositions at Dawn D-day 1944.

Figure 9—*Enemy Commanders on The Western Front.* *Conference of the two leading figures, Field Marshal Gerd von Rundstedt (right), Commander in Chief West and Field Marshal Erwin Rommel, Commander of Army Group B.*

the differences is arguable and, in fact, the numerous historical works of World War II carry on the discussion *ad nauseam*. However, the crux of the matter bears on the employment of engineers during landing operations and cannot be neglected in this account. Firstly, it should be noted that the two commanders had some important thoughts in common; neither was satisfied in early 1944 that the Atlantic Wall was adequate for its intended purpose. Also, they were both highly disturbed that the panzer divisions constituting the western strategic reserve, probably the best trained and equipped units on the front, were under a separate command and were responsive to instructions directly from Berlin.

The differences in their thinking grew out of Rommel's experience in the Mediterranean campaigns. He knew that the German loss of airspace control made for difficulties in moving Army units. He was certain that Allied air power would successfully intervene if the defensive tactics depended primarily on counterattack. Distant control of the key reserve forces further compounded the problem. He was forced to the conclusion that the invaders had to be stopped at the waterline. But, the differences should not totally mask some thinking that the two commanders had in common. Both believed that up to some reasonable level, fortified positions were a valid defense measure and also that some degree of mobile artillery should be part of the plan. Rommel was not totally negative in regard to a mobile reserve but wanted these to be positioned within four to five miles of the beach, this being a very close-in position by von Rundstedt standards. Rommel's thinking was more in accord with Hitler's policies, as stated in Directives No. 40 and No. 51, than with his superior's.

MINE WARFARE MEASURES AT THE BEACH SECTORS

The final form of protective measures along the invasion beaches was a reflection of the energy and thought processes of Field Marshal Rommel. His attitude can be summed up concisely. He believed that the first 48 hours of the battle would be decisive and that the prospect of getting his reserves into action would be slim unless these forces were deployed in proximity to the shore. Even though his position as Commander of Army Group B, with responsibility for defending the most probable target beaches, was the key to German fortunes, he had no control over the strategic reserves, which included the most able panzer formations. He was inclined to expect an invasion in the Pas-de-Calais sector, but would not neglect the defenses of Normandy. He considered that his time for final preparations would definitely be inadequate.

In these circumstances, Rommel was forced to get the maximum benefit from all the existing fortifications and upgrade defenses wherever possible by expedient means. Construction of concrete fortifications had been in progress for two years. Emphasis at this point would be on mines, obstacles, and entrenchments.

The previous campaigns fought by Rommel had convinced him that land mines were effective weapons both when used by the Allies and by his own forces. His objective for the invasion beaches was a quantity of 50 million mines to be sown in overlapping belts to a depth of several miles, reaching inland from the shoreline. This quantity turned out to be overly ambitious and the actual achievement by the time of the D-day landings was approximately one-tenth the goal. However, the magnitude of the mine laying was still formidable. There were variations is type, style, and design features, and additionally there were diverse national sources. A great deal of ingenuity was apparent in the installation of the mines and the booby traps which were intended to complicate the removal of mines. Also, an innovation in design had turned up by 1944 in that non-metallic mines were in widespread use thereby complicating the detection of mines with standard U.S. equipment. Regardless of the new difficulty, it was possible to locate these new mines by finely tuning the detectors, especially if the depth of burial was not extreme.

Tellermines dominated the antitank category of German mines; the name was derived from the overall appearance of the mine, resembling a large dinner plate (teller in German) (Fig. 10). For the model variations, diameter was in the range of 12 to 13 inches and thickness (height) was between three to four inches. The weight of bursting charge was in the range of 10 to 12 pounds while the total weight was on the order of 19 pounds. Explosive material through the evolution of model specifications was primarily TNT, but others such as amatol were used. The mine housing was made of pressed sheet steel. Pressure plates were primarily steel, but in some cases aluminum, either flat or corrugated depending upon the model.

Tellermines function in a straightforward manner. A pressure plate is installed atop the main body housing the explosive with a compression spring incorporated in the plate suspension design. Obviously the stiffness of this spring controls the force required to detonate the mine. The force required for ignition varies between 200 pounds

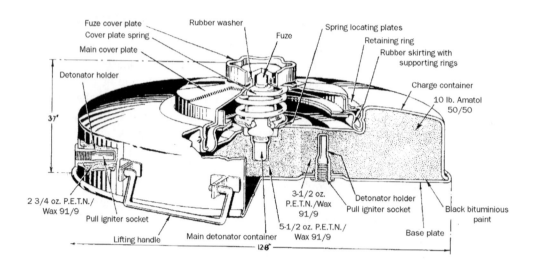

Fuze cover plate
Cover plate spring
Main cover plate
Detonator holder
Rubber washer
Fuze
Spring locating plates
Retaining ring
Rubber skirting with supporting rings
Charge container
10 lb. Amatol 50/50
37″
2 3/4 oz. P.E.T.N./ Wax 91/9
Pull igniter socket
Lifting handle
Main detonator container
3-1/2 oz. P.E.T.N./Wax 91/9
5-1/2 oz. P.E.T.N./ Wax 91/9
Detonator holder
Pull igniter socket
Black bituminious paint
Base plate
128″

Figure 10—*Tellermine—Type 2.*

when applied to the edge of the plate and 400 pounds when applied centrally. A pressure fuse is fitted in the central fuse well and is actuated by failure of a shear pin as the pressure plate is forced downward. Following failure of the shear pin, a striker pin is released to detonate the percussion cap, the detonator, the booster, and the main charge. Early models of the fuse had two safety devices: a safety bolt was in parallel with the shear pin and needed to be removed when the mine was laid, and a restrictive cam which blocked the striker pin and which was turned to the *armed* position when the mine was laid.

As a result of field experience a number of design changes were made which produced a series of models from T.Mi.29 through T.Mi.43; the number indicates the year of introduction. The performance of the early models showed an excessive rate of sympathetic detonation, that is to say that the mines had been set off by a nearby explosion rather than by the action of a vehicle. This discrepancy was corrected by reduction in the size of the pressure plate from the full diameter of the mine to a size of about one-quarter the original area. The smaller pressure plate did not accumulate enough of the blast pressure to produce the force to detonate in most cases, but still had the original detonation force when subjected to a vehicle passing over. The first model with reduced pressure plate dimensions was T.Mi.42. In addition to the reduced susceptibility to artillery detonation, the improved pressure plate design enabled closer spacing of mines in patterned mine fields and roadblocks.

German mine fields could be doubly difficult to clear since the mines were provided with recepticles for pull-type detonators. Two wells were provided, one on the side wall and the other on the bottom. Standard firing devices were readily available. A wide variety of booby traps could be quickly rigged to the mines under field conditions. The available components especially favored use of trip wires.

With Allied engineers progressively better equipped and trained with magnetic-type mine detectors, a German response appeared. Wooden box antitank mines (Holzmine 42) were developed with about the same explosive capacity as Tellermines and with a similar actuation force. A pressure block of wood was installed on the upper surface of the mine to provide a similar function as the pressure plate did for Tellermines. Even with the essentially all non-metallic construction, there remained some traces of metal, as for example in the few nails and in the detonator pins, so that a possibility did remain for detection by expert personnel.

Antipersonnel mines within the German arsenal were numerous and effective. The best known was the S-Mine, popularly called the Bouncing Betty. The action of this mine is a two-step function which commences when a force of about 10 pounds is applied to the exposed part of the pressure fuse. This part consists of three, approximately one inch high, flared prongs which are difficult to see when the mine is set into the ground. When detonation is initiated a propelling charge fires the main body out of a surrounding casing which acts as a sort of mortar tube while at the same time setting off a delay train to fire the lethal charge. When the propelling phase has lifted the main body to a height of about four feet, the main charge is detonated and scatters some 300 steel balls, or other shrapnel-like material, in all directions, in a nearly horizontal plane. As an alternate to the usually installed pressure fuse, an adaptor could be used to fit one or two pull-type fuses which made this mine diabolically useful in booby traps. These antipersonnel mines had taken a heavy toll in the Mediterranean Theater, especially prior to the general availability of mine detectors.

Antipersonnel mines had a non-metallic counterpart analogous to the situation in antitank mines. The Schumine 42 was housed in a small wood box about three by five inches and about two inches high. The box lid served as a pressure plate and under a force in the range of six to ten pounds disengaged a protruding pin of a firing device to detonate the demolition charge in the box. The charge was the standard block of TNT at 200 grams (seven ounces), not greatly unlike the U.S. standard TNT block. The consequence of an engagement with one of these mines was usually not fatal but did cost a foot or a leg or in some cases both feet. As in the case of the Holzmine 42, the Schumine 42 could also be detected by a U.S. mine detector tuned to a high sensitivity and operated by an expertly trained engineer soldier, due to the small metal content in the fasteners and in the fuse.

OBSTACLES—PRIMARILY ON THE TIDAL FLATS

It must be emphasized that Field Marshal Rommel arrived on the western front very late in the evolution of defense planning and in the construction of the Atlantic Wall. He was assigned to a command with the heaviest responsibility, but with severe limitations on his authority, particularly with regard to disposition and control of reserve forces. Furthermore, his prior experience against Allied forces had demonstrated that mobility of reserves was sorely impaired by the failure of the Luftwaffe to hold off hostile air activity. His voracious desire for mine fields of maximum density between fortified positions was far from being realized. Above all, he clung to his policy of stopping the invasions at the shoreline.

In these circumstances Field Marshal Rommel, driven to improvise, introduced the obstacles into the tidal zone, referred to by many military analysts as underwater obstacles. The term antilanding obstacles has also been applied to these structures and is clearly descriptive. Rommel's logic had forced him to expect a landing at high tide. He was certain that invading troops would not be put through the long trek ashore from a low tide debarkation during which they would be most vulnerable to weapons fire from sheltered and entrenched defenders. The placement of obstacles in the tidal zone fits well with Rommel's concept of placing the main line of resistance, generally referred to as the MLR, at the shore line. Additionally there were some practical justifications for launching into the obstacle construction program. This effort was relatively sparing of time, labor, and materials, all of which were in short supply. In fact, some of the obstacles already existed having been placed at inland locations for use as antitank defenses. This was particularly the case for hedgehogs and tetrahedra.

Initially these obstacles were placed rather close up to the high water line and then distributed more to seaward as additional quantities became available. The obvious intention was to cover the entire tidal zone of all potential landing beaches as shown in the sketch (Fig. 11). Of course, highest obstacle density was applied to the most probable target beaches. As noted previously, the principal commanders in the west were inclined to expect the invasion at the Pas-de-Calais sector, but the Normandy coast west of the Orne River was not neglected. It appears from the limited evidence available that by the spring of 1944 Rommel was focused more to the west. Clearly the sketch is more in the nature of an objective rather than a depiction of obstacles at any specific location. At installations along the beaches of Normandy, the density of obstacles was generally less than shown when D-day arrived.

The primary categories of tidal zone obstacles were: adaptations of antitank obstacles such as hedgehogs and tetrahedra; timber poles frequently tipped with Teller-mines; ramps of timber members; and fabricated steel structures known variously as Belgian gates or Element Cs. While these obstacles all functioned to impede safe debarkation of troops from landing craft, there are differences in their design approach. Some tend to tear the bottom of craft as would be the case when the sharp corners of hedgehogs contact the skin of the bottom. The action of ramps is to stop the craft and thus present an attractive target to artillery on shore, particularly if the unarmored bottom becomes exposed. Photographs taken at various other beaches (Figs. 12–15) show that a standard distribution of obstacles did not prevail. Yet other patterns of obstacles can be found on the maps (Appendices A through D) originally prepared for early waves of landing forces (classified Bigot) and updated with intelligence from aerial photographs as of mid-May of 1944.

Hedgehogs were conspicuous among the Normandy tidal obstacles. Some de-

A German Sketch of Beach Obstacles Lined Up on D-day

Figure 11—*General Layout of Tidal Zone Obstacles.* *Reproduction of a German sketch showing mix of various types of obstacles.*

tails of their construction can be seen in the illustration which shows their disposition after being cleared from the tidal flats by bulldozer. The primary structural members were three lengths of angle-iron, about six feet in length, joined at their midpoints by means of riveted gusset plates. It can be seen from the photographs that the hedgehogs were anchored into position by attachment to concrete base plates, and that the base plates were carried away as the metal structures were dozed ashore. The clearing operation also caused many of the angle members to separate from the gusset plates. The construction and anchoring of hedgehogs indicates they were adequately robust to crush the bottom of most landing craft.

Tetrahedra had several operational features in common with hedgehogs. They had four plane sides which were of triangular form where the edges were of equal length or nearly so. The most common material of tetrahedra was reinforced concrete with a hollow core. The apex of the obstacle was capable of piercing the bottom of most landing craft. These were also used as antitank obstacles and a fairly useful quantity was collected when the program was intensified to obstruct landing operations at the shoreline.

Figure 12—Details of Some Tidal Zone Obstacles. *A slanted pole tipped with a Tellermine of the reduced pressure plate type is shown in the upper left view. The upper right view shows a typical hedgehog. These were initially land-based antitank obstacles of simple but effective construction with three primary members of an angle shape joined at their centers with a gusseted connection, either riveted or welded. Note also concrete pads used as anchors. In lower view a unit of Element C, a fabricated steel structure with good area coverage for the amount of material, is shown. This obstacle was also known as a Belgian Gate because of its appearance.*

Figure 13—*Emplacement of Element C.* *Note that soldier performing task is older than those found in most effective units and is using a team of horses rather than more efficient powered equipment.*

Ramps were in place on many of the potential landing beaches. Their effectiveness can be judged by examination of photographic information. The view of ramp installations in the Pas-de-Calais sector shows that these were built to a much more robust design than those on Normandy beaches. For example the inshore support of the heavier ramps was in the form of a tripod versus a single pole for some of the lightweight ramps. Also the density of ramp installation varied widely. It would be a reasonable estimate that the more fragile ramps would not stand up to their intended purpose. When the construction of ramps was begun troops were sent off to nearby woods to retrieve poles, probably without specific instructions as to the required dimensions.

Poles were readily emplaced but of doubtful value for impeding landing craft unless they were used as mounts for mines or explosives. There are reports to the effect that poles did not stand up well under wave action and that a high level of maintenance was required to keep a field of poles upright. A cursory examination of the use of poles leads to the conclusion that the intention was that poles would serve as mounts for specially waterproofed Tellermines but that the supply of mines could not keep pace with the cutting of poles.

Element C was a fabricated steel structure having the general appearance of an ornate gate-like object, hence the use of the name Belgian gate. The general characteristic of these obstacles was a good stopping power for the mass of material employed but probably requiring excessive manufacturing manpower for general use in the tidal zone. These units were, in fact, more usually placed in such critical locations as obvious beach exits. Structural effectiveness of Element C was frequently augmented

Figure 14—*Example of Heavy Ramp Construction.* *Timber diameter and density of obstacles exceed those found on Normandy beaches, probable location is toward Pas-de-Calais.*

Figure 15—*Tidal Zone Obstacles Bulldozed Ashore.* *A post-D-day view of obstacles cleared by dozer, mainly hedgehogs with concrete anchor pads.*

by the supplementary use of waterproofed Tellermines. Appendices H and I provide additional details on obstacle construction and placement on the beaches.

Not only is Rommel credited with the instigation of obstacles in the tidal zone, his frequent inspections assured that maximum benefit would be derived from the investment of materials and labor. One recorded item has it that he usually carried several accordions in his touring car and awarded them as gifts to units which were making good progress toward their objectives. Another anecdote relates that he visited the Normandy beaches about mid-May and assured the troops that Allied landings would be made at high tide and that the obstacles in the tidal zone would be crucial in turning back the invaders (Fig. 16).

FIELD MARSHAL ERWIN ROMMEL
COMMANDER ARMY GROUP B
APRIL 1944

"In the short time left, before the great offensive starts, we must succeed in bringing all defenses to such a standard that they will hold up against the strongest attack. Never in history was there a defense of such an extent with such an obstacle as the sea. The enemy must be annihilated before he reaches our main battlefield. We must stop him in the water, not only delaying him, but destroying all his equipment while it is still afloat."

There has been no clear answer to the question of how far along toward completion was the installation of tidal zone obstacles. It is well established that resources available on the Atlantic Wall were strained to the limit as the year 1944 unfolded. Organization Todt had some unfinished work on port defenses and was also being used to keep some rail links in operation under the steady pounding of Allied air forces. Cement was in short supply and what little could be found had to compete for limited transportation space. Troops were being used for defense labor, but this practice had an adverse result on training, especially in the case of those divisions which were new or were being refitted after a mauling on the Russian front. In mid-May, the Seventh Army (the field army with responsibility for the Normandy and Brittany coasts) reported that disposition of obstacles was complete. Rommel's estimates were vastly different from all the optimistic levels. He believed that the work accomplished up to that time was merely the start of the effort and that much more depth, in the seaward direction, was required and also that a greater density of the obstacles was necessary. Adm. Theodor Krancke, naval commander in the west and von Rundstedt's counterpart, never subscribed to the postulation of a high tide landing and therefore con-

Figure 16—*Field Marshal Rommel Inspects Obstacles at Low Tide.* Graphic illustration of the frequent trips of Rommel along the coast.

cluded that the placement of tidal zone obstacles commencing at the high water area was a terrible mistake. He would have preferred the work to begin in the low water area and to progress toward shore. As for von Rundstedt himself, as already observed, he was not keen about the effort being expended on fortifications, mines, and obstacles. He had, nevertheless, initiated some early work at inland sites in order to add depth to the defenses, only to have Rommel's priorities supersede his own. It is indeed difficult to fathom the command alignment.

GERMAN TROOP DISPOSITIONS

A survey of the quality, organization, and readiness will complete the description of enemy capabilities. Various analysts have assigned quality levels to German forces which span the spectrum from one extreme to another. This, of course, is what might be expected when an observer's focus is permitted to wander. It is also a fact that many foreign military establishments favored the creation of elite units to a much greater degree than is the practice among U.S. forces. Indeed, much of the U.S. high command was definitely negative about non-standard divisions within each category of organization.

As time passed during the two-year period prior to the invasion exactly the opposite of elitism was taking hold of the German Army in the west. This is the period during which the quality and size of defensive forces was expected to improve along the Atlantic Wall. The proportion of non-German personnel was increasing. Supposedly anti-communist soldiers fighting against the advancing Red Army were steadily growing less reliable and were being transferred to the west. The German draft was bringing in the very young and the very old, as the pool of eligibles was running low, and these untrained candidates were filling vacancies in the west. And, the need for recruits in the west was growing as most units were being drained of capable manpower to supply needs in the east. To appreciate the drain of forces in the west, note that from October of 1942 until October of 1943, there was a transfer to the east of 36 infantry divisions, 12 panzer divisions, and five panzer grenadier divisions. The gaps were filled by transfer to the west of the so-called "East Battalions" composed of non-German personnel. Additionally, since the time of the withdrawal of Italy from the war there were demands for troop units to take over assignments previously held by the Italian Army, including numerous locations in the Balkans.

The use of static coastal divisions was one approach to alleviating the manpower problem. These units had a large proportion of older age classes, physical disabilities, non-German nationals, and recuperating wounded from the eastern front. In the case of the 709th Division, a static division on the east coast of the Cotentin Peninsula, the average age of the troops was 36 years. It was expected by the German high command that the high state of fortification on the Atlantic Wall would make troop quality less of a decisive factor in the outcome of the battle.

In any consideration of the German troops on the western front, note should be taken of their make-up. During the six months or so prior to the invasion, several processes were put into motion to cope with the manpower problem. The division structure in the German Army was comparable in general with that of the U.S. division, being triangular in form. The *static division* had its nine rifle battalions, the same as the field divisions, but lost its transport capability, its reconnaissance battalion, and some of its artillery. The *field division*, after a reorganization in 1943, was trimmed to just under 14,000 total personnel by eliminating one of the battalions from each of the three infantry regiments. Concurrent with the manpower reduction weaponry was augmented with increased use of machine guns to maintain fire power with fewer troops. By comparison with a U.S. infantry division structured in accordance with the then current table of organization, the German counterpart had fewer personnel, less mobility equipment, but was a nearly equal match in firepower. Within the forces manning the Atlantic Wall, there were further variations due to local conditions and a tendency to improvise. The situation on the coastal sectors actually assaulted is a prime example. At the time of the landings, the 716th Division, a static division, had only one regimental headquarters controlling six rifle battalions. Not far away, but on a coastal sector more than twice as long, the 709th Division, another static division, contained 11 rifle battalions organized into three regiments.

There was also the matter of national composition of the divisions on the western front as transfers of non-German personnel accelerated during late 1943 and early 1944. The trend was to exchange German personnel from the west to the east and replace them by moving battalions of eastern peoples (Cossacks, Georgians, and Azerbaijanis) from the east to the west. As Red Army successes multiplied, the eastern units of German forces were becoming increasingly unreliable. The overall result of the troop shuffling was that the German Seventh Army, defending on the sectors under assault on D-day, contained 23 rifle battalions of eastern, non-German personnel, this number representing about one-sixth of such units.

To round out the survey of defending forces manning the Atlantic Wall, note should be taken of the more capable formations. The mix of divisional structures within the Seventh and Fifteenth Armies can be seen in the accompanying table, and their locations are on the map showing dispositions (Fig. 8). Field divisions were manned with far fewer under-par personnel based on age, wound status, and other physical limitations, as compared to the static divisions. They were trained to a more rigorous standard and contained at least a limited degree of mobility. Some of the equipment regarded as mobile was horse-drawn and some troops were equipped with bicycles.

A notch above the infantry division was the parachute division. Its personnel were more numerous, met superior selection standards, and were volunteers. While the units were not qualified for airborne warfare, their training was intensive and they could be regarded as elite troops. Weaponry of the parachute divisions included generous allotments of heavy mortars, rocket launchers, and antiaircraft artillery. Structure of the divisional regiments included 15 rifle companies which produced a strength for the division in excess of 17,000. This type of division suffered from a shortage of mobility equipment, along with other infantry divisions, at least by Allied standards.

Note should be taken of German panzer forces, definitely in the category of superior military effectiveness. Intelligence information seems to place a great deal of significance on the matter that all the panzer divisions were understrength, as compared to organization tables, in their allotment of tanks of all types ranging from Mark III to Mark V (Panther). The standard called for a tank regiment in each panzer division which would be comprised of one battalion each of Mark IV and Mark V, the battalions to have four companies of 22 tanks each. Panthers mounted 75-mm high-velocity guns, weighed about 50 tons and were rated as generally superior in armor and armament in comparison to the U.S. Sherman. The redeeming features of the U.S. design were seen as superior mobility and a more reliable power plant.

German Army Group B

(Shortly before D-Day)

Commander—Field Marshal Erwin Rommel

SEVENTH ARMY
Generaloberst Friederich Dollman
(Normandy, Brittany)

LXXXIV Corps
716th Inf. Div.—Static
352d Inf. Div.—Field
709th Inf. Div.—Static
243d Inf. Div.—Static
319th Inf. Div.—Static
Reserve
 91st Airborne Div.—Field

LXXIV Corps
77th Inf. Div.—Field
266th Inf. Div.—Static

XXV Corps
265th Inf. Div.—Static
275th Inf. Div.—Field
343d Inf. Div.—Static
Reserve
353d Inf. Div.—Field

II Parachute Corps (Army Reserve)
2d Parachute Div.
3d Parachute Div.
5d Parachute Div.

FIFTEENTH ARMY
Generaloberst Hans von Salmuth
(Pas-de-Calais, Le Havre,
Netherlands)

LXXXI Corps
711th Inf. Div.—Static
 17th Luftwaffe Div.—Field
245th Inf. Div.—Static

LXVII Corps
348th Inf. Div.—Static
344th Inf. Div.—Static

LXXXII Corps
 49th Inf. Div.—Static
 47th Inf. Div.—Static
 18th Luftwaffe Div.—Field

LXXXIX Corps
 48th Inf. Div.—Static
712th Inf. Div.—Static
165th Inf. Div.—Refitting

LXXXVII Corps (Netherlands)
719th Inf. Div.—Static
 16th Luftwaffe Div.—Field
327th Inf. Div.—Static

ARMY GROUP RESERVE
XLVII Corps—Panzer
21st Panzer Div.
116th Panzer Div.
 2d Panzer Div.
Panzer Group—West (OKW Control)
I SS Panzer Corps
1st SS Panzer Div.
12th SS Panzer Div.
17th SS Panzer Grenadier Div.
Panzer Lehr Div. (Training)

Most of the intelligence information states that Mark VI Tigers, a 63-ton tank mounting an 88-mm main gun, but with an underpowered engine, were diverted to the eastern front and did not appear in Normandy. However, more factual information has it that shortly after the invasion, Allied commanders were inspecting Tigers captured during the battle. It seems that engine failure was a hallmark of this model also. In any case, the confused picture of the state of equipage within German forces is undoubtedly traceable to the exigencies of the times. An even further complication was the fact that a large proportion of panzer divisions were SS (Schutzstaffel or Elite Guard), and the resulting superiority in training and fighting spirit set them apart. Aside from the matter of armament, the 1st SS-Panzer Division enjoyed a special reputation of having fought hard on the Russian front.

The difficulties confronting German forces described in the preceding sections were, of course, formidable, but it should not be concluded that their military capability was completely second-rate. The German military establishment had a corps of competent and experienced commanders at all levels. Their achievements on all battlefields of the European Continent, and beyond, have been rated, in military terms, as impressive. But for a few erratic decisions on the part of the Fuehrer, the campaign into Russia might have gone differently and the consequences on the Atlantic Wall would have been markedly disadvantageous to the Allies. As things did turn out, the German command fielded an effective fighting machine with well-trained and disciplined personnel and with experience widely distributed. Most of the materiel was well designed, had some unique superiorities, and was well apportioned. Certainly the Allied invaders had to wage a fierce struggle to achieve success in the invasion.

Before leaving the general subject of German capabilities to defend against the impending Allied invasion several matters pertaining to intelligence must be addressed. The primary item is the movement of the 352d Infantry Division into positions along the Normandy coast between Port-en-Bessin and Vierville-sur-Mer, which was to become Omaha Beach. This highly regarded attack division had been positioned in the vicinity of St.-Lô and constituted an important reserve resource to be employed in the event of an assault anywhere in Normandy. During March of 1944, when Rommel was fighting the problem of reserve elements being too far inland, some redistributions were made. Obviously, the Omaha landing force confronted defensive units of unexpected strength in what has been judged one of the more serious intelligence failures of the war. During April, the reserves were further depleted for all practical purposes by movement of the 21st Panzer Division from Rennes (central Brittany) to the vicinity of Caen, which was a D-day objective of British forces.

Finally, it is interesting to note on the map of German Army dispositions (Fig. 8) that troop concentrations are decidedly more dense in the Pas-de-Calais sector than along the Normandy coast. Much of the research on this subject has found that von Rundstedt was more inclined to expect the main effort of the Allies in the Calais sector. While Rommel's thinking is not quite as overt, he obviously did not upset the preponderant troop strength in the Pas-de-Calais sector.

CHAPTER IV

LANDING FORCE PREPARATIONS

The main thrust of the engineer amphibian story will now resume, following the diversion to examine the enemy thought process, fortification construction and other measures to repel a breakthrough of the Atlantic Wall. We previously had recounted the early planning activities within the British and American high commands looking toward a recrossing of the English Channel. This led us to the later joint planning, particularly including the work of COSSAC. There was virtual unanimity among Allied planners that the Normandy coastline contained the most feasible landing beach candidates. Beyond that there was substantial disparity in planning approach. The crux of the matter was the required strength of the landing force. Obviously the COSSAC draft outline was based on an inventory of amphibious lift specified in directives which guided the planning. Conditional approval of the outline plan granted by the Quadrant Conference in August of 1943 attached the condition that a strengthening of the invading force by 25 percent should be incorporated into the plan. While Prime Minister Churchill was fully in support of the strengthening, there was much deliberation at the Conference as to whether all the alternatives to Overlord had been fully considered and when the operation might be launched. A matter of prime importance to preparation of the landing force was discussion at the Conference of the transfer of seven battle-hardened divisions from the Mediterranean to Britain. In the succeeding months, continued critique of the COSSAC draft outline pointed to a need for force strengthening and for expansion of landing beach frontage.

In late 1943, the introduction of commanders into the invading force structure enabled the planning activity to intensify and move to the command levels, mainly field army and corps, where operational details could be introduced. For the most part, the leadership of the invaders would be in the hands of those who had held the senior positions of the Mediterranean armies and their air and sea support. The immediate problem facing the commanders was assembly, final training, and equipment for the expanded assault force.

It is a moot point as to exactly where preparations for Overlord commence. Bolero, the build-up of supplies in the United Kingdom during 1942, was intended to support a cross-Channel operation, but of course these resources were diverted to North Africa in support of the Torch landings and subsequent campaigns in Tunisia and Sicily. The supply build-up under Bolero needed to commence afresh. Facilities for amphibious training up to division-size exercises were created in the continental U.S. and under Fifth Army direction in North Africa, all of which had carry-over benefits to the cross-Channel operation. Similarly, there were a number of technical developments as the total war effort progressed which had application to amphibious tactics and they will be noted. As a consequence, the chronology in this chapter may appear to be disjointed at times.

FINAL PLANNING—COMMAND LINE-UP

Above all else, the appointment of a Supreme Commander to the Allied Expeditionary Force (AEF) was crucial to final planning. There were numerous reasons for the delay. On the British side, Prime Minister Churchill favored his Chief of The Imperial General Staff, Gen. Sir Alan Brooke, and had, in fact, promised him the position. It was clear, however, that during the build-up of the invading force, American troops would quickly become dominant and that American public opinion would not accept a British General in the position of Supreme Commander.

On the American side, the problem was more difficult, but in a much different sense. President Roosevelt believed that Gen. Marshall had earned the position on the basis of his achievements in the rapid expansion of American forces. However, the overwhelming argument presented to the President by his most reliable advisors was that Gen. Marshall simply could not be spared from the Washington command post. Furthermore, pressure was being applied by the Russians to resolve this problem once and for all. Early during the Teheran conference commencing on 28 November 1943, Marshal Stalin made pointed remarks to the effect that without a Supreme Commander, the prospect was for continuing procrastination in launching Overlord. Promptly after the conclusion of the conference, during a stop-over in Cairo, the selection of Gen. Eisenhower was made final. It may seem an incidental item but the Russians in their continuing effort to ensure that Overlord was not postponed beyond early May of 1944, gave assurances that a major effort on the eastern front would be made to coincide with the time of the landings.

Undoubtedly there was an implicit understanding that with an American Supreme Commander there would be a strong British presence in the next command level. The framers of the Overlord draft outline seemed to have in mind an arrangement under which the land, sea, and air commanders would be a sort of committee of directors for the campaign while the Supreme Commander would be forced to devote much of his energy to intergovernmental affairs and to communication with the combined staff. There is no evidence, however, to support a notion that Gen. Eisenhower's role was in any way less than a Supreme Commander, in the usual connotation of the term.

The overall command arrangement (Fig. 17) was less than ideal from an American point of view, but the ample war experience and qualifications of the British candidates were compensation. The position of Deputy Supreme Commander went to Air Chief Marshal Sir Arthur Tedder. This appointment was an indication of the importance which Gen. Eisenhower attached to the air contribution to the invasion. Also, during his service as commander of Allied air forces in the Mediterranean, Air Marshal Tedder had performed well and developed cordial working relations with American Gens. Eisenhower and Spaatz. Some military historians have detected a dislike on the part of Tedder towards Montgomery on the grounds that the credit for victory at El Alamein had not been equitably shared. He also had little regard for his

Figure 17—Overlord Commanders at Supreme Headquarters. *Gen. Dwight Eisenhower, Supreme Commander, Allied Expeditionary Force; (middle row) Maj. Gen. Walter Bedell Smith, Chief of Staff; Air Chief Marshal Sir Arthur Tedder, Deputy Supreme Commander, Allied Expeditionary Force; (bottom row) Adm. Sir Bertram Ramsay, Commander in Chief, Allied Naval Expeditionary Force; Gen. Sir Bernard Montgomery, Commander 21st Army Group (in effect all Allied ground forces); Lt. Gen. Omar Bradley, Commander First U.S. Army; Air Chief Marshal Sir Trafford Leigh-Mallory, Commander in Chief Allied Expeditionary Air Force.*

service colleague Air Chief Marshal Sir Trafford Leigh-Mallory, mainly on matters of doctrine.

The responsibility to command all Allied ground forces went to Gen. Sir Bernard Montgomery, not by choice of Gen. Eisenhower. His command position would more accurately be described as Commanding General of 21st Army Group, consisting of the First U.S. Army and the Second British Army. The plan called for the activation of a U.S. Army Group to operate under an American commander just as soon as U.S. strength ashore reached the level of two field armies. The main characteristic of Montgomery's philosophy was that all battle preparations should be totally ready before any operation was launched and the assurance of victory was present. His reconstruction of a demoralized army in North Africa and his success in a series of campaigns vindicated his military approach. His mannerisms were regarded as irritating by most of his colleagues throughout his long career. However, both Prime Minister Churchill and Gen. Brooke insisted he was the best choice. Thus, Gen. Sir Harold Alexander, Gen. Eisenhower's preference for the ground commander position, was passed over and remained in the Mediterranean Theater. Before leaving the subject of ground command, there is an interesting distinction to be emphasized from an American perspective regarding the exact definition of the position held by Montgomery. His preference to be the Ground Commander would have given him continuing control of the entire battlefield, including all U.S. forces. On the other hand, if he commanded only the 21st Army Group and additional Army Groups were activated, then the Supreme Commander would have direct control of all ground forces. Montgomery maneuvered for the broadest degree of control throughout the European campaigns, but without success, except when during the Ardennes action some U.S. forces briefly came under 21st Army Group.

The position of Allied Naval Commander Expeditionary Force was relatively free of controversy and went to Adm. Sir Bertram Ramsay. Adm. Ramsay enjoyed good relations with his associates in both the Royal Navy and the U.S. Navy and was recognized for his breadth of view of overall military affairs. Early in the war he was recalled from retirement and had been a dominant figure in the Dunkerque rescue of the British Expeditionary Force. He was the chief naval planner during the North African landings working under the direction of Gen. Eisenhower. He was in key roles during the subsequent Mediterranean amphibious operations.

The nominee of the British high command for the position of Allied Air Commander was Air Chief Marshal Sir Trafford Leigh-Mallory and his approval for the position was granted by the Combined Chiefs. On first sight, his qualifications appeared to be first-rate. However, he could not have been Gen. Eisenhower's selection since the Leigh-Mallory appointment dates from 25 November 1943 prior to the Eisenhower appointment. His background was in Fighter Command of the R.A.F. During the Battle of Britain, he was in command of a Fighter Group operating in the vicinity of London. His operating tactics did not foster cooperative relations with nearby units, thus leading to a lack of depth in the respect and support he enjoyed among colleagues. Notwithstanding any doubts about his abilities, he went on to head up Fighter Command. From this position, he moved to the COSSAC team where he was in charge of air planning. Obviously, his career moves were monitored in high places, possibly in the office of the Prime Minister.

The position of Allied Air Commander came to be a source of difficulties for Gen. Eisenhower. It is well established that the heavy bomber forces believe their destiny is to operate under strategic bombing plans and not to be at the beck and call of a ground commander, or even a theater commander. An opposite problem faced Gen. Eisenhower since he had past experiences when the battle situation on the ground dictated support from heavy bombers only to find that such support was not promptly forthcoming and the negotiations and arrangements were then extremely time-consuming. Therefore, early after moving into the Supreme Commander position, he set about to resolve the question of incorporating heavy bomber support into an air plan. Without relating the merits of the diverse approaches to pre-invasion air operations such as the oil plan versus the transportation plan versus the interdiction plan, it can be noted that a solution was found by which the Supreme Commander and the Deputy had a direct influence on strategic air missions while bypassing Air Chief Marshal Leigh-Mallory. Incidentally, this achievement, along with many others, certainly negates any notions that Gen. Eisenhower would be so burdened by ceremonial types of functions that all operational matters would be handled at the second echelon of command.

GENERAL DWIGHT D. EISENHOWER
SUPREME ALLIED COMMANDER
ON OVERLORD—COMBINED CHIEFS OF STAFF—23 JANUARY 1944

"Every obstacle must be overcome, every inconvenience suffered and every risk run to ensure that our blow is decisive. We cannot afford to fail."

All U.S. ground forces were organized into the First Army for landing operations under the command of Lt. Gen. Omar Bradley. The assignment came in September of 1943 at which time Gen. Bradley was instructed to organize both a field army and an army group headquarters, the latter to be activated at the point following the invasion when American forces ashore reached the level of two field armies. Here again a key subordinate to the Supreme Commander is in place prior to the selection of Gen. Eisenhower. Of course, the acumen of Gen. Marshall had much to do with the progress of candidates for high command on the American side. There was a period when Gen. Bradley was on the faculty at The Infantry School concurrently with the time when Gen. Marshall was the assistant commandant and maintained records on personnel performance, which in the case of Gen. Bradley had been superior. Later, Gen. Bradley was in command of the 82d Infantry Division and brought the unit to such a high level of proficiency that it was selected for conversion to an airborne division. Later, in Tunisia, he played a crucial role in the measures taken to upgrade the floundering II Corps after the Kasserine disaster. He commanded the corps through the victorious final phase of the campaign and again in Sicily. His command performance established him as fully qualified to lead a major organization of the Army. As events unfolded during the preparation period and the landing operations, the presence of an all British second level in the SHAEF command structure did not inhibit Gen. Bradley's access to Gen. Eisenhower.

The initial make-up of the First U.S. Army was V Corps and VII Corps. The influence of Gen. Marshall shows up here again with the selection of Maj. Gen. Leonard Gerow and Maj. Gen. Lawton Collins to be the corps commanders. Gen. Gerow had been a classmate of Gen. Bradley at The Infantry School where they finished first and second in the period when Gen. Marshall was on the staff of the school. Gen. Gerow went on to head the War Plans Division of the General Staff prior to the point when Gen. Eisenhower was put into the post and the office was redesignated the Operations Division. Gen. Gerow headed V Corps during the period when it was the only field command in the European Theater and, as such, attempted to monitor the planning activities of COSSAC. Gen. Collins had served in the Philippines drawing up defense plans under the directions of Gens. MacArthur and Eisenhower. After hostilities commenced, he was in command of the 25th Infantry Division which, in early 1943, relieved the 1st Marine Division on Guadalcanal and performed well in finishing off Japanese resistance, much to the credit of Gen. Collins.

On the American line-up of naval commanders, Rear Adm. Alan Kirk headed the Western Task Force, the grouping of U.S. forces afloat for the invasion. Adm. Kirk assumed this command in mid-November 1943. His background in amphibious operations was especially strong. During the landings in Sicily, he had developed effective working relations with Gen. Bradley. Subordinate elements were Force "O" destined for Omaha Beach and Force "U" for Utah Beach, commanded by Rear Adms. John Hall and Don Moon respectively. Adm. Hall, in addition, exercised overall command of XI Amphibious Force. It was Adm. Hall who played a prominent role in augmenting the naval fire support plan from levels that were proposed in the early planning documents.

Command problems arising in air support for the Normandy landing forces were substantial. The main thrust of the difficulties was the existing tradition that strategic bombing was best controlled according to a master plan created by and for strategic forces. These forces succeeded in remaining outside the Overlord organization, except for a brief period during the final preparatory bombardment of the target beaches. In these circumstances, Gen. Eisenhower especially desired to have Gen. Spaatz nearby. Thus, Lt. Gen. Carl Spaatz was appointed as Commander, U.S. Strategic Air Forces—Europe and moved from the Mediterranean to Britain, from where he directed strategic bombers operating in both areas.

Working relations between Gen. Eisenhower and Gen. Spaatz were excellent and the two men had great personal respect for each other. Maj. Gen. James Doolittle also came along from the Mediterranean and was placed in command of Eighth U.S.

Air Force, primary operator of the heavy bomber units. Commander of the Ninth Tactical Air Force was Lt. Gen. Lewis Brereton, later to be supplanted by Lt. Gen. Hoyt Vandenberg. The Ninth had been created in Britain in October of 1943 so as to separate the tactical air elements from the heavy bombers of the Eighth Air Force and thereby contribute to a solution of the command problems. However, in the pre-invasion training period, the commitment of tactical air units to joint air-ground operations was less than the expectations of Gen. Bradley. The redeeming factor during the period when priorities seemed to favor other missions was the presence of Maj. Gen. Elwood Quesada who, more than most airmen, viewed ground support as a vital air mission and worked diligently to perfect tactics.

In view of the main theme of this account, some coverage of the principal engineer commanders is in order. The Provisional Engineer Brigade Group provided a single command over all shore party (essentially the 5th and 6th Brigades) activities at Omaha Beach and was headed by Brig. Gen. William Hoge. He had a varied Corps of Engineers career including duty with troops and on construction assignments. He was in charge of the establishment of the Engineer Replacement Training Center, which incidentally built the first military obstacle course. This asset to training was duplicated at practically all U.S. Army training facilities. He was in charge of construction of the ALCAN highway commencing in March of 1942, which included command of a 9,200-man provisional engineer brigade. In command of the 5th Engineer Special Brigade was Col. Doswell Gullatt. His headquarters was the first brigade level organization ashore at Omaha Beach which put him in overall charge of shore party activities until the other headquarters arrived later on D-day. Later, he commanded the U.S. 13th Port organization. In command of the 6th Engineer Special Brigade was Col. Paul Thompson. He contributed greatly to engineer doctrine as a consequence of his experience during the German sweep through the Low Countries and France. He established and commanded the Assault Training Center, which will be covered later.

The divisional engineers were conspicuous on Omaha Beach and should be noted. Col. William Gara commanded the 1st Engineer Combat Battalion and, during a three year period was at all command levels from platoon leader to battalion commander through the campaigns in North Africa and Sicily. Col. Robert Ploger commanded the 121st Engineer Combat Battalion. Previously, he had served as a company commander in the 10th Engineers of the 3d Infantry Division when the Division was part of the Pacific Fleet Amphibious Corps. Also, he had been on duty at Fort Belvoir for the training of engineer officer candidates. He was on the staff at First Army immediately prior to joining the 121st. Later, he was in command at Fort Belvoir.

At Utah Beach, Brig. Gen. James Wharton commanded the 1st Engineer Special Brigade for a brief period spanning two months, just before and just after the D-day landings. He had been in the 80th Infantry Division, assigned as Assistant Division Commander. Subsequent to his duty with the 1st ESB, he was in command of the 28th Infantry Division during action at the Falaise gap where he suffered a fatal battle wound. The anomalous nature of his duty with the 1st ESB will come up for further examination during consideration of a Brigade training exercise later in this chapter. Col. Eugene Caffey was placed in command of the Brigade in May of 1943 at the time of preparation for the invasion of Sicily (Operation Husky). At that time, the Brigade had responsibility for three regimental-size shore parties in support of the three assault divisions, the total U.S. seaborne landing force. When Col. Caffey retired from the Army some years after the war, he held the rank of Maj. Gen. and the position of Judge Advocate General.

FINAL PLANNING—TROOP SELECTION

The strength of the assault forces has been highlighted as the major problem to be attacked in developing a workable Overlord plan. With the command and staff installed at Supreme Headquarters Allied Expeditionary Force (SHAEF) the vital decisions were quickly reached. Previously, at the urging of Prime Minister Churchill, the Quebec Conference had concluded that the strength levels proposed in the COSSAC draft outline for Overlord needed to be increased by at least 25 percent. An agreement was quickly reached by Gens. Eisenhower and Montgomery that even that level of increase was not adequate. The initial draft plan calling for three seaborne assault divisions would be revised to provide five divisions in the initial assault. The airborne force would also be augmented with an additional division.

Concerning the exact number of divisions involved an element of potential confusion needs to be clarified. An examination of historical accounts and also the memoirs of the prominent commanders show that the American contribution to seaborne landings is variously described as two or three divisions. Landing diagrams show that the divisions in assault placed only one regiment forward. Otherwise described, this could be called a landing with divisions in column of regiments. In prior major amphibious landings, the general practice had been to land divisions with two regimental landing teams abreast. As the plan evolved for the Omaha force, there would indeed be two regimental teams abreast, but one would be from the 1st Division and the other from the 29th Division. Moreover, with only two regiments ashore, there was no reason to allocate early boat spaces to put two divisional headquarters teams ashore. Thus, the regiment of the 29th Division was officially attached to the 1st Division for the landing, and this could be called a one division assault. Certainly one division headquarters was fully responsible for all action on Omaha Beach. But it is beyond doubt that a grave injustice would be done if the 29th Division were not included among Normandy assault units. In short, a case can be made to categorize the American side of the seaborne assault on Normandy as either a two or a three division effort. Note also that the 4th Division Utah landing was executed with two battalions of the 8th Infantry Regiment (four abbreviated rifle companies) in the initial assault. This is a further example of the application of regiments in a column formation.

To continue with revisions to the draft outline plan produced by COSSAC the next aspect tackled by the newly installed commanders was the matter of landing beach frontage. The original concept called for close spacing between units and rather narrow assault fronts for all units in the early assault, with a compact 20-mile total front being the result. With emphasis on the early capture of Caen, this attack would have been on the beach segment from Ouistreham to Arromanches-les-Bains, the segment later assigned as the British target. Two problems caused concern: the American objective—following beachhead establishment—was to be the taking of the port of Cherbourg. To facilitate this operation, it was evident that a landing on the east coast of the Cotentin had several advantages. The distance from the site of initial landings to Cherbourg was greatly reduced. Moreover, a landing at the base of the peninsula enabled the severance of the peninsula and an attack on Cherbourg from the landward direction with minimum opportunity for the German defenders to reinforce. The second problem was an irritation, particularly to Gen. Montgomery. He feared that the compact landing frontage would not provide the necessary space for rapid build-up ashore of the follow-up forces and he had the benefit of experience during the landings at Sicily to condition his outlook.

The consequence of all these considerations was an expansion of landing beach frontage to a distance of approximately 55 miles. The British sector would extend westward from the Orne River to Arromanches (approximately the original 20-mile front) and include beaches Sword, Juno, and Gold. Omaha was planned to cover the beach sector from in front of Colleville-sur-Mer and extend westward to the beach in front of Vierville-sur-Mer with an extension to include the heights at Pointe du Hoc. Utah was planned to cover the beach sector at the base of the Cotentin between les Dunes de Varreville and la Madeleine.

Obviously, the revised layout of target beaches left a number of gaps that would need closing as the battle progressed. The American commanders preferred this arrangement by far to the original plan of a single narrow front wherein the invading force would be vulnerable to a German counterattack. However, the introduction of a landing force on the Cotentin brought about a new problem. While the newly conceived landing scheme would make an important contribution to the capture of Cherbourg, and the rather flat terrain of the proposed Utah Beach landing sector favored assault operations, there was also a negative factor. The low-lying ground inshore from the dunes was traversed only by several causeways (generally referred to as beach exits). As a countermeasure to the potential vulnerability of the Utah landing force, First Army planners proposed that one of the two U.S. airborne divisions drop in a position to seize the inland exits of the causeways. A second airborne division would drop farther south to cover the exposed extremity of the Utah force, to facilitate the link-up of the two separated U.S. beachheads, and to deny enemy passage through the key road junction at Carentan.

The proposed use of the airborne divisions met with stern opposition from Air Marshal Leigh-Mallory and was in jeopardy. He preferred to divert the American airborne divisions to the Caen area which was a D-day objective of the British Second Army. Gen. Bradley was firm on the point that without airborne support, the risk of failure at Utah Beach was excessive and, in fact, he could not proceed on planning for the Utah Beach landing without assurance that the airborne troops would be assigned. Gen. Bradley was adamant that he assumed responsibility for success of the Cotentin venture. Finally, with the support of Gen. Montgomery, the First Army proposal became a firm element of Overlord plans.

Final planning included detailed attention to troop assignments. By early in the year 1944, the build-up of U.S. forces in the U.K. was reaching a crescendo. Among the decisions reached at the Quadrant Conference (Quebec, August of 1943) an important policy issue was the rate of force build-up in Britain for Overlord and the withdrawal of battle-hardened troops from the Mediterranean Theater. At the completion of the campaign in Sicily, three divisions became available for transfer: 1st and 9th Infantry Divisions, and the 2d Armored Division. Through the fall of the year, these units, to which was added the 20th Engineer Combat Battalion, made the move. The 531st Engineer Shore Regiment was hastily inserted into the Avalanche (Salerno invasion 9 September 1943) force just prior to embarkation and therefore did not reach the U.K. until late November. The 82d Airborne Division similarly was involved at Salerno and not only was detained, but also left an important part of the division with Fifth U.S. Army. British forces withdrawn from the Mediterranean were roughly the same magnitude as those of the U.S. At the end of 1943, American divisions in Britain numbered 11 and included, in addition to those already named, the 101st Airborne Division, and the 3d Armored Division. The arrival rate for additional divisions was two per month.

Selection of the assault divisions absorbed the attention of Gen. Bradley for an extended period. The 29th Division had been in Britain for more than a year and was mentally conditioned for a prominent role in a cross-Channel operation. It had filled the void created by the embarkation of the North African center and eastern task forces for the landings in October of 1942. In addition to training within the division, regimental combat teams of the division were all put through the course at the Assault Training Center. In fact, the 116th Regimental Combat Team (RCT) returned later for a refresher period. This training activity commenced in September of 1943, when the ATC was ready to receive troops. Meanwhile, and also in September, the 4th Infantry Division was going through an intensive amphibious training program. The site for this training was Camp Gordon Johnson, in Florida, to which the 4th Engineer Amphibian Brigade had moved, and where it was prepared for joint training with the division. After arrival in Britain, all regiments of the 4th Division went through the program at the ATC. Thus, two divisions were splendidly prepared for assault duty with the landing force.

Notwithstanding the availability of these two divisions, Gen. Bradley grappled with a dilemma. Neither of the two had yet come under fire. On the other hand, the thoroughly seasoned 1st Infantry Division was also available. To Gen. Bradley, it made no sense to omit his most valuable resource from this most difficult and important undertaking, even if there was some injustice in calling on the Big Red One time and again. His final solution was to place both a regiment from the 29th and a regiment from the 1st in the Omaha Beach landing force with the former on the right and the latter on the left. As the two divisions built in strength ashore, the 1st would force the link-up with the British while the 29th would force the link-up with the Utah Beach force. Undoubtedly, the desire on the part of Gen. Bradley to get all these three divisions into action at the earliest possible moment helps to explain the complicated command arrangement on Omaha whereby the 116th Regiment of the 29th Division operated under control of the 1st Division in the initial phase of the assault.

At this point, a brief digression will intrude on these preparations for Overlord-Neptune. Readers may recall that shortly after the creation of the COSSAC organization, it was directed to plan an expedition to reenter the Continent in the event that the German government was on the verge of collapse. The code name for the proposed operation was Rankin and obviously the plan was filed away to be forgotten. However, in early 1944, the contingency was revived and the 1st Division prepared for a landing in the vicinity of Le Havre. Plans were issued on 1 March for Operation Rankin "C". The 1st Engineers had assignments which matched very closely the typical role of shore party engineers. After landing as a component of Ranger Force, the engineer assignment included preparation of beaches, docks, and assembly areas for landing the remainder of the task force. Further duties included reconnasissance, mine clearing, and removal of obstacles. This plan must have met the same fate as the earlier Rankins.

Among engineer units, the 1st Engineer Special Brigade had both training and operational experiences to warrant a prominent role in a cross-Channel plan. At the Amphibian Command on Cape Cod in mid-1942 it had overcome the difficulties of hasty organization and deployment overseas. In Scotland it had participated in joint exercises with the 1st Infantry Division and had gone on to North Africa with an assignment in the Center Task Force. Its responsibilities at the Fifth Army Invasion Training Center further polished its skills in amphibian operations. During operational assignments with the Husky and Avalanche landing forces, the units of the Brigade developed a skill to overcome obstacles of most any sort (see following box).

The 5th and 6th Brigades had been formed by transformation of Engineer Combat Groups, but they each had some significant training experiences in amphibious operations. The 5th was organized in Britain during November of 1943, out of the 1119th Group and consisted of the 37th, 336th, and 348th Engineer Combat Battalions. The Group had been at Camp Carabelle in Florida after the move of the Engineer Amphibian Command south from Cape Cod. The 6th Brigade was organized in January of 1944 out of the 1116th Group and consisted of the 147th, 149th, and 203rd Engineer Combat Battalions. This group had participated in training programs at Fort Pierce in Florida, after the U.S. Navy gained control of all amphibious training. The group also was in landing exercises in the Chesapeake Bay thereby acquiring a wide range of shore party skills.

The naval far shore components, as distinct from the forces afloat, were closely integrated into the Army landing forces. The 2d Naval Beach Battalion had been in the Mediterranean Theater and during operations at Gela and Salerno had developed effective working relations with the 1st ESB. As noted at the end of Chapter VII, the 2d Beach Battalion seemed to be pleased that they were again teamed with their partners in earlier campaigns. Coordination between the two units was further polished during exercises in leading up to the events of Neptune in preparation for landing on Utah Beach. Forces of V Corps included two new units, the 6th and 7th Beach Battalions which had been formed at Fort Pierce, Florida, and assigned to the sectors of the 5th and 6th ESBs, respectively, at Omaha Beach. Additionally, units of the 25th Naval Construction Regiment were assigned to Normandy landing forces. D-day responsibilities were primarily centered on operation of rhino ferries, with the 81st Construction Battalion being responsible for 12 ferry units assisting in offloading LST vessels at Utah and the 111th responsible for 20 units at Omaha. Lastly, both the Naval Beach Battalions and the Naval Construction Battalions provided personnel and support to the forces assigned the mission of clearing obstacles in the tidal zones of both invasion beach areas.

FINAL PLANNING—AMPHIBIOUS LIFT

At every turn in the planning process, the supply of amphibious lift had been a critical input data item. The work performed by the COSSAC team derived from a specified fleet of ships and craft; which, as it turned out, was not adequate to deliver the

531st Engineers Show Versatility in Combat

An Extract from: *Sicily—Salerno—Anzio*; Volume Nine
History of United States Naval Operations in World War II;
by Samuel E. Morison

Pertaining to Salerno Landings: "Thirty DUKW's hit Beach Green as early as 0525, one in every 12 bringing in much-wanted 105-mm howitzers, and other ammunition. They unloaded in good order behind the dune line and most of them returned to the transports. No fewer than 123 DUKW landings were made on the American beaches between 0530 and 0730—a remarkable achievement. The 2d Battalion of the 142d Regiment here had a hard time getting through barbed wire and lost men from exploding land mines; but it managed to reach the same assembly area as the Battalion from Beach Red. The southern half of Beach Green was interdicted by enemy gunfire throughout D-day.

Much of the trouble here and on the next beach (Yellow) came from machine guns mounted on the 50-foot stone tower and from one or two tanks that lurked behind the farm buildings attached to it. This tower was too near the beach for naval gunfire to take on. It was finally captured, the tanks put out of business, and all German defenders killed or made prisoner by the 531st Shore Engineers, who had already lost a number of officers and men in the early air attacks . . . Company D of this engineer regiment, commanded by 1st Lt. G. L. Shumaker did fine work preparing the beaches . . . under heavy fire from the tower . . .

strength of landing force required for the mission. At least that was the evaluation of all leadership echelons downward from Prime Minister Churchill. The Overlord staff estimates of the additional required amphibious lift were:

APA (attack transports)—6   LCI (landing craft, infantry)—71
LST (landing ships, tank)—47   LCT (landing craft, tank)—144.

There would, of course, be a large number of LCVP and LCM; the smaller landing craft, to complement the larger types enumerated above. The reader should be reminded that the various types of ships and craft are not interchangeable. The smallest landing craft, the 36-foot LCVP with a capacity of 30 troops, is preferred for the early waves since it presents the smallest target and enables the assaulting force to be dispersed for the (relative) safety to be thereby gained.

Sources for the additional ships and craft were not easy to come by. U.S. Navy requirements for Pacific operations had been restrained and the production rates at shipyards were at the limit. An interacting problem was the landing on the south coast of France (code-named Anvil) which was originally planned to be concurrent to Overlord. Gen. Eisenhower was expecting the two-sided envelopment of the total French land mass to benefit the penetration of the Atlantic Wall and to limit the concentration of German defenders while the Normandy landing force was in a build-up period. He was a keen proponent of the simultaneous attacks on both coasts. The landing craft problem, however, convinced him that it would not be feasible for the two landings to be concurrent. By setting Anvil one month behind Overlord, lift for a full division could be brought up from the Mediterranean for the cross-Channel operation. For the full requirements of a second add-on division there would need to be a postponement of Overlord from early May to the June moon period. This would permit an extra month of production to be added to the fleet of ships and craft. It would also cause consternation among the Russians who had been assured of a May date for Overlord.

By way of summary, a few figures are interesting. These numbers apply to the ships and craft in service on 1 June 1944, in the assault fleet for Overlord: LSTs in the U.S. 11th Amphibious Force numbered 168 and in the Royal Navy 61, all of which were built in American shipyards; LCIs numbered 124 U.S., and 121 British; LCMs numbered 216 U.S., and 265 British; and finally there were 1,089 U.S. LCVPs, and the British had 649 LCAs, their small boat equivalent.

FINAL PLANNING—TACTICAL MATTERS

The Neptune Initial Joint Plan settled many major questions, but at the same time left much planning to be done at field army and corps levels. The plan was issued in early February of 1944 by the committee of chiefs and covered the augmentation of the landing force by two additional seaborne divisions and broadening of the target beaches from 20 miles to something in excess of 50 miles. The code name "Neptune" was introduced and applied to all operational communication involving critical security data of the highest level, such as planned location and timing of the landings. Later, the Neptune name was applied to the amphibious phase of operations within the larger scope of Overlord. There was no conflict between the two connotations of Neptune since the landing information was of the highest security level.

Much of the tactical planning had a profound impact on the conduct of engineer operations. There were a number of issues that had no precedent from operations in the Mediterranean and therefore needed analysis and empirical solutions. The first matter was whether the seaborne landings should be made under cover of darkness or in broad daylight. In the case of the airborne landings, darkness was preferred, but that operation did not face prepared defenses and benefited from the darkness to achieve surprise. In the case of landings on the beaches of Sicily, the landings were made in darkness and complete surprise was achieved. The fixed defenses were relatively thin and occupied by ineffective troops. The primary defenders were first-rate German mobile forces. Had there been a preparatory bombardment, the element of surprise would have been sacrificed for no tangible gain. In the case of the British operation at Dieppe, the lessons are not totally clear, but a number of well-regarded military analysts believe that an adequate preliminary bombardment was not applied and that all measures to achieve surprise did not compensate for the absence of the softening of defenses by fire power.

The uniqueness of the situation at Normandy was that defenses provided by the Atlantic Wall were orders of magnitude stronger than encountered in any other amphibious operation. On the other hand, superior naval and air forces provided the Allied invaders with weapons to offset, to some degree, the advantage of well-engineered fortifications. The situation argued for a daylight landing. In fact, the preferred time was believed by the commanders to be approximately one hour after dawn, so as to allow this amount of time for preparatory bombardment. The time was divided about equally between air and naval forces. The solution to the problem was then along these lines. Leading waves of assault troops would commence transfer from transport shipping to small landing craft early enough so the transit to shore would gain the cover of darkness to the maximum extent possible. Preparatory bombardment would commence at the point after dawn when sunlight permitted. After the necessary length of time for softening of shore defenses, weapons would cease fire and then after a gap of time, for safety purposes, the ground forces would attack their assigned targets.

In the tradeoff of duration of preparatory bombardment versus the surprise factor, a fine line had to be drawn. As the plan turned out, the bombardment was toward the minimum side. The advantage was obviously that the defenders, after realization that this was to be a full-scale invasion, had practically no time at all to reposition reserve elements into useful defensive positions. Additionally during the weeks and months of general harassing bombing along the Atlantic Wall, no special concentration against Normandy defenses had been permitted lest the German defenders be alerted to the location of the target beaches.

From the engineer point of view, the argument for a daylight landing was even more compelling. Among engineer tasks of high priority was neutralization of the anti-landing obstacles in the tidal zone. The obstacles, previously described in some detail, were of fairly substantial construction and a portion were mined. Even with a rigorous training program, the level of expertise of the engineer troops probably never reached the point where these obstacles could have been reduced in darkness. The task was simply too large and complicated and required coordinated effort of hundreds of troops so that the burden of darkness was unthinkable.

The matter of tides was another vexing issue for planners and one that impacted on the action to neutralize the obstacles in the tidal zone. These obstacles are often referred to as "underwater obstacles", which they obviously were at high tide. An overview of the various types of obstacles was presented in the previous chapter describing how emplacement of the obstacles was commenced near the high water mark, based on Field Marshal Rommel's confident assumption that landings would be made at high tide.

Army and Navy attitudes toward the optimum landing conditions differed markedly. It was clear that landing craft passing over the obstacles at or near high tide could have their bottoms torn. Obviously, the Navy made a strong case for landing at low tide. The Army position favored high tide to avoid the long trek of troops debarking from craft which would beach at positions well seaward from the low water mark, during which time the heavily loaded engineer troops, many carrying loads in excess of 75 pounds, were vulnerable to fire from shore weapons. To appreciate the peril consider some data on English Channel tides. During the planned landing period, the rise and fall of the tide was in the range of 18 to 24 feet. At Omaha Beach, the high-water to low-water horizontal distance was typically greater than 400 yards. At Utah Beach, the bottom gradient was even more nearly flat, with the typical high-water to low-water distance being 900 yards. On the left flank of Utah, at the location of the actual landings, the distance reached approximately 1,700 yards. To these distances must be added the traverse through water from the grounded positions of the landing craft, in some locations more than four feet deep.

Since sunk landing craft at high tide are also a danger to invading troops, the Army had to yield. However, Gen. Bradley struck a compromise under which the initial landings would be timed for just past extreme low tide and would allow approximately 30 minutes for the demolition teams on Omaha Beach to work before the water depth reached two feet. Trials had shown these to be practical values. Whether this was a judicious compromise, or whether a more conservative allocation of working time for the demolition team should have been planned will remain one of the topics for long-term military history debates. The situation at Utah Beach was more favorable to the demolition teams as there was no such limitation on the time available for work on the obstacles due to the more nearly flat bottom in the tidal zone. In both cases, successive waves of landing craft would then ride the rising tide nearer to the high water mark before grounding. A further benefit to landing on the rising tide was the ease of retracting landing craft as contrasted to the possibility of landing craft being stranded during a falling tide.

Since engineer shore operations generally, and obstacle work in particular, were so profoundly influenced by tidal conditions, planners used very detailed data on tides. An English Channel Handbook prepared by the British Admiralty was included as an annex to U.S. Navy operational orders and covers pertinent locations between Cherbourg and Le Havre. The tidal stream along the French coast is quite strong in the vicinity of the landing beaches and reached its maximum of 6 knots at Pointe de Barfleur just east of Cherbourg. The tables of tides use Dover in the east and St. Helier in the west as reference points. Extracts and extrapolations from the tables for 6 June 1944 show the following data (time is double daylight saving):

Location	*St.-Vaast-la-Houge* (N. of Utah)	*Port-en-Bessin* (E. of Omaha)
First low water	0504 hours	0521 hours
First high water	1004 hours	1036 hours
Second low water	1728 hours	1745 hours
Second high water	2240 hours	2257 hours
Mean high water	22 feet	23 feet

See also Fig. 18 for tidal data for Omaha Beach.

To sum up the rationale in the derivation of the favorable landing time consider these few input items. Leading waves of the assault forces would rendezvous in the designated transport area about 12 miles from the French coast and then proceed toward the beach under cover of darkness for much of the way. Then, for approximately the first hour of useful daylight, bombarding forces would be in action against the beach. With low tide falling roughly at dawn, H-hour would be set for about an hour later, coinciding with the lifting of preparatory bombardment. For early June of 1944, three days, the 5th, 6th, and 7th had low tide close enough to the optimum to serve as feasible landing dates. These dates also provided satisfactory moonlight to facilitate air operations.

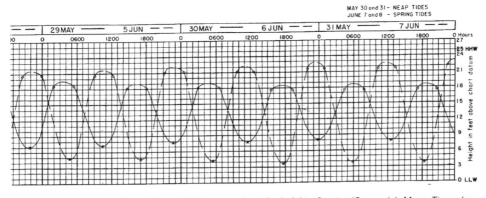

Figure 18—*Tidal Stage Data.* *These tidal curves show the height of water (Greenwich Mean Time plus two hours) above approximate level of lowest low water for Omaha Beach.*

Referring to the table of tides, it can be seen that the cycle is about twelve and one-half hours, making the day to day variation in the occurrence of low tide about one hour. It thus becomes apparent that the decision to sail for a landing on the 5th of June, or to postpone one day was simple while the decision to sail for a landing on the 6th of June was much more difficult. By postponing for another day, the occurrence of low tide was off by one hour from the preferred timing. Also, the prospect for better weather on the 7th was shaky at best.

A Typical Landing Plan

Much of the accepted doctrine on amphibious operations was to be modified to meet the situation prevailing on the Normandy beaches. Use was to be made of daylight conditions to exploit preparatory bombardment and to cope with obstacles both in the tidal zone and ashore. Thus followed the preference for a daylight landing. Another tactic introduced in Overlord was the very early landing of tanks. The more conventional practice had been to delay the arrival of armor to such time as infantry had eliminated the most dangerous antitank weapons. The availability of amphibious, dual-drive (DD) tanks was one point of motivation for early employment of armor. These tanks used a fabric envelope surrounding the vehicle to create a buoyancy chamber and could be driven by their normal treads or by a stern-mounted pair of marine propellers (Fig. 19). The primary objective of these DD-tanks was to assure the landing force of some substantial fire power between the time the bombardment lifted and until the beach could be readied for conventional artillery. Development of the duplex drive tank built upon a British-inspired concept and was pursued on a compressed schedule. A serious school of thought among American observers questioned whether the DD concept would prove to be adequately seaworthy for service in the Channel environment. Nevertheless, the key commanders directed that a mix of Shermans be modified to the DD concept and those conventionally waterproofed be incorporated into the landing force. The latter were capable of submerging in seven feet of water depth.

From among the three regimental landing plans (8th Infantry, 16th Infantry, and 116th Infantry), the 116th on the western sector of Omaha is presented here as an example (Fig. 20). Before focusing on the anomalous features, observe that there are some conventional items about the plan. First, the Regiment is to land with two battalions abreast, or in line, for a total of four rifle companies in line. Since the rifle companies had been reorganized into 30-man boat teams and six boats are allocated to each company, the infantry strength of the initial assault appears to total 720 officers and men. No distinction is made between LCVPs and LCAs since they are of similar size except to note that Company A of the 116th was brought ashore by the Royal Navy. It is somewhat strange that of the four companies, only Company A, on the extreme right flank, is from the 1st Battalion.

The mix of armor and engineers with the assaulting rifle companies is shown on the 116th Regimental Combat Team typical landing plan. The DD-tanks are only with

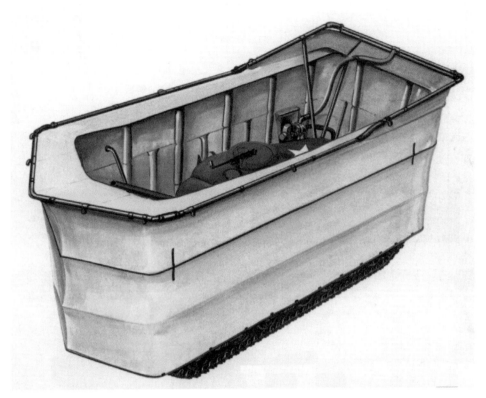

Figure 19—*Dual Drive Tank with Flotation Gear in Sea-going Position.* *DD-tanks achieved an amphibious capability by means of a watertight appendage to a Sherman tank consisting of a fabric shell on a folding steel framework, along with a pair of marine propellers and a small rudder. The abbreviated development cycle for the flotation system proved to be inadequate for assurance that the DD tank could cope with the rough water frequently encountered in the Channel. The decision to include DD-tanks in the early waves was made at high levels of command with limited technical evaluation.*

the right-side battalion on Dog White and Dog Green beaches. Each of these beaches was assigned a tank company which consisted of 16 tanks in three platoons of five tanks each, plus one command tank. However, on Easy Green and Dog Red, the tank company is landed by LCTs. A question naturally crops up as to the feasibility of landing tanks off of LCT craft at low tide. If the answer is that it can be done, one must wonder whether the inherent risks of DD-tanks swimming in to shore were warranted. A related question raised by the plan is why the right side tanks are scheduled to arrive five minutes before those on the left. Clear answers to these questions have not been uncovered.

Engineer units are prominently positioned in the typical landing plan (see Fig. 20 on following page) which covers the initial assault and more than three hours of scheduled arrivals on the beach. The four early waves, due to land within a span of about 10 minutes, include an allocation of 13 LCMs for the 146th Engineer Combat Battalion. This number of craft can accommodate approximately 500 troops, which

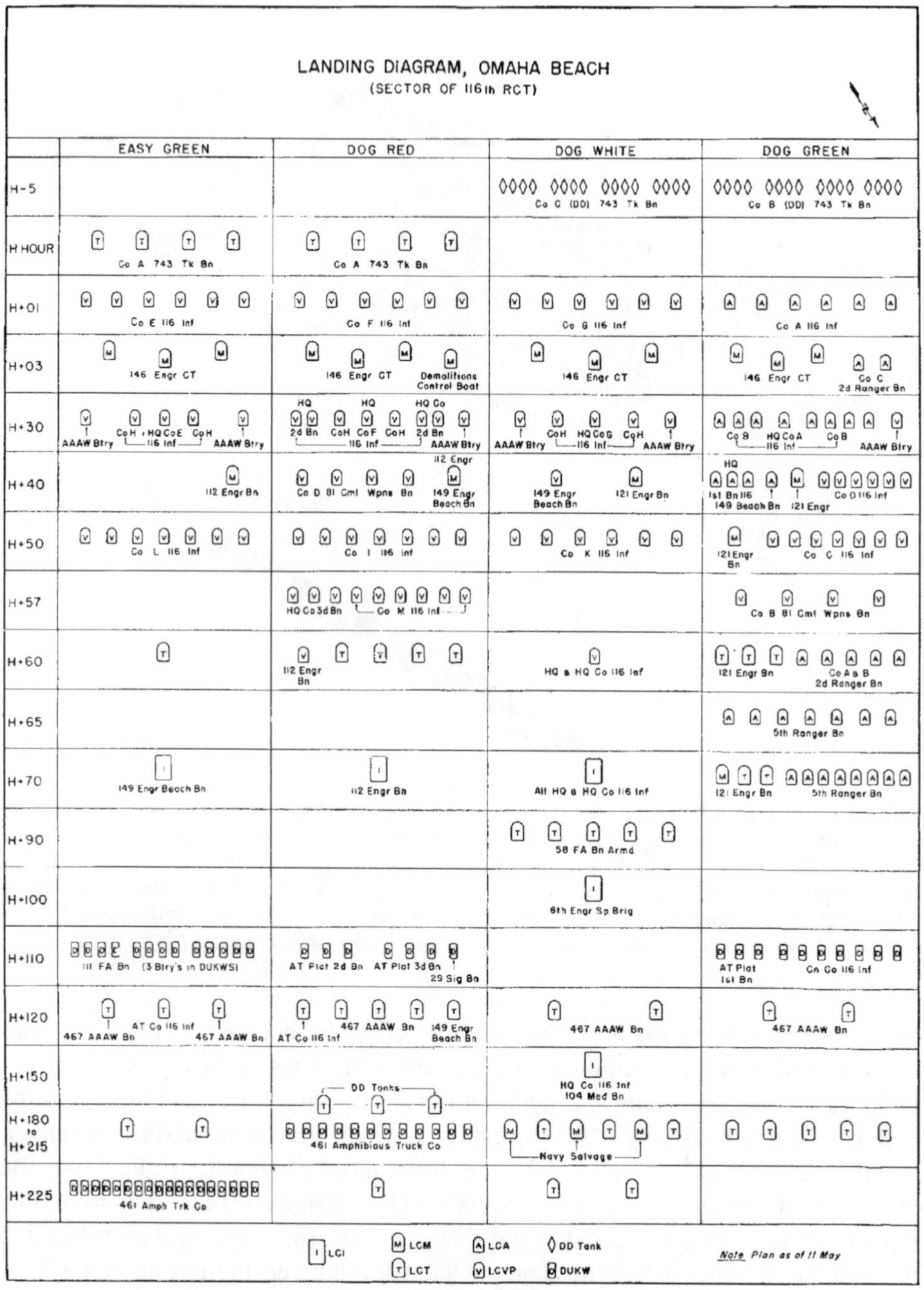

LANDING DIAGRAM, OMAHA BEACH
(SECTOR OF 116th RCT)

	EASY GREEN	DOG RED	DOG WHITE	DOG GREEN
H-5			◊◊◊◊ ◊◊◊◊ ◊◊◊◊ ◊◊◊◊ Co C (DD) 743 Tk Bn	◊◊◊◊ ◊◊◊◊ ◊◊◊◊ ◊◊◊◊ Co B (DD) 743 Tk Bn
H HOUR	Co A 743 Tk Bn	Co A 743 Tk Bn		
H+01	Co E 116 Inf	Co F 116 Inf	Co G 116 Inf	Co A 116 Inf
H+03	146 Engr CT	146 Engr CT Demolitions Control Boat	146 Engr CT	146 Engr CT Co C 2d Ranger Bn
H+30	CoH · HQCoE CoH AAAW Btry —116 Inf— AAAW Btry	HQ HQ HQ Co 2d Bn CoH CoF CoH 2d Bn —116 Inf— AAAW Btry	CoH HQCoG CoH AAAW Btry —116 Inf— AAAW Btry	Co B HQCoA Co B HQ —116 Inf— AAAW Btry
H+40	112 Engr Bn	Co D Bl Cml Wpns Bn 112 Engr 149 Engr Beach Bn	149 Engr Beach Bn 121 Engr Bn	Ist Bn 116 Co D 116 Inf HQ 149 Beach Bn 121 Engr
H+50	Co L 116 Inf	Co I 116 Inf	Co K 116 Inf	121 Engr Bn Co G 116 Inf
H+57		HQ Co 3d Bn Co M 116 Inf		Co B Bl Cml Wpns Bn
H+60		112 Engr Bn	HQ & HQ Co 116 Inf	121 Engr Bn Co A & B 2d Ranger Bn
H+65				5th Ranger Bn
H+70	149 Engr Beach Bn	112 Engr Bn	All HQ & HQ Co 116 Inf	121 Engr Bn 5th Ranger Bn
H+90			58 FA Bn Armd	
H+100			6th Engr Sp Brig	
H+110	III FA Bn (3 Btry's in DUKWS)	AT Plat 2d Bn AT Plat 3d Bn 29 Sig Bn		AT Plat Cn Co 116 Inf Ist Bn
H+120	AT Co 116 Inf 467 AAAW Bn 467 AAAW Bn	AT Co 116 Inf 467 AAAW Bn 149 Engr Beach Bn	467 AAAW Bn	467 AAAW Bn
H+150		DD Tanks	HQ Co 116 Inf 104 Med Bn	
H+180 to H+215		461 Amphibious Truck Co	Navy Salvage	
H+225	461 Amph Trk Co			

I LCI M LCM A LCA ◊ DD Tank
T LCT V LCVP B DUKW

Note Plan as of 11 May

Figure 20—Landing Diagram, Omaha Beach (Sector of 116th RCT). Distribution of landing force is shown for each subsector of the western beaches, along with scheduled time of arrival ashore.

just happens to be about one-half the strength of the Special Engineer Task Force. The Task Force, under command of Lt. Col. John O'Neill, was assigned the mission of creating gaps, each 50 yards wide, on each beach segment, except that on the broader Easy Red beach there were to be six gaps. Col. O'Neill's Task Force included another engineer battalion, the 299th, the source for the teams designated to operate in the sector of the 16th Infantry. The structure of the teams was slightly complicated, being a mix of both Army and Navy personnel. This subject will be treated in more detail later.

The major units of engineer troops were due ashore shortly afterward. The sector of the 116th Infantry Regiment was to become the 29th Division sector when division headquarters arrived ashore and assumed command of its elements which had been operating initially under 1st Division control. In the meantime, the engineer build-up resembled that for a full division. Referring to the typical landing diagram, it can be seen that there were two battalions of combat engineers arriving ashore rather early: the 121st Engineers (organic to the 29th Division) and the 112th Engineers (attached to the 29th Division). Each of the two battalions had two teams scheduled for H plus 40 minutes, arriving by LCM craft. The 6th Engineer Special Brigade, assigned to operate in support of the 29th Division, also had two teams arriving at that same time. These would be reconnaissance and command personnel. At H plus 60 minutes, the build-up of the battalions continued. At H plus 70 minutes, a sort of peak was scheduled with the arrival of two LCI craft with engineers of the 149th and 112th Battalions and several LCT craft with elements of the 121st Battalion.

There are numerous and diverse values published on the proportion of engineer troops in the assaulting force during the Normandy invasion. The variations in these figures can be readily understood by reference to the typical landing plan. The initial waves, that is to say those landed by H plus 3 minutes, contain a proportion of engineers at about 50 percent. Then, the wave due at H plus 30 minutes brought in additional infantry along with some anti-aircraft artillery but no engineers. At that point the proportion of engineers dropped to something on the order of 30 percent. Thereafter the proportion started to climb when at H plus 40 minutes a wave landed which included about one-half engineers. This brought the cumulative proportion back over 40 percent. This proportion, in round numbers, held to about H plus 100 minutes at which time there was a steady decline until the long term average set in with the continuing build-up of forces ashore. Certainly, an overall view would lead to a conclusion that engineer troops were represented in the opposed landing at the Normandy beaches in much greater proportion than their field army strength would have predicted. As to an exact numerical value on the proportion of engineer troops in the assault force, an analyst would first need to define the precise point at which the assault was complete and this process leads to endless, pointless speculation.

APPLICABLE TECHNICAL DEVELOPMENTS

A few technical developments in military hardware contributed to the success of the Normandy invasion. In some cases, a new item was useful in general ground warfare, mine detectors for example, and in other cases an item which would be useful in general amphibious operations fortuitously became available in time for the Normandy invasion. Probably the only developmental equipments prepared specifically for Normandy were a collection of appendages, worked up by British technicians to be fitted to armored vehicles. Among these, the dual-drive tank was the only type which found acceptance among American forces.

The concept of the DUKW (an amphibian truck) originated in the Office of Scientific Research and Development (OSRD) in the effort to improve amphibious logistics. The head of transportation research within OSRD, Hartley Rowe, had been with United Fruit Company before the war and had faced the problem of getting banana ships loaded in remote places where the closest port was not an ideal solution. Apparently his vision sparked the project. However, it remained for Palmer Putnam to make the concept work. He recognized that the General Motors two and one-half ton truck would be a feasible chassis and that a means to incorporate buoyancy was to build into the body a series of sealed, empty tanks. A pair of small marine propellers would drive the vehicle when afloat. The very large tires were to operate at low inflation pressure when traversing a sandy beach and then to be re-inflated, from the driver's cab, when operating on hard surface roads. One asset of the proposed design which made the vehicle attractive for the military environment was that 90 percent of its parts were common with the GMC two and one-half ton truck. Performance-wise, the vehicle was reasonably seaworthy, could do five knots in calm seas, and could travel on roads at 50 mph. The nomenclature came from General Motors where the 'D' indicated the year (1942), 'U' stood for utility, 'K' described the four-wheel drive, and 'W' meant that there were two rear-driving axles. General Motors produced four prototypes and early testing yielded encouraging results (Fig. 21).

Unfortunately, acceptance of the new amphibian vehicle at some key Army agencies was not immediately forthcoming. There were a few enthusiastic sponsors scattered around the Pentagon. The main problem confronting the protagonists was that several early attempts to produce an amphibian cargo carrier had been clearly unsuccessful. Finally, Col. Anthony McAuliffe (later to be conspicuous at Bastogne in the Ardennes) put on a presentation before Gen. Brehon Somervell, commander of Services of Supply. Immediately following this session an order for 2,000 vehicles was placed. Most of these were directed to the Engineer Amphibian Command at Camp Edwards, Massachusetts. A development section had been established at the EAC in late August of 1942. A test program covered both the General Motors' DUKW and the Alligator, a track-laying vehicle in wide use throughout the Marine Corps. Both vehicles performed well in the test, but the edge went to the DUKW as a work-horse cargo transporter. Later, in the winter of 1942, a Coast Guard boat foundered in seas off Cape Cod. A DUKW was dispatched from Camp Edwards and succeeded in a difficult rescue.

Figure 21—*Amphibious Truck (DUKW).* *The vehicle was developed primarily as a cargo carrier in logistic applications but served also as a tactical vehicle with five-knot speed in moderate seas and 50 mph overland.*

This event proved to be a clincher and the DUKW went on to a role in amphibious operations in all theaters. The vehicles demonstrated superior versatility and indeed exceeded all expectations. While they were intended to be logistic equipment applied to shuttling cargo from offshore ocean-going ships to locations behind the beach, they also filled a tactical role. At Normandy on D-day, DUKWs served as an artillery platform and appeared quite early in landing plans. In the Southwest Pacific Theater they served as launching platforms for heavy rocket bombardment during landings on hostile shores.

Tank dozers reached the development phase in 1942 as an outgrowth of several related tactical equipment requirements. The first came from reports on British experiences in their Eighth Army operations in North Africa, which eventually reached the Mechanical Equipment Section of the Engineer Board. The problem faced was an excessive rate of losses among bulldozer operators working in forward, exposed locations. The first approach to solve the problem attempted to install shields of steel plate in critical locations on the dozer. In due time, similar reports began to arrive from U.S. forces in Tunisia and New Georgia in the Pacific. However, the more effective the protective measures became, the closer the result began to resemble a tank. Concurrently, the idea of fitting a dozer blade to a tank hull was evolving. In this case, the problem being attacked was the rapid removal of mines. The process of ex-

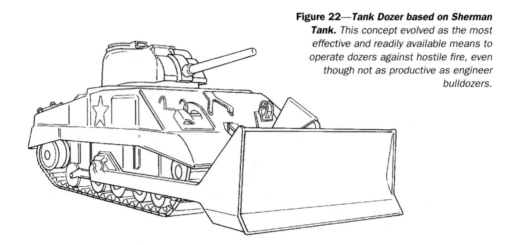

Figure 22—*Tank Dozer based on Sherman Tank.* *This concept evolved as the most effective and readily available means to operate dozers against hostile fire, even though not as productive as engineer bulldozers.*

ploding mines in place never proved as fast nor as safe as desired so, an alternative approach was under consideration by which the mines would be excavated. The addition of the dozer blade to a tank was expected to enable coverage of large areas rapidly using a small crew, with the crew in a protected environment.

For the application to excavation, various dozer blade configurations were tested. Initially, the emphasis was on blades with teeth; these produced a plowing action. Industrial concerns cooperated with the development project and supplied the blades for experimentation. In particular, the LeTourneau and LaPlante-Choate organizations made valuable contributions. The general trend of testing showed that a medium tank could operate very well as a dozer, that a conventional blade was a satisfactory compromise as compared to special-design blades, and that the tank dozer produced adequate traction to overcome substantial barriers. However, the productive work rate for a tank dozer did not match that of a conventional bulldozer. A general conclusion can be drawn that the tank dozer would be a great asset to engineer units in extremely high risk applications even though its cost would mean that limited numbers of units could be expected. Operations on the beaches of Normandy were just such an application and the presence of tank-dozers solved many difficult obstacle problems (Fig. 22). Meanwhile, efforts to produce an armored cab appendage for conventional bulldozers were successful, and the armored tractor entered service in the Pacific theaters.

Note has been made in this account of the extensive use of mine fields on the shores of Normandy as a consequence of Field Marshal Rommel's conviction regarding their effectiveness. The Atlantic Wall defenses contained many millions of units of all types: antitank and antipersonnel, metallic and non-metallic. Engineer planners at Fort Belvoir, while somewhat lagging behind their European counterparts, did also anticipate the coming importance of mine warfare, even in the pre-war years.

Under the auspices of the Engineer Board, a request was made to the National Defense Research Committee (NDRC) for assistance in developing a countermeasure for antitank mines. Tentative specifications called for detection of a typical antitank mine buried at a depth of 18 inches, along with such standard requirements as simplicity of operation and resistance to the field environment. This project was launched in September of 1940. During the period of NDRC cooperation, the Board continued its in-house efforts. Both groups pursued improvements in commercially available detectors which were in use in such fields as prospecting for mineral deposits. By the summer of 1941 both lines of investigation resulted in the firm Metal Locators submitting a unit with reasonable sensitivity in a rather lightweight package. The NDRC product came from the Hazeltine firm and by comparison was heavier and more bulky in form. Notwithstanding the evaluation results the latter organization was selected for further development on the basis of greater capability to see the project through to production.

The service item came to be called the SCR-625 by virtue of procurement through Signal Corps channels. Its configuration may be seen in Fig. 23. A search coil, in the form of a thin disk, is mounted on the lower end of an exploring rod, six feet in length. The search coil, operating in the audio frequency range, contains both transmitting and receiving elements, being an echo-type of device. When a metal object is encountered a signal is generated, then converted to a warning sound by a shoulder-mounted amplifier. While the capability for detection to a depth of 18 inches was never at-

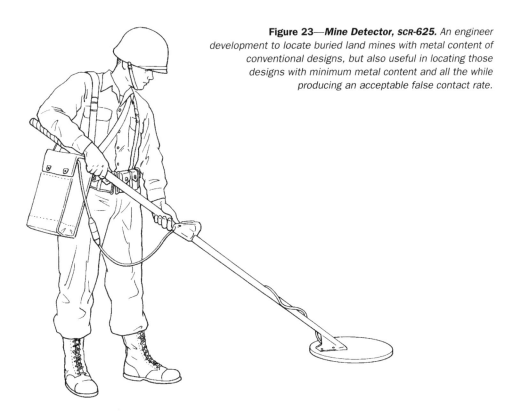

Figure 23—*Mine Detector, SCR-625.* *An engineer development to locate buried land mines with metal content of conventional designs, but also useful in locating those designs with minimum metal content and all the while producing an acceptable false contact rate.*

tained, the instrument was an overall success and a great contributor to speed and safety in mine detection.

Some limitations did become apparent after service experience began to accumulate and, therefore, development activity continued. When the detector did malfunction the most likely source of the problem was found to be moisture entering the electronic assemblies. Otherwise, engineer soldiers found that sweeping large expanses of terrain for hour after hour with the 7.5 pound detector could tax one's endurance. Also, the long-handle design was not adaptable to operating in the prone position. Lastly, operation of the detector in soils with high concentration of magnetic substance produced a high rate of false signals and slowed operational progress. None of the models expected to supersede the SCR-625 were available for service during Normandy landing operations.

TRAINING AT THE ASSAULT TRAINING CENTER

It was not a new experience for American military personnel to be put through intensive training experiences. That had been the primary means for building an Army of some 90 divisions and numerous separate units, and their support elements, in the amazingly short span of time up to May of 1944. Several of the training venues were especially relevant to this account. The establishment on Cape Cod of the Engineer Amphibian Command, and its neighbor, the Amphibious Training Center for joint exercises at the divisional level, was the initial effort to formulate doctrine and create proficient troop units. The 1st Engineer Amphibian Brigade benefited immeasurably from its short stay with the Command. Later, the Command moved to Camp Carrabelle on the Florida Gulf Coast where the later Brigades continued their training. When the Navy assumed control of all amphibious activity, this training shifted to Fort Pierce, also in Florida. Still later some of the units destined for the Normandy landing force participated in practice landings on the shores of the Chesapeake Bay.

Meanwhile there was continuing amphibious training activity in the Mediterranean Theater where further landings were constantly being contemplated. In the spring of 1943 Fifth Army established an Invasion Training Center at a site just south of Arzue on the Algerian coast east of Oran. The 531st Engineer Shore Regiment provided school troops which conducted demonstrations and supported infantry divisions. Fifth Army also established an Engineer Training Center at an abandoned French Foreign Legion fort in the Moroccan desert which concentrated on realistic mine warfare, including a final exercise with extensive live fire. This course served to send qualified instructors back to their units and propagate a high level of expertise. The units which joined the forces building in the U.K. following their transfer from the Mediterranean brought the benefits of these training experiences to First Army.

The requirement for an Assault Training Center in Britain grew from two prevailing problems. First, the invading troops needed to complete their training under the most realistic conditions that could be prepared. There is an implication here that the staff of the Center would need to study the fortifications and obstacles along the

German-held coast to determine what would be encountered during an invasion. The second area to be covered at the Assault Training Center was the development of doctrine for the conduct of landing operations against specific target beaches. There were numerous tactical issues not included in the planning studies of COSSAC, typical items being daylight versus darkness landings, the mix of weapons for assault troops, formations best suited to overcome defenses, and the like. The Theater Commander of U.S. forces preferred that the staff at the Center use its own resources, including experimentation where appropriate, rather than wait on guidance from planners as to doctrine for the invasion.

Assignment as Commanding Officer for the new Assault Training Center went to Lt. Col. Paul Thompson then (January 1943) on duty at the Office of the Chief of Engineers. His contributions on the subject of assault of fortified positions were previously noted as was his duty as observer of German Army performance. In the new position, he had to quickly become familiar with the situation at European Theater headquarters including a review of voluminous existing documentation and a sampling of official thinking. Among the high priority tasks were preparation of a plan, selection of a training site, and assembly of a staff. The approval process for the plan was expedited by discussion and submittal of increments as progress was achieved. The plan was complete by mid-April and approved in due course.

Site selection proved difficult. The general situation was that the British Combined Operations Command, the Royal Navy, and the U.S. Navy had occupied all the most suitable locations for amphibious training during the four years of war. Nevertheless, a feasible site was found at a place called Appledore-Woolacombe, Woolacombe for short, on the northwest shore of Devon in southwest Britain. Probably the site had not been taken because of prevailing stormy weather and rough water. Overall, Woolacombe satisfied requirements enumerated in the plan. It was accessible to areas where U.S. troops would concentrate for training prior to the invasion. The 10,000 yards of beach, beach exits, and surrounding area were adequate for maneuver of regimental-size landing formations. Similarity to probable, but unknown at the time, landing beaches of Normandy was striking; the range of tides was up to 26 feet, the surf was strong, the horizontal distance from low tide to high tide was in the range of 400 to 500 yards. The nearby harbor of Appledore was adequate for use by supporting naval contingents. Finally, extensive billeting facilities were available in the vicinity.

In the matters pertaining to doctrine which would guide landing force tactics, the approach was to form a Special Doctrine Board. The Board Chairman was Col. Louis Chase, Chief of Staff at the ATC. Composition of the Board was broadly based, extending to all services both American and British and including representation from both continental U.S. agencies, as well as those of the European Theater. Apparently, the deliberations of the Board were spirited and ranged widely over reasonably pertinent topics. The main issue was determination of the most favorable tactics for success in the *Fight for the First 1,000 Yards*. The origin of this term is not certain so it is most likely a coincidence, but Field Marshal Rommel maintained a strong objective that the first 1,000 yards of beach be densely mined. A prominent discussion item was analysis of the outcome of the Dieppe raid. The British view held that the disaster forced one to the conclusion that the fight for a beachhead against strong defenses, as were building along the Atlantic Wall, had an inherently low success probability. The consensus of American thinking had it that the negative position was based on incomplete study. It was a fact that Canadian tanks did make shore and at least initially were abreast of the infantry. Therefore, given control of air and sea, and with a strong follow-up to the leading waves, the prospects for a successful invasion could reach acceptable levels.

Two of the findings of the Special Doctrine Board led to solutions of practical problems and were immediately significant to ATC planning. The Board recommended that tanks should accompany assaulting infantry and therefore be included in the first wave. The ratio would be two tanks for each infantry team. It has been noted earlier in this account that the early landing of tanks was a departure from tactics employed in the previous major amphibious operations and that the extent of fixed defensive measures in the Atlantic Wall required heavier fire power under local control. Obviously, the Board drew its own conclusion from the Dieppe experience on the benefits of bringing tanks ashore in the early waves. The second matter pertained to the structure of an infantry assault team. The difficulty stemmed from the size of the standard infantry platoon consisting of three 12-man rifle squads plus a platoon leader, and possibly several overstrength members. The smallest and most appropriate landing craft for the leading waves was the LCVP which could accommodate 30 troops. Therefore, organizational integrity would be lost during the most critical phase if the standard platoon was to be maintained. Moreover, a revised team structure would enable a new emphasis to be placed on military specialties most suited to the cross-Channel assault.

The new organization for the infantry assault team not only adjusted the numbers of troops to match its landing craft, it also redistributed the assets of the standard infantry company and added additional capabilities of an engineer-type. The revised 30-man structure was comprised of an 8-man Rifle Section, 4-man BAR Section, 4-man Light Mortar Section, 4-man Bangalore Torpedo Section, 4-man Bazooka Section, 4-man Explosives Section, and a 2-man Flamethrower Section. The main loss, but not a severe one, compared to the standard infantry small unit, was in Browning automatic rifles which were normally one per 12-man squad. In the modified unit structure there were two per 30-man unit. But, the offsetting gains were substantial. New capabilities were integrated into a small infantry unit by the flamethrower, explosives, and bangalore torpedo sections. Also, the bazooka and light mortar placed in the team were from the standard infantry company, but, under the new structure, were immediately available to the small unit commander.

In keeping with the objective of realistic experience for troops going through the program, creating suitable facilities at the ATC was a major undertaking. Col. Thompson made an effort to have nearby civilians evacuated but was not successful. Shortly after the site was turned over U.S. occupation moved forward with gusto. Not only were tactical facilities required, but a host of housekeeping necessities were provided ranging from shelter, roads and water supply to waste disposal.

The necessities for training were full-scale and extensive. A replica of a German fortified position was built including concrete structures with walls six feet thick. The position occupied an area in excess of one square mile. Continuous attention was placed on accurate reproduction of fortifications and obstacles so that when aerial photographs showed any new development, the facility was upgraded accordingly. At one point, a new concrete sea wall was detected by aerial reconnaissance and promptly duplicated on the practice beach. In fact, two walls were built so that they could alternately be breached and repaired, in tandem, to meet training schedules. Individual ranges were provided for demolitions practice, mine clearing, and booby trap and flamethrower training.

Operating procedures were spelled out in the approved planning document. A complement of school troops would be on duty at the Training Center for the purpose of test and demonstration of assault techniques and to assist in training the combat teams. Cadres from the combat teams were to have advance training prior to the arrival of their units at the Center, and would assist in the training of their units. The training program for a Regimental Combat Team would be three weeks. A fitting conclusion to the total experience was the climactic, realistic landing exercise with live fire for the full Regimental Team.

The distribution of effort within the total training period illustrates the intensity with which the student soldiers were immersed in the subject matter. Individual training covered the skills comprising the Infantry Assault Team and received 25 percent of the training time. An example of the level of detail is seen in the topics taken up by the explosives section. They were drilled with pole-type and satchel-type charges, and advised on use of recommended and improvised charges. They worked with various combinations of fuzes and explosive materials. The weapons sections worked on such matters as target designation and coordination of fires. Demonstrations and critiques took up 22 percent of the program. Problems associated with Navy cooperation and familiarization with landing craft were treated to the extent of 20 percent of training. Company and battalion-size exercises received 14 percent of the program and the balance of 19 percent went to the regimental landing.

Operations at the training center were conducted to highly professional standards. The crucial deadline for starting training was met when the 116th Regimental Combat Team of the 29th Division arrived on 1 September 1943. The 29th Division sent all its regiments through and the 116th even returned later for a refresher program. The 4th Division sent all its regiments. The 1st Division sent only its 16th Infantry, but this variation was justified by the Division's accumulated service and training in amphibious operations. The commendations from the 29th regarding the effectiveness of the program were extremely high (as noted in the quote on the following page). Later, a large group of key commanders at Field Army and Theater level made an inspection visit at one of the final regimental-size graduation exercises. They were especially laudatory regarding the realism built into the program.

GENERAL C.H. GERHARDT
29TH INFANTRY DIVISION
DECEMBER 1943

"I desire to commend the U.S. Assault Training Center, and members of its staff for the superb training facilities and opportunities afforded the 29th Division during the past three months. . . . I am confident that this Division which has taken full advantage of the facilities at this Center will be capable of a successful landing on the shore of Fortress Europe."

EXERCISES AT SLAPTON SANDS

Despite the successful program at Woolacombe, an assessment at the highest command levels found that even larger scale exercises should be conducted to test and continually improve the readiness of landing forces. It was particularly required that preparatory bombardment by air and naval units and movements of ground forces be closely coordinated. Only a very large training site would serve the purpose. Satisfactory characteristics were found at a location on Start Bay on the south coast of Devon, specifically Slapton Sands. The British government took control of the site under war powers and directed the evacuation of 30,000 acres, along with a local population of 3,000 people, in the short space of six weeks. On 20 December 1943, the site was turned over to military authorities.

By any standard of comparison the exercises at Slapton Sands were major events. A characteristic of this series of training actions was their comprehensive nature ranging as they did from planning, transport and marshalling of troops, embarkation, transit to the naval transport area at the far shore, transfer to landing craft and related evolutions leading to the assault, and finally to the establishment of a beachhead. These large scale, detailed exercises enabled the high command to feel confident that no stone had been left unturned.

The first landing exercise was Duck I in January 1944. The units involved were the 29th Division and the 1st Engineer Special Brigade with the number of troops at a total of 10,000. The Brigade was back from Italy for only a few weeks and had not yet been through a refit. A minimum of equipment was quickly gathered together and the force sailed intact on schedule. Following the completion of the exercise an extended critique produced voluminous observations: that landings were made quite close to the assigned positions; assault waves bunched up one against another, and troops within a wave needed more teamwork and initiative; insufficient fire was placed on known enemy positions; equipment loads inhibited the movement of troops across the beaches; vehicles failed to pass through an assembly point to remove waterproofing; radio voice procedure was faulty, particularly in the maintenance of security; and so forth. In February, the succeeding exercises, Duck II and Duck III, were held for the training of those elements of the two organizations which were not included in Duck I, with results that were somewhat improved.

Early 1944 was also the time when the new Overlord command was installed and promptly set about reworking the existing COSSAC draft outline plan. With the incorporation of a second U.S. landing beach in the new plan, the 1st Engineer Special Brigade was moved to VII Corps and its subsequent encounters with Slapton Sands were in team with the 4th Infantry Division. Thus, in March, the force destined to land at Utah Beach began its large scale practice landings with Exercise Beaver. Several of these included regimental landing teams and a full complement of engineer shore party support from the 1st Brigade.

Meanwhile, details were emerging from the new Overlord plan on the formation for the Omaha Beach assault. The first major test for this force was Exercise Fox, also in March, and involving 17,000 troops. Two RCTs landed. The 16th Infantry team included elements of the 1st and 20th Engineers plus shore parties from the 37th Engineers of the 5th Brigade. The 116th Infantry team included elements of the 121st and 112th Engineers plus shore parties from the 149th Engineers. The period for preparation of Exercise Fox was quite short since arrangements were contingent upon what could be learned from the revised Overlord plan. As a consequence the exercise did not proceed as smoothly as expected, neither in the mounting, nor in beach operations. Nevertheless the comments that came out of the critique did not represent serious flaws in the qualifications of the troops. For example, the waterproofing of vehicles could have been more effective and the available DUKWs could have been used more efficiently.

The first of the two final exercises at Slapton Sands was planned for the Utah Beach landing force. Generally known as Exercise Tiger this was to be full-scale, realistic, and to include live fire naval support. The schedule allotted the period 22–30 April to Tiger. This is the event about which much has been written, both in popular journals and in serious military history, and which has been erroneously described in both essential matters and in peripheral details. Sensational accounts, which charged that high-level defense authorities had attempted to conceal scandalous facts, appeared in profusion at about the time of the 40th anniversary of the D-day landings. Several objective attempts to piece together a picture of events have been made, but appear only in specialized journals, and are difficult to locate. Since one of the major engineer units of the Normandy landings was at the center of the Tiger affair, a brief effort will be made here to set the record straight. First, consider the dates, which are quoted over a range of 10 days to two days. The variation can be explained by the intention of most of the Slapton Sands exercises to include preliminary events such as marshalling the troops, briefings, embarkation, and an excursion in the English Channel. There are any number of points at which the exercise can be said to have begun. Several days were devoted to actual operations ashore. The simulated H-hour was fixed at 0730 hours on the morning of 27 April, with further unloading scheduled for numerous times throughout the day. A convoy of LSTs bringing in follow-on elements of the force was scheduled for the morning of the second day of operations ashore. In summary, the operation included one day devoted to a D-day rehearsal followed by building the beachhead.

At the time of the exercise, the Royal Navy carried the major burden of tasks at sea. For the D-day (simulated) convoys, channels were swept free of mines and the attack transports of the landing force were covered by destroyer escorts. The danger of enemy interference with the exercise was certainly not simulated. At about 0400 hours, the transports anchored, these being mainly U.S. APA-type ships that were assigned for Normandy duty. Lowering of landing craft (LCVP-type) for the assault waves commenced promptly and was accomplished without a hitch. However, it later developed that the LCTs bringing armor ashore were behind schedule and the best solution to this problem was to delay H-hour by one hour. Since the troop commanders had left for shore to witness the assault, the naval commander made this decision without consultation and attempted to notify all ships, landing craft, bombarding forces, and assault troops. This was not completely accomplished and the resulting confusion flawed the early phase of the landing. The naval bombardment was canceled for safety reasons. Nevertheless, performance improved through the morning and by afternoon the exercise had recovered to schedule.

Meanwhile, a more serious problem was developing. Follow-on convoys were sailing from Plymouth on a schedule to land the next morning, the morning of 28 April. One of these was Convoy T-4; consisting of eight U.S. tank landing ships, (LSTs), specifically numbers 515, 496, 511, 531, 58, 499, 289, and 507. At the time of sailing H.M.S. *Azalea*, a corvette, was the only escort vessel with the convoy. H.M.S. *Scimitar*, an old WW I destroyer, had been scheduled as the main escort, but had been rammed the night before and was ordered to remain in port for repairs. A message reporting the accident went to Commander in Chief, Plymouth, but no copy reached Commander Force "U" (transporting the VII Corps landing force), who would have been the authority to dispatch a relief vessel to substitute for the damaged destroyer.

German E-boats based at Cherbourg were more active than usual on the evening of 27 April. The heavy volume of radio traffic had caught their attention. These E-boats packed a powerful punch for their size. They were 108-footers driven by Daimler-Benz diesels capable of speeds up to 35 knots, except for a few which were supercharged and even faster, had a range of 700 miles, and a crew of 21. Main armament consisted of twin 21-inch fixed torpedo tubes with two reloads, supplemented by small cannon which were 20-mm on most boats, but included 37-mm guns on some others. Seven boats in a formation of two columns slipped out of the harbor and eluded a Royal Navy patrol of three motor torpedo boats. Additionally, a line of vessels was distributed between Start Point (close by Slapton Sands) and a point near Portland Harbor to provide a defensive screen and again there was a failure to detect the E-boats.

Around midnight of 27–28 April the E-boats made contact with the LST convoy, after the convoy position had been fixed by radio location. Initially, one section of E-boats identified a target at 3000 meters as a pair of destroyers (obviously a misidentification) and one boat launched a double salvo while a second boat followed with single torpedoes. Both target vessels were hit. Shortly afterwards, the second section of E-boats arrived on the scene and launched torpedoes, all of which failed to explode. At this point it became obvious to the attacking E-boats that they were dealing with shallow draft vessels, probably tank landing ships, and cannon fire commenced. Later a third section of E-boats arrived and found one ship burning fiercely and putting out heavy black smoke, causing the boat to report a tanker on fire. Both these E-boats launched torpedoes and a third LST was hit (see quote below).

OBERLEUTNANT ZUR SEE HANS SCHIRREN
CAPTAIN, E-BOAT S-145
LYME BAY, 28 APRIL 1944

"We approached the convoy from the Northwest (coast side) and had no problem attacking from the rear on convoy in view of our superior speed. We normally did 34 to 36 knots out of the harbor, even when dropping mines. Only when firing torpedoes did we have to bring speed down to around 10 knots. The high speed was needed to avoid radar plotting by the escorts. We met several LST's and launched two torpedoes at each vessel at close range, the majority of which must have passed harmlessly under the bottom of the shallow craft. Two LSTs (531 and 507) were hit squarely, while one of the torpedoes launched by S-145 (around 0228 hours) developed depth control problems and became a 'surface runner' yet somehow it hit an LST which later was reported to have been LST 289."

The survivors accounts of the action were even more confused. A summary of events shows that flares were first seen at times between 2352 hours (27 April) and 0020 hours (28 April), with the later time showing up more frequently among tabulated data; an underwater jar was felt at times between 0104 hours and 0128 hours (28 April); observation of the first torpedoed and burning ship is reported between 0202 hours and 0215 hours; observation of second torpedoed and burning ship was between 0208 hours and 0221 hours, and observation of third torpedoed and burning ship was between 0221 hours and 0230 hours Actually, the record of events reconstructed from survivor reports is somewhat more comprehensive than these extracts, but a few salient items in the sequence can be inferred. Probably, the first torpedoes impacted their targets at a few minutes after 0100 hours, the time at which underwater jars were felt nearby. The LST reporting this observation was next in line to LST 507, the first stricken ship. Burning was observed an hour later aboard LST 289, probably indicating that the fires were building before they became visible to other ships in the convoy.

The main incontrovertible facts are the losses. LSTs 507 and 531 were sunk. LST 289 took a torpedo hit on the stern, promptly launched its LCVPs, and by skillful maneuvering of five of these craft was kept on course to reach Dartmouth. Personnel losses totalled 639 killed and missing distributed as follows: LST 507—Navy–71, Army –131; LST 531—Navy–114, Army–310; LST 289—Navy–13. Nearly all the Army losses were from the 1st Engineer Special Brigade, organic and attached units. The types of units aboard the LSTs were to prepare for and operate dump and depot facilities as these were established during the phase of the exercise devoted to beachhead building. Typical units included amphibian truck companies, quartermaster truck companies, quartermaster railhead companies, chemical decontamination companies, and the like. Cargo losses per ship amounted, on the average, to 22 DUKW vehicles and several dozen other vehicles ranging from one-quarter ton to two and one-half ton trucks. When the report on the losses reached Gen. Eisenhower, he passed the word to the Combined Chiefs that his reserve of LST vessels had reached zero.

Leo Gross—Corporal
818th Engineer Aviation Battalion,
3d Platoon, Company C
1st Engineer Special Brigade
Operation Tiger, 28 April 1944

"It was almost dark when we boarded an LST. Several hours after leaving the dock we were roused by what sounded like an approaching thunderstorm. Going on deck, we could see that the flashes had to be gunfire and other ground-level explosions. I asked someone what the shooting was about and he replied that it was possibly to make 'dry run' more realistic. It was not long, however, before we were ordered to go below deck, behind the heavy equipment and tanks."

Alarm developed in the aftermath of the catastrophe that some of the missing personnel may have been recovered by the attacking E-boats with extremely sensitive invasion information in their possession. Immediately, severe security measures were enforced. All information pertaining to the event and to the lost and missing personnel became classified at the highest level. An investigation disclosed that possibly a dozen officers with Bigot classification, the level which included information on time and place of landing, scattered throughout the convoy could have been picked up by the E-boats. Fortunately, all of those with Bigot clearances either survived, or their bodies were recovered. It was in this atmosphere that all sorts of rumors flourished, ranging from stories about hidden bodies to vastly inflated numbers of casualties. In the search for scandal over passing years, the following main facts were disregarded: the killed were publicly interred at the U.S. Military Cemetery at Cambridge England, in a timely way, and after the landings at Normandy were successful, the servicemen's newspaper *Stars & Stripes* carried an accurate account of the story. Also, when the memoirs of prominent wartime figures were published the general public finally had ready access to first-hand information. Thus, the main facts were in the public domain as early as the period 1945 to 1951.

From the description contained in his memoirs, *A Soldier's Story*, an impression is created that Gen. Bradley witnessed only the events of the second day ashore. For example, this statement appears: "It was already April 28 . . . later that afternoon, I was told by Collins that German E-boats had broken through the naval screen offshore to attack his convoy en route to Slapton Sands. A ship, or ships, it was reported, had been hit. I asked if there were any losses. Some, I was told, but no one yet knew how many . . ." Gen. Bradley drew a conclusion that the beach engineer organization had broken down and that a new commander should be assigned to the Brigade, and suggested so to Gen. Collins. Gen. Bradley's account does not explicitly state whether he went ashore to observe events or spent all his time on the LCT cruising off-shore.

Gen. Collins acted on Gen. Bradley's suggestion for a change of command, and shortly afterwards, Brig. Gen. James Wharton was installed as Commander of the 1st Engineer Special Brigade. However, in an unusual and fortuitous arrangement, Col. Caffey, who had been in command for over one year, remained in the Brigade and served as Deputy Commander, while performing essentially the role he had up to that time. No word of explanation, nor justification for the change of command was given to Col. Caffey. Gen Bradley relates that it was four years after the war when he learned that the naval engagement had been one of the major tragedies of the war, rather than a minor brush with the enemy, and that it might have affected the conduct of the exercise. When Col. Caffey read Gen. Bradley's book after its publication in 1951, he learned, for the first time, some of the reasoning behind the change in command. He subsequently wrote to the Adjutant General of The Army, requesting that his military record reflect Gen. Bradley's admission. Col. Caffey, who served with great distinction before, during, and after D-day, later retired from the position of Judge Advocate with the rank of Major General. The letter sent by Col. Caffey to the Adjutant General can be found in Appendix G.

JOHN A. PERRY—T/5
462 AMPHIBIAN TRUCK COMPANY
1ST ENGINEER SPECIAL BRIGADE
OPERATION TIGER, 28 APRIL 1944

"[April 25, 1944] was the first time we saw the LST. We were instructed to put 22 DUKWs in the bottom deck—three across and two men to a DUKW. It was LST 531. I drove the 22nd DUKW in with my buddy T/5 Lawrence R. Flynt from Texas. . . . On April 28, around 0230 hours in the morning, Flynt and I were in the front seat of our DUKW when the first bang was heard. All we saw was a ball of fire. The center of the truck deck was hit. My buddy got out of the right side of the DUKW and hollered 'Get your gas mask on, you can't breathe.' I got my mask on and made it to the escape hatch and climbed to the top deck. That's when the second explosion hit me in the legs and blew me overboard . . . Popping up and down in the water, I could see another LST to my right on fire. It was like a red hot dog. I saw bodies floating all around and the bow of our ship sticking up about ten feet out of the water. I swam and climbed onto it. There were seven or eight other men on the bow but I didn't recognize any of them. I was numb from the forty-degree water. I never saw my buddy Flynt again. He never made it."

A recapitulation of the salient issues surrounding the Tiger exercise follows. This write-up concentrates on those areas where misinformation has been most rampant.

- If there is to be a search for malfeasance it would have to commence with naval security measures. Commander in Chief, Plymouth was the responsible agent for protection of the exercise. The Allied patrols operating off Cherbourg failed to detect the German E-boats departing port. The destroyer H.M.S. *Scimitar* was damaged and not available to sail with Convoy T-4, the eight LSTs in question. The ship was not replaced with another, thereby leaving only corvette H.M.S. *Azalea* on duty as escort. The LSTs were not informed of a radio frequency for communicating with escort vessels, a deficiency which detracted from effective rescue operations. Apparently, a thorough investigation was not pursued because of the potential for an inter-Allied dispute on the very eve of the invasion.

- The question has been raised as to whether the performance of the 1st Engineer Special Brigade was at a satisfactory level during Tiger, mainly due to the impact of the losses. Gen. Bradley, in his book *A Soldier's Story*, states his displeasure with the conduct of shore operations and his inclination to relieve the Brigade commander. A careful reading of the book, however, conveys the impression that he was not present for the simulated D-day performance and that he witnessed the second day operation (28 April) only from an offshore vessel, hardly a platform for accurate observation. The book contains this statement: "Not until four years after the war did I learn that these engineer troubles during the Utah rehearsal had been caused not by a breakdown in command, but rather by the S-boat ("S" designation from the German useage for schnell or fast) attack. . . ." This statement certainly calls into question the action to replace the Brigade commander. It does not, however, deal with the validity of the assessment of Brigade performance during Tiger. Notwithstanding the uncertainties, the "green book", *The Corps of Engineers: The War Against Germany,* carries the evaluation to a new extreme (despite its publication in 1984) with the statement: "Shattered by the disaster, which reduced it to little more than it's assault-phase elements, the 1st Engineer Special Brigade made a poor showing in Tiger. . . ."

- The response of Col. Caffey to the indignity of the new command arrangement was commendable. He accepted the role of deputy brigade commander without question. Obviously, his loyalty to the unit and to the Army was the motivating factor. That he was able to serve on D-day in substantially his former function was a recognition of his prior superior performance by those most closely involved.

- Searches for scandal came along much later. The accusation that the U.S. Army had orchestrated a massive cover-up was widespread in both British and American press and broadcast mediums. Unquestionably, there was bonafide classification of all information surrounding Tiger during the period when landing targets and timing were under Bigot controls. When the security classification was lifted during the summer of 1944, there was prompt publication of the essentials in *Stars & Stripes*, the service newspaper. Col. Ralph Ingersoll, in his book, *Top Secret,* published in 1946, relates considerable detail based on his direct involvement in accounting for personnel with Bigot security clearances who were lost on the sunken LSTs. Of course, the publication of Gen. Bradley's book in 1951 is widely known. At about that same time, Gordon Harrison's *Cross-Channel Attack* was published, also presenting the main items pertaining to lost personnel and ships. Adm. Morrison's book, *The Invasion of France and Germany* was published in 1957 with a rather complete picture of the Tiger events. Most of the highly outlandish stories, as for example the items pertaining to mass graves, are refuted by Charles MacDonald in his paper appearing in *Army Journal* of June 1988. Treatment of survivors at the 228th Station Hospital located in Dorset, not Devon, is related in an article of *American Heritage* published February/March 1985, "What Happened Off Devon", and indicates that transfer of any bodies back to Slapton Sands would be most unlikely. *Exercise Tiger,* published in 1990, contains details of research on the movement of surviving LSTs to Chesil Beach on the western shore of Portland Bill and the recovery of some bodies at that location.

Fabius I was the final rehearsal for Force "O", the Omaha Beach landing force. Preparations proceeded rather smoothly, leading up to a simulated D-day on 3 May. The particular objectives of Exercise Fabius I were the deployment ashore of 25,000 troops, including three regimental landing teams, two Ranger battalions, two tank battalions, three engineer combat battalions, and some other support units. The revisions possible to correct such faults as did show up had to be kept to the minor level since the actual D-day was only one month off. Some changes were made in the landing schedule with a military police detachment, engineer brigade headquarters, and the signal company being advanced to earlier positions. Similarly to Tiger, a second day was included in the exercise devoted primarily to beachhead building. The plan called for delivery ashore of 300 tons of equipment and materials, including treadway bridge sections, Sommerfeld track, and other beach road items. At the conclusion of Fabius, most of the units were ready for movement to marshalling areas.

CHAPTER V

MARSHALLING— EMBARKATION—TRANSIT

That the Allied high command attached great importance to a smooth mounting of the invasion was evident throughout the preparations. The major exercises included enough of a simulation of actual movement, assembly, and loading to accumulate hard empirical data for planning the preliminary phases of the invasion. Time, space, facilities, and movement requirements were all factored into the solution of gathering and delivering the invasion force.

ASSEMBLING THE FORCE

A number of environmental factors introduced special difficulties into the problems of assembling and dispatching the landing force of Neptune-Overlord. The geography of southwestern England was a major contributor to these difficulties. The region was crowded and its road network consisted of narrow and twisting lanes. Early planning had anticipated that there would be difficulties in assembling the force. For example, precautions were taken early in the process of locating major units to segregate American units into the southwestern counties, primarily Cornwall, Devon, Dorset, and Somerset. The British units were concentrated more to the southeast. Units were also positioned with regard to their movement to embarkation ports with the least interference to each other.

One feature of the marshalling plan to head off the possibility of traffic congestion was the movement to ports in phases. Marshalling areas were created to hold troops between the time they left billets and later went aboard ships and craft. For the most part, these areas were camps of various sizes composed of standard pyramidal tents. Small camps could accommodate company-size units. A collection of perhaps a dozen of the small camps could hold about 3,000 troops. Large camps reached a capacity on the order of 9,000 troops.

Since the troops had to exist without their organic transportation and equipment, a host of facilities and services had to be provided. This operation was in itself a major undertaking. Consider that vehicles needed final waterproofing before loading aboard ship and once waterproofed were not available for administrative purposes. Loading schedules dominated all other priorities. Extensive use of personnel from the Services of Supply troop units coped with many tasks of operating the camps. However, it became evident that large manpower pools would be required to assist troops bottled up in the camps without access to their everyday necessities. Major formations of field force units, for example armor divisions, were applied to housekeeping chores. It was not at all unusual for tank crews from the 4th Armor Dvision to operate a mess line in one of the marshalling camps with personnel having no skill nor experience in food preparation. Needless to say, troops awaiting embarkation survived the ordeal. As a matter of nomenclature the camps were widely referred to as sausages. The origin of the term came from the appearance of the camp layouts on area maps where the small unit camps were sketched in by a sausage-like symbol and then might be linked together in various numbers.

Port capacity was an important problem which surfaced rather early in planning for the orderly dispatch of the invasion force. Berthing space for the thousands of ships and craft was simply not there in the small harbors dotting the coast line, even when such ports as Plymouth were included. The solution to shiploading was to ferry loads out by lighterage to ships standing in a roadstead. This in turn led to a requirement for extensive space to get troops and cargoes out to the anchored ships. Concrete aprons were put in place to bridge the gap between existing paved roads and the water's edge, such as along a river bank. There was no shortage of river bank space. The concrete aprons were built up with precast concrete units which had a scored checkerboard surface to assure traction on sloping and wet surfaces. The concrete slabs were generally 10 inches thick and several feet on an edge. The hardstanding surfaces were extended well out into the water what with the tidal problem entering here again. For short, these facilities became known as hards (Fig. 24).

Security was a factor in site selection and design of the camps. Initially, the emphasis was on camouflage and other natural vegetation. As the most favorable sites became taken, another approach evolved. It became an assumption that sooner or later German aerial reconnaissance would produce photographs which would reveal the existence of the camps. Then, since the camps were used for rehearsals from time-to-time through the spring of 1944, there was a continual filling and emptying of the camps. The possibility was worked up that with deceptive marks planted about the camp area, it might not be possible to detect from the air whether the camps were occupied or not. Of course, if the camps were vacant, a cross-Channel operation could not be considered imminent. As it happened, enemy air activity was not strong enough to pose either a physical or an intelligence threat.

Another aspect of security covered the possibility that troops might not be adequately careful with classified information. Briefing of troops on matters of destination and timing was withheld until shortly before sailing. Nevertheless, simply by virtue of participation in the large-scale rehearsals, the individuals with key roles became security risks. To avoid the possibility of leaks all troops in the marshalling centers were confined to camp.

There were situations during the marshalling procedure where an intermediate move was both feasible and advantageous. In the case of some troops scheduled to embark at Torquay, there was abundance of hotel space in town, enabling the transfer of personnel from tent camps into more comfortable quarters. From a military view, the advantage was a superior facility for intense briefing, table space suitable for map study, an opportunity for final check-out of personal weapons and tactical loads including mine detectors, marking devices, wire cutters, explosives and fuzes, and the like. A further advantage was the short hiking distance down to the hardstanding site for lightering out to the attack transport. Of course, there is no implication that personnel who remained in the tent camps had a less than satisfactory briefing experience.

Great care was taken that all personnel were fully apprised of the situation to be

Figure 24—*Hardstand Sites for Embarkation at River Ports.* *Adequate port capacity was expeditiously created by hard surfaces installed along river banks using precast, concrete blocks. Note equipment items standing by for loading in correct sequence.*

encountered on the far shore, and that all assignments were completely understood. The primary briefing aid was a set of maps containing the utmost detail. Maps were at a scale of 1:12,500 (approximately 5 inches to 1 mile), or of 1:10,000 (approximately 6.3 inches to 1 mile). At such scale ratios, all natural and man-made features of the area show up distinctly, down to and including individual buildings such as farm houses.

Terrain features were very readable including such detail as hedgerows, tracks, and paths having military significance. Copies of Bigot maps for Omaha and Utah Beaches are to be found in Appendices A through D.

Overprints on the maps proved especially useful for troop briefings. One set of maps contained data on beach obstacles as of mid-May 1944 covering obstacles in the tidal zone. On shore, the data covered mine dispositions including such detail as whether there were scattered mines or a mine field pattern, and if the latter, the number of rows and spacing between rows. The obstacle overprint maps included a panoramic shoreline sketch primarily intended as an aid to coxswains of small landing craft, but also useful to Army small unit commanders. The second set of maps also carried a May date, but these maps concentrated on weapon installation information, thus complementing the first set described above. On the assumption that the overprinted intelligence data was reasonably accurate, the needs of the troops were fully satisfied. Aerial photographs were the prime source of the overprint data.

DILLON H. MERICAL—T/4
149TH ENGINEER COMBAT BATTALION
OMAHA BEACH

"When we were finally briefed on the landings and we studied the models of the landing beaches at the staging areas, we asked if this was the 'real thing' and our officers told us that we had a one-way ticket and that we would be going to stay.

A full array of briefing aids was available to the troops, varying of course with the mission of the units. As noted in the two accompanying quotes the briefings were intensive and reached personnel of all ranks. Among the engineer shore parties the reconnaissance elements had the greatest need for rapid orientation to the ground once reaching shore. These platoon-size teams had the task of clearing lanes through obstacles and mine fields so as connect up with planned beach exits. Sand tables were provided as a briefing aid and did indeed contribute to familiarization with terrain features to be met on the far shore. The difficulty these engineer troops would face upon reaching shore would be one of immediately locating their position on maps to accomplish any meaningful reconnaissance. Considering the number of instances where landing craft crews mislanded Army troops both in practice exercises and in actual operations one can appreciate the necessity for the troops to have the utmost familiarity with landmarks.

Joseph Anderson Hicks—Captain
531st Engineer Shore Regiment
1st Engineer Special Brigade
Utah Beach

"Several weeks before the invasion, we were called together, company commanders and upward, and shown sand table models of our actual sector of the beach. This model showed in detail enemy gun fortifications and beach obstacles. . . . We were one engineer company on an LCI. This was a rather sober and subdued group, [we] were all veterans of three previous D-day landings: North Africa, Sicily and Salerno. As one GI phrased it, we all felt like fugitives from the law of averages."

Boarding Ships and Craft: Embarkation

Diversity was the hallmark of the invasion fleet assigned to transport the landing force to the far shore. All types of amphibious transports and landing craft that had seen action in the transatlantic theaters of operation were called into service for Neptune-Overlord. The attack transports included veterans such as U.S.S. *Samuel Chase*, which had seen action at Gela, Sicily along with new ships such as U.S.S. *Bayfield* which had participated in Exercise Tiger, but not in any combatant actions. Among the other attack transports were *Dickman*, *Barnett*, *Henrico*, *Carroll*, and *Jefferson*. Also within the task forces transporting American forces were H.M.S. *Empire Gauntlet* and *Empire Javelin*.

Engineer troops, by the nature of their scheduled arrival ashore and their varied equipment loads, were distributed throughout the fleet. To illustrate the rationale of amphibious lift assignments a few salient tactical considerations need to be scrutinized. From earlier consideration of the structure of an Engineer Amphibian Brigade it was seen that a cross-Channel operation in a shore-to-shore mode was judged not feasible by the key commanders. Thus, the Army reorganized the Brigades to be used in the transatlantic theaters of operation and deleted the boat units. Also when examining typical landing plans it was found that LCVP and LCM-type craft dominated the early assault waves. These small boats would enable broad distribution of troops and offer the smallest targets. Means for delivery of the small boats would be the ocean-going attack transports which would mount the small boats on davits.

Attention needs to be focused on the distinction between *tactical* and *administrative* loading plans. All things being equal, one would expect that an efficient loading plan is one that stows the maximum quantity of equipment, vehicles, and stores in the limited space aboard ships and craft. For amphibious operations this is definitely not the case. The loading plan is governed by the needs of the tactical situation ashore. The first requirement is that unloading be accomplished in the least amount of time so as to minimize vulnerability of the landing force. Of practically equal importance is that the needs of the troops ashore govern the scheduled arrival of all personnel, equipment, and vehicles. The experience gained in actual operations and in large scale exercises should be sufficient guidance on exactly what is needed and when. Nevertheless, an ideal tactical loading plan is not easily achieved. A number of reasons can be cited. The logistics personnel working up loading plans may not be familiar with all details of the operations ashore. They may have been indoctrinated with the notion that higher tonnage deliveries are better than lower tonnages. Actually, the arrival of any item not absolutely required is likely to cause clutter on the beach and delay arrival of urgent needs.

Several types of engineer units were transported to shore in the small boats. The teams of the Special Engineer Task Forces assigned to neutralize the obstacles in the tidal zones were organized into units which averaged 41 personnel, combined Army and Navy. At this size, these units were a good match to the capacity of LCM-craft, with sufficient space remaining for explosives for demolishing the tidal obstacles. Many of these craft were towed to the transport area about 10–12 miles from the French coast by LCTs where the troops made a transfer to smaller craft for the final run into the beach. The reconnaissance teams of the shore party engineers were scheduled to land at various times, on the order of H plus 30 minutes to H plus 45 minutes. These teams were of platoon-size, but in most cases were reinforced to a strength of about 50 men. At this size of unit they exceeded the capacity of LCVPs and were, therefore, subdivided for loading. They became parts of mixed boat teams in which there could be included an assortment such as a 4.2-inch chemical mortar, a signal detachment, or a medical-aid detachment.

Those of the engineer reconnaissance teams which had an assignment including a breach of the seawall had to personally carry extremely heavy loads (Fig. 25). The explosives alone were 40 pounds per man, issued in a pair of 20-pound containers. The teams carried, in the aggregate, over and above a standard infantry load and the explosives such items as mine detectors, wire cutters, beach markers, safe lane markers, and some bangalore torpedoes. The standard load included a rifle, cartridge belt of rifle ammunition, two extra bandoleers of ammunition, grenades, bayonet, entrenching tool, two days supply of rations, and water. The load had to be carried down to hard-standing areas, aboard lighters, and then up rope ladders to board the attack transports. Of course upon reaching the far shore the transfer to landing craft meant a repetition in reverse of the process this time in darkness and rough sea conditions.

The divisional engineer units were somewhat better able to maintain unit integrity among their advance elements. These were similarly scheduled for landings in the range of H plus 30 minutes to H plus 40 minutes. They had assignments on board attack transports and would be transferred to LCVP and LCM-types of landing craft in the transport area. These arrangements applied to the 1st and 20th Engineer Combat Battalions on the eastern sector of Omaha Beach, and to the 112th and 121st Engineers on the western sector. On Utah Beach, the pattern of assignments did not con-

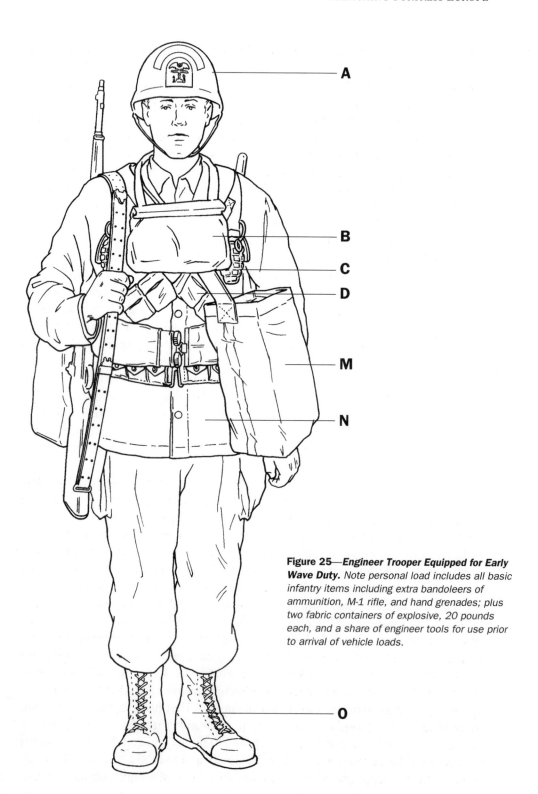

Figure 25—Engineer Trooper Equipped for Early Wave Duty. *Note personal load includes all basic infantry items including extra bandoleers of ammunition, M-1 rifle, and hand grenades; plus two fabric containers of explosive, 20 pounds each, and a share of engineer tools for use prior to arrival of vehicle loads.*

Representative Uniform Details

A. M-1 steel helmet with insignia of Engineer Special Brigade and arc

B. M5 waterproof assault gas mask

C. MK II A1 fragmentation grenade (two)

D. M-1 bandoleer (two) with six pouches, each pouch containing one eight round clip of .30 caliber cartridges

E. .30 caliber M1 Garand rifle

F. M1 bayonet with long scabbard

G. M-1928 haversack with suspenders and meat can pouch attached

H. M 1943 entrenching shovel and carrier pack (worn under the meat can pouch)

I. M-26 life belt, dual type

J. M1923 cartridge belt (worn under life belt) with ten pouches, each pouch containing one eight round clip of .30 caliber cartridges

K. M1942 canteen with cup and cover

L. M1942 first aid pouch. In addition, a parachute first aid kit (not shown) containing tourniquet, wound dressing and morphine syrette was carried usually on the front suspender

M. Ammunition bag, M-1 (two), each carrying twenty pounds of TNT or composition C blocks of explosives

N. Herringbone cotton twill special fatigue jacket and trousers (worn over field jacket, OD and trousers) impregnated with CC-2 chloroamide antigas compound

O. Parachute jumper boots

form to those prevailing at Omaha, with the 4th Engineer Combat Battalion scheduled to reach shore at a later point.

The main bodies of the engineer battalions, both divisional and shore party, embarked directly aboard landing craft. Bulldozers and other heavy mobile items went aboard LCT-type craft at the hardstanding sites. These craft, at 105 feet in length, were capable of crossing the Channel on their own bottoms with heavy and bulky loads. Most bulldozers were prepared to come off the LCTs towing sleds or trailers with surfacing materials for improving the traction properties on sandy beach roads. The tradition of the 1st Engineer Special Brigade was formulated during the early period at Camp Edwards, and progressively refined through testing at the Fifth Army Invasion Training Center and subsequent operational experiences. Essentially, sleds were flat bed structures constructed of heavy timber members with broad runners. The main cargo brought to shore on the sled was Sommerfeld track for road surfaces. These were prepared by attaching heavy burlap fabric to wire mesh, and then coiling the assembled surfacing product for transportation. Rope nets provided a lashing so that sled loads maintained their integrity under the most rigorous transportation conditions. The later engineer brigades, having been derived from a different table of organization, were equipped with Athey trailers, a general purpose unit with a track-type suspension. Among the cargoes brought ashore on these trailers was a considerable quantity of explosives.

An out of the ordinary use of the LCT-type craft involved the obstacle-gapping teams of the Special Engineer Task Force. The landing plan shows the teams arriving ashore in LCM-craft and it was earlier noted that the size of the teams was a good fit to the capacity of the LCM. However, most of these craft were towed to the transport area by LCT-craft whereupon there was a transfer of personnel, equipment, and stores to the LCMs for formation into assault waves and the run into shore.

Large numbers of dismounted, main body engineers embarked in LCI-type landing craft. These craft, approximately 150 feet long, appear in the landing plans at H plus 70 minutes. Two ramps are provided, one on each side of the bow, suited for personnel only. Outsize loads were not brought ashore by troops embarked on LCI-craft.

The largest of the beaching vessels, LST-types at about 300 feet long were much more suited to follow-on operations rather than the assault phase, but did have limited participation on D-day. There were several engineer transport requirements that required the capability of the LST to cope with outsize cargoes. The case of heavy, track-laying cranes is an example. These cranes were also appropriate to movement by Navy rhino pontoon ferries. These flat structures were constructed by the bolting together of seven-foot cube modules with the primary function of expediting debarkation from LSTs. Fig. 26 shows how several heavy cranes can easily adapt to the broad space on the deck of the ferry. Several of the shore engineer battalions brought in cranes at the rate of one per company.

Probably the final chore for D-day troops before going aboard the invasion fleet was the donning of uniforms resistant to poison gas agents. A survey of protective

Figure 26—*Rhino Ferry Aids Offloading of LSTs*. *This ferry has taken a full load of vehicles and mobile equipment off an LST standing offshore for the final transfer to the beach. Note construction of ferry with cube elements bolted together to form flat platform. The rhino ferry complements the capability of LST vessels when tide, beach bottom, or hostile resistance are unfavorable to beaching LSTs.*

uniforms indicates that several variations were in use. A commonly found type was the standard woolen olive drab uniform impregnated with defensive agents.

For the boarding procedure, plans were prepared to the utmost detail, nothing was left to chance. The conditions of tide, dawn, and moon phase led to the conclusion that three days in early June were satisfactory for landing operations: Monday the 5th through Wednesday the 7th. Obviously, the initial preference would be Monday. Also various convoy serials had different sea-going speeds, with the early classes of LCT (for example: LCT-5 at 105 feet long) being capable of a maximum speed of only seven knots, with load. Therefore, serials of LCT craft would be dispatched early in the sequence. A *typical loading schedule* for LCTs called for troops to reach their assigned hardstanding site around midday Saturday, the 3rd of June. After all vehicles were loaded aboard the craft and lashings checked, the troops were ready to sail. Generally, each LCT required 30 minutes at the hard-standing to get cargoes and troops aboard. The final item was a topping off of fuel and water. The craft would then cast off from the hard and proceed downstream to an assigned anchorage. Sunday morning would be the sailing time for the convoy serial. However, those slow serials sailing from ports with the greatest distance to the invasion beaches would be the first to depart and some would leave as early as Saturday the 3rd of June.

IN TRANSIT TO THE FAR SHORE

At this point there was a period of approximately 40 hours until the scheduled H-hour of 0630 hours (Double British Summer Time) on the 5th of June. The slowest serials and those with the greatest distance to go were forming up and heading to sea. These convoy serials were composed primarily of LCT landing craft, and included a large proportion of engineer troops. Sailing orders had been confirmed at SHAEF.

ARTHUR FROMMER HOFFMAN—CAPTAIN
1ST ENGINEER COMBAT BATTALION
EASY RED, OMAHA BEACH

"[During the crossing] the rumors on board ship were that the beaches were so heavily barricaded and mined that thousands of us would be killed while clearing the fields for the rear echelons to come in. We also feared that the large ships would pull away after we had landed and that we would all be marooned."

A weather problem was also setting in at this time. Through Saturday, the predictions were turning unfavorable and there was a prospect for severe conditions over the next several days. The next decision point was set for 0400 hours early Sunday morning the 4th of June. The forecast presented to the commanders during the very early morning session was totally negative. It appeared unlikely that the air bombardment would be effective through the heavy cover. It was also likely that landing craft attempting to reach shore would be swamped by the rough sea conditions. Gen. Eisenhower, with the concurrence of all his subordinates except Gen. Montgomery, reached a decision to postpone the scheduled landing by 24 hours to the 6th of June.

With a number of convoy serials already at sea, and secure communications in force, the turn-around problem was no simple matter (Fig. 27). The Western Task Force, supporting the U.S. component of the invasion and under the command of Rear Adm. Alan Kirk, consisted of Assault Force "U" for Utah Beach, Assault Force "O" for Omaha Beach, and Follow-up Force B. In the van of Force "U" was the LCT convoy which had originated in Plymouth harbor with the destroyer *Corry* leading

Figure 27—*Landing Craft Underway on Channel Crossing.* *An LCI, with debarkation ramps elevated follows behind two serials of LCTs in column. Main bodies of engineer units arrive ashore, with bulldozers and sled loads, in these craft in the time period after about H-hour plus 120 minutes.*

the escort. Having been at sea all night they had made more than 80 miles and by 0900 hours Sunday morning were roughly 25 miles south of the Isle of Wight. The turn-around message reached the lead destroyer at this time. All indications were that the minesweepers up ahead and the other destroyers of the escort had as yet failed to receive the turn-around message, prompting the *Corry* to rush ahead and use blinking signal lights to get the sweepers turned around. This maneuver succeeded and there had been no radio transmission within the convoy. In the meantime the other escort destroyers had turned the LCTs, with no reason to believe the convoy serial had been detected even though it was only about 40 miles from the French coast. Despite a few moments of relief no one was aware of the reasoning behind these events and it was natural for a feeling of apprehension to prevail over both Navy and Army personnel.

All ships and craft of the early serial convoys did manage the turn-around and headed for their emergency postponement ports, but not without some mishaps. The weather was worsening. Troops on board the open LCTs were soaked by lashing rains which were compounded by the severe motions of the flat-bottomed hulls. Rations for the troops were mainly ten-in-one packaged, dry and cold. Casualties began to accumulate even before the invasion force met the enemy. The minesweeper *Osprey* while working to clear and mark a channel struck a floating mine. Shortly thereafter fires broke out and the vessel was abandoned with the loss of six sailors. The last convoy back ran into crowded conditions off Portland and while attempting to find safe anchorage LCT-2498 suffered engine failure, lost control, and went down in treacherous waters.

Command attention focused intently on the weather problem as the decision point for a 6th of June landing neared. Gen. Eisenhower had two meetings per day throughout this period during which the meteorologists presented the evolving movement of weather systems and their predictions for specific times ahead. All the principal commanders were in attendance. The meeting at 2115 hours. Sunday evening was especially dramatic. Despite the continuing bad weather and the grim picture conveyed by the charts, the chief meteorologist, Group Capt. J.M. Stagg, R.A.F., predicted that a favorable break would occur on the 6th of June, and that even the preceding night would clear to the extent required for the planned bombing operations. The next weather briefing and decision point would be at 0400 hours, Monday morning, the 5th of June. However, the Navy could not wait until the firm decision but had to factor in the departure timing of the slow convoys.

Thus the slow convoys, hardly recuperated from the ordeal of Saturday night and Sunday, were ordered to sea again. These convoys composed primarily of LCT craft were assigned mainly to transporting the heavy engineer loads such as their bulldozers. Also included, however, were the DD-tanks and other Shermans waterproofed for moderate depths of immersion. The weather continued to be stormy, and the rain was wind-blown to the extent that it appeared to be driven utterly horizontally.

At the 0400 hours commanders' meeting early on the morning of the 5th of June, the choices were difficult to the utmost degree. The slow convoys had sailed on their second attempt at crossing. What started as a set of three feasible days for landing operations had now become only two. If the slow convoys were again turned around and ordered to emergency postponement ports they would need to be refueled, and this could not be accomplished in time for a departure to land on the 7th of June. The state of the prevailing weather at the time made it obvious that the first postponement had been a wise decision. If a second postponement were to be ordered numerous problems would surface immediately. The 8th of June might be a possibility but would lead to an adjustment in H-hour to get usable tidal conditions. Such a move could be a forerunner to chaos. A postponement of about two weeks would bring tidal conditions into the preferred range but only a postponement of about four weeks would bring both tides and moon into the preferred configuration. In the meantime it would be necessary to keep all troops pent up in secure camps for fear of an intelligence breach. So the preponderance of argument favored a decision to sail and the weather prediction called for a short spell of improving conditions on the 6th of June with a probability of more foul weather later. The momentous decision came after Gen. Eisenhower had listened to final comments from subordinates. At 0415 hours, he said, "I am quite positive we must give the order . . . I don't like it, but there it is . . . I don't see how we can do anything else."

The handling of the difficult decision process regarding landing date by Gen. Eisenhower is generally regarded as masterful. His performance in the extremely tense, high pressure environment clearly put to rest once and for all the notion that as Supreme Commander he would be removed from operational control. He emphatically rejected the position of Gen. Montgomery to sail for a landing on the 5th of June and thereby forestalled what could have been a disaster of the greatest magnitude. Similarly, he rejected the advice of Air Chief Marshal Leigh-Mallory to postpone beyond the 6th of June and this would have produced terrible complications with no sure benefit in sight.

Thus the initial sailing orders of the slow convoys were confirmed, and the rest of the convoys proceeded to load their troops for a landing on Tuesday, the 6th of June. The attack transports, U.S. Navy APA-type ships, carried the leading waves of infantry and most of the early-landing engineer parties. The obstacle gapping teams of the Special Engineer Task Force were aboard LCTs, towing their LCMs. The main body of most of the engineer companies were also aboard beaching craft, especially those arriving with the heavy equipment. An example of an APA is U.S.S. *Bayfield*, of Force "U". This ship was new to amphibious operations and did not have the experience of Mediterranean operations, such as the seasoned U.S.S. *Chase* and most of the others. The *Bayfield*, 492 feet long, had a troop capacity of 1,650, and carried on davits 18 LCVPs, four LCMs, and several other craft assigned to command and control. It was the flagship at Utah Beach. These ships comprised the convoy serials traveling at comparatively high speed, and were the last to be boarded by troops.

An excellent description of the picture at sea is available in the work of Adm.

Samuel Morison. In his Volume XI of the *History of U.S. Naval Operations in World War II: The Invasion of France and Germany* he presents a well researched summary (see box on the following page). Strangely, several of the contributions from key participating individuals touch upon the matter of landing craft rendezvous, but neglect to mention a matter of considerable discomfort to troops. Discipline of the landing waves is a well-established tradition in amphibious operations. While mislandings have been a plague to landing forces, at least the naval crews make every attempt to have all boats properly loaded and formed into waves precisely according to plans and schedules. This is accomplished by the rendezvous procedure. As boat teams go overboard from attack transports and fill the small craft, boat operators cast off and proceed to search for their wave. This is not a simple procedure under conditions of darkness and unfavorable weather. The early arrivals commence making circles while subsequent cast offs search for their wave. An hour or more can be consumed in the searching. All this while the boats, which are circling, lay down a dense cloud of diesel exhaust. Even with a prevailing breeze, the troops cannot escape from the shortage of breathable air. Thus, the troops are prone to seasickness even before the motion of the flat bottom craft takes its toll. Obviously, coxswains of small craft eventually become acclimated to the difficulty. Some pertinent remarks by key engineer commanders are also included on the following pages.

The Crossing—as recorded by Adm. S. E. Morison

Extract from: *The Invasion of France and Germany,* Published by Little, Brown, & Co., 1968.

Swept channels . . . were wide enough for two convoys to sail abreast up to . . . "Piccadilly Circus" (13 miles S.E. of the Isle of Wight) . . . thence five swept lanes were provided, one for each task force. About halfway across the Channel each lane became two, one for the fast and one for the slow convoys.

Let us first follow the fortunes of Capt. Sabin's slow convoy for Omaha Beach. This was one of those that had started on the morning of 4 June, reversed course . . . and dashed madly back to Portland. Sabin's convoy made its final start, in four columns 100 yards apart. The wind was still strong and the sea became rougher the farther they sailed into the Channel. Under such conditions, LCT are not easy boats to handle . . . the bow both high and light, they are almost impossible to hold on a course in a strong wind.

Now let us turn to the heavy gunfire ships and transports . . . the parade forms up, each group in single column. . . . Attack transport Bayfield . . . slips into her place in the column off Plymouth at 1045. . . . Three other transports for Utah join off Dartmouth.

During the afternoon Deyo's column overtakes those of the beaching craft. He is impressed by "an air of cheerfulness, even jauntiness, in their crowded human cargoes."

At 1800 5 June, off Portland Bill, Deyo's column changes course to S.E. The sky is still overcast and the wind a fresh N.W., but the sea is moderating. As far as the eye can reach, the Channel is covered with ships and craft, . . . the small ones tossing and heaving, the great ones steadily advancing . . . An hour before midnight battleship Nevada . . . behemoth of this fleet . . . turns to starboard. This is the entrance to swept channel No. 2, one of 10 into which the approach lanes have now separated . . . columns will pass to their initial positions for the landing. High overcast obscures the moon, but light filters through the clouds.

There were indeed things so remarkable in this crossing as to suggest divine guidance. The crowded movement of these thousands of vessels . . . ran off very close to schedule in spite of the foul weather . . .

. . . The other amazing circumstance was the enemy's complete unawareness . . . no planes discovered anything . . . E-boats failed to make their routine patrol . . . commander thought the weather was too foul . . . and . . . the tides were not right.

A Sampling of Some Engineer Experiences In Cross-Channel Transit

Col. Paul Thompson; Commanding, 6th Engineer Special Brigade.
Extract from remarks delivered at Ft. Belvoir; October, 1987

The fourth of June, we move to the loading hards, units and detachments of the 6th Engineer Special Brigade move aboard their specified ships and craft. With a small contingent of my staff I board the designated LCI (landing craft, infantry) . . . I had the peace of mind of the pro golfer who knows that he has brought with him all that is necessary to win.

Came the orders postponing the launching of the invasion by 24 hours . . . I don't recall any major impact on morale; I recall looking at the skies and the waves and remarking to my Ensign friend that at a place called the Assault Training Center weather like this would not have deterred us from any planned landing exercise.

Came the dawn of 6 June. LCI 2 is approaching the French coast. So far as I can discern all goes according to plan. It's an hour after dawn and, on the bridge alongside the young Ensign, I make a dismaying discovery: our Ensign has no idea what those disc-shaped objects atop long poles sticking out of the water are. I explain Tellermines. Bump into one of those, I told the Ensign with an air of urgency, and we're blown out of the water. What luck, that the Germans spaced their Tellermine poles so thinly as to make it easy, even for poorly trained craft operators, to avoid them.

It must be close to 40 minutes after H-hour, it's "rampdown", and we step off into water arm-pit deep. My short-lived experience in combat is beginning. I have no idea how short-lived it is due to be.

Across maybe 300 yards of beach, men are bunched under scant cover, with seawall and wire just ahead. I note the blockhouse ahead and to the left, I think I recognize it and I head for the bunched group of soldiers apparently engaged in attacking it . . .

Lt. Col. William Gara; Commanding, 1st Engineer Combat Battalion
Extract from remarks delivered at Fort Belvoir; October, 1987

D-day came with exceptionally bad weather—it was gray and overcast
with heavy waves, anywhere from four to eight feet, northwesterly
winds at least 20 miles per hour, the tide was flowing easterly. Upon
loading into LCVPs we made rendezvous with our landing wave and
finally headed into shore. The overall time from loading to arrival at
the shoreline was one and one-half to three hours depending upon
the difficulties and the direction taken by the craft, heading for their
assault objectives. In our experience, the landing craft deliberately
ran into the tidal obstacles . . . it was high tide and the obstacles
were concealed. There were no gaps marked.

Lt. Col. Robert Ploger; Commanding, 121st Engineer Combat
Battalion
Extract from remarks delivered at Fort Belvoir; October, 1987

The move to the ships and craft took place the 3rd of June and
the night of 5–6 June saw us afloat. Training and planning had
ended. . . . Eating a quick breakfast at about 0200 hours, climbing
over the side on a cargo net at about 0330 hours into a wildly pitching LCM, bouncing on board while the craft joined a rendezvous circle
and waited for the last of our wave to join. Thus started D-day for . . .
54 occupants of LCM 1098. Finally, we ceased circling; started the
straight run to the beach, still in the dark.

While we travelled the 12 miles to the shore line, the dawn came up.
. . . Everyone soon was experiencing the pangs of seasickness,
wanting to get off that pitching and rolling boat no matter what might
come next. I positioned myself right at the front . . . believed it
essential to be the first member of the command on the beach . . .

In our craft we could feel the bottom scrub some sand, jar to a
grounded halt. I plunged forward, jumped into about eight feet of dark
water. Obviously, the boat had struck a sand bar. My lifebelt brought
me back to the surface, already swimming. Soon my feet touched
bottom and I was able to begin splashing and running out of the
water. Winded, paused kneeling in the shelter of a steel hedgehog,
then lunged ahead . . . dove into a depression filled with water.
Suddenly, my ankle felt as if hit by a baseball bat . . . I hobbled the
remaining 50 yards, I lay down against the stony rubble. . . . There
was no one in front of me, beside me, nor behind me that I could see
or hear.

CHAPTER VI

THE FIRST ONE THOUSAND YARDS AT OMAHA BEACH

Bluffs and cliffs at Omaha favor defenders

Formidable weapons include batteries at Pointe du Hoc

Allied intelligence misplaces strong defender, 352d Division

Air bombardment, for safety reasons, misses defenders

Phasing of operations proposed in paper by Col. Thompson

Run in from transport area through stormy seas

Initial infantry-tank assault pinned down at shingle

Engineers in tidal zone produce valiant effort; small benefit

Losses within 116th Infantry at Vierville upset landing zone progress

Main bodies of engineers lose heavily in shore debarkation

Mislandings scatter engineer and infantry units among sectors

Early engineers join infantry in fight up the bluffs

Antipersonnel mines planted densely, slow movement up bluff

1st Engineers provide first egress from beach at Exit E-1

Explosive demolition by 121st Engineers opens Vierville draw

Engineer missions accomplished—if a bit late

From the time that plans for landing at Omaha Beach began to take their final form, it was apparent that this would be the main seaborne effort for American forces. The assignment would be difficult by any standard of measurement. Selection of troops was a carefully crafted piece of work by First Army, and did, in fact, occupy Gen. Bradley's attention for a substantial period. The size of the force was roughly double that which was allocated to Utah Beach. The level of support from bombardment elements, both sea and air, was in proportion to the magnitude of the effort. And of course the engineer contribution to mission success—the primary focus of this account—was on a similar scale.

Omaha Beach is situated centrally on the Normandy invasion front. It is roughly midway between Le Havre on the east and Cherbourg on the west. The British beaches Gold, Juno and Sword lie to the east of Omaha, and are separated by approximately eight miles. Utah Beach, the other American landing site, is across the Carentan estuary from Omaha about 14 miles to the west.

GEOGRAPHICAL CHARACTERISTICS OF OMAHA

Omaha Beach is a stretch of coastline decidedly out of the ordinary. Whereas Utah Beach is often described as similar to much of the east coast of the continental U.S., it is not so easy to find a simple comparison for Omaha Beach. The target beaches were tucked between two regions of stark cliffs rising abruptly to a height of more than 100 feet. On the left (to the east), commencing at the boundary between First U.S. Army and Second British Army which runs through the coastal village of Port-en-Bessin, there is rocky shoreline backed by cliffs reaching beyond Arromanches. From Colleville-sur-Mer west to Vierville-sur-Mer, a distance of some 6,000 yards, there is a shingle embankment just above the high water mark. This bank is about eight feet high and extends about 15 yards inland, thus resulting in a 1:6 slope. Of course there is variability in the properties of the embankment. But for most all of its length, the shingle embankment is an impediment to both track and wheel vehicles even though at some locations traffic may move across the shingle bank. A close-up view of the texture of the shingle is provided in Fig. 28. Note that the principal dimension of the pebbles making up the shingle is in the range of four to six inches. The only redeeming feature of the shingle embankment was the cover it afforded to troops in the assault landing. On the western end of the region cliffs reappear on both sides of Grandcamp. A characteristic of this area is the rocky shale bottom just seaward of the high water mark. An included terrain map (Fig.29) shows the onset of these regions. The accompanying photographs (Fig. 30) show a comparison of the sheer rise of cliffs at the extremities of Omaha with the bluffs making up the center.

Figure 28—*Typical Views of Omaha Beach Terrain.* *Upper view shows the Exit E-1 draw on the Eastern sectors of Omaha Beach where the abrupt transition from cliffs to the flat upland is clearly visible. The lower view shows an example of the shingle embankment, this being in front of the Exit D-3 draw, with the slope steepness being plainly visible. Readers can appreciate the difficulty of moving military vehicles ashore through the poor traction and slope presented by the embankment.*

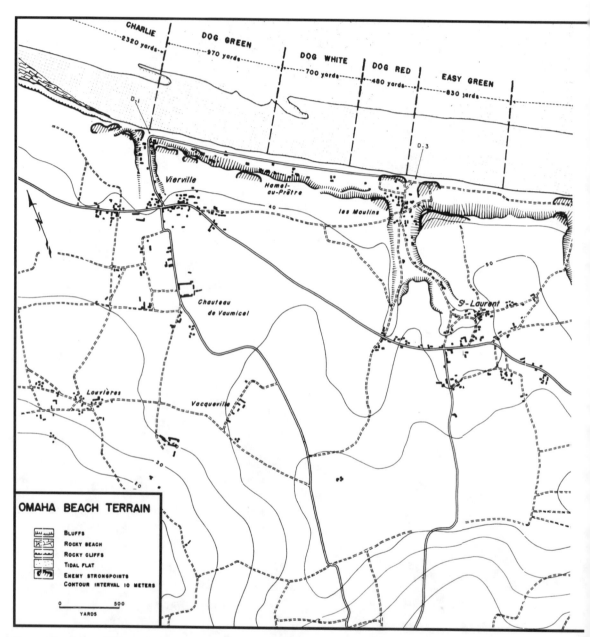

Figure 29—*Terrain Map.*

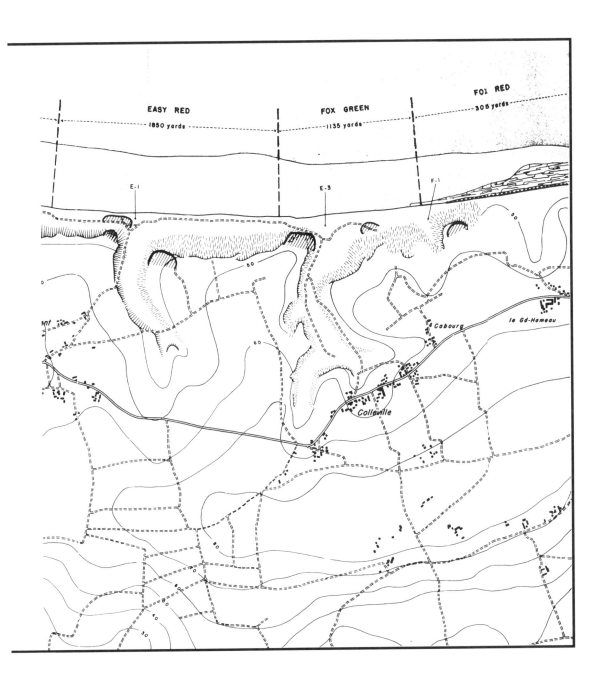

Figure 30—*Omaha Beach Terrain Views.* *Upper view shows extreme western end of beach and merging of bluffs into cliffs toward Pointe de la Percée. Cliffs contain pillboxes and other gun positions which commanded substantial areas of Omaha Beach. Lower view shows western sectors from Exit D-3 draw onward to the right flank. Note the topography in the vicinity of the draw.*

With the Vierville-Colleville (the suffix *sur-Mer* sometimes found in place names is often disregarded) stretch being the only feasible landing site for a corps-size operation, further attention will be given to its terrain features of military importance. The tidal zone has a quite gradual slope, leading to a high tide to low tide distance of 500 yards, more or less. The overall grade corresponding to this tidal range is 1:75 but actually the bottom is more nearly flat in the low water region and becomes a bit more steep inshore. Navy data gave values of gradient at 1:190 for most of the tidal zone but reaching a ratio of 1:47 inshore. The comparison of the Omaha tidal zone with that on Utah Beach is illustrative of the effect of this tidal zone property. Since the topic is discussed at several other points in this account, only the main conclusions will be presented here. On Omaha, the farthest offshore obstacles are out approximately 250 yards which is about one-half of low-tide to high-tide distance. The map enclosed here (Fig. 31) shows the location of obstacles in the tidal zone with respect to the low water mark. With low tide on D-day at about 0530 hours and the interval between low tide and high tide being roughly five and one-half hours the incoming tide reached the obstacles in the tidal zone at approximately 0800 hours. Obviously, where the obstacles were farther seaward they were in contact with the incoming tide at an earlier time. Whether the allocated time was adequate for the obstacle neutralization task will remain one of the imponderables for military historians to grapple with over the years. Advancing H-hour to get an earlier start on the obstacle task would not have been a practical measure since that approach would have subtracted from the daylight period set aside for preparatory bombardment of enemy defenses. At the location on Utah where landings were actually made the high tide to low tide distance ranged between 1,700 and 1,100 yards. In this case, the tide reached the obstacles about 0930 and 1000 hours on the right end and left end of the beach respectively.

The terrain inshore from the shingle embankment presented a whole set of difficulties to the landing force. While the shingle provided some defilade to assault troops it reduced trafficability of vehicles virtually to zero, even track vehicles. Next came the problem of a masonry seawall. The wall ran westward from a point just west of les Moulins and was in the range of four to eight feet high. Toward the western extremity of Omaha, the wall extended even higher. Immediately inland of the seawall there was a paved road paralleling the beach and extending from the beach exit at Vierville to les Moulins. Thereafter, the road became an unpaved track and extended eastward to a point beyond the beach exit running inland to Colleville. Inshore from the beach road a sandy beach flat extended to meet the commencing rise of the bluffs. The beach flat contained areas of marsh and high grass and it also was not conducive to the passage of military traffic. At its widest, near the center of the target beach, it was about 200 yards deep and at each end became quite narrow.

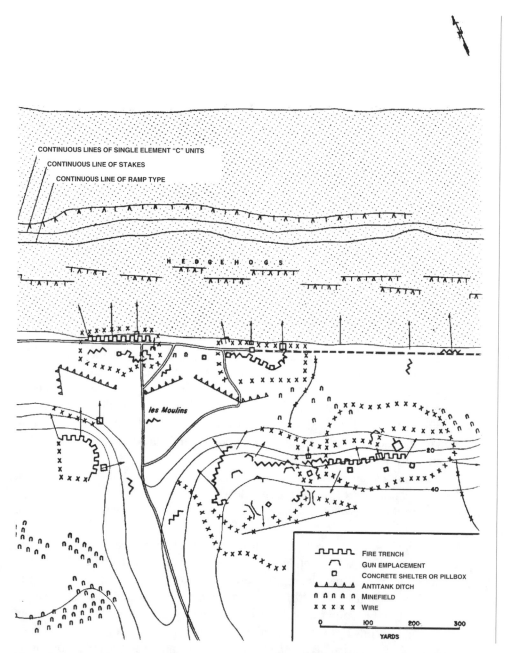

Figure 31—Diagramatic Representation of a Set of Integrated Defenses. This arrangement of concrete fortifications, mine fields, barbed wire, trenches, ditches, and tidal zone obstacles was at les Moulins draw, Exit D-3. It proved to be a difficult target for the V Corps landing forces.

The dominant feature of Omaha Beach was the bluffs. These bluffs provided defending troops with the classic military advantage of high ground. The entire beach area, with the exception of the very easternmost extremity, was backed by these bluffs. The bluffs rose rather sharply and reached a height of 100 to 170 feet, thus presenting a nearly continuous obstacle to track and wheel vehicles and restricting their movement to the draws, as identified on the accompanying terrain map. The draw at Vierville, marked as Exit D-1 on the map, contained a paved road which linked up with the main coast road running through Vierville. Exits D-3, E-1, and E-3 carried unimproved roads but also reached to the highway though their distances were roughly one mile, more than double the distance by way of Exit D-1. It may also be seen that the ground beyond the crest of the bluffs continued to rise; then beyond the villages there was a leveling and a gradual descent. The sampling of the terrain covered by the photographs includes an example of the merging of the bluffs into the cliff areas which flank the landing beaches. An overall summary of the terrain characteristics at Omaha Beach should certainly note that there were more than ample opportunities to site fortified positions for the attempt to fight off landing forces.

DEFENSIVE MEASURES AT OMAHA BEACH

A general principle stated in describing the Atlantic Wall fortifications was that the distribution of defensive assets would be in proportion to the probability of Allied attack. The application of the principle can be seen at Omaha Beach. There were 12 fortified positions along the landing beaches concentrated at beach exits. The German defenders obviously appreciated the attraction that these avenues over the bluffs would have for the invaders. If the coastal areas adjacent to the landing beaches are included there were altogether 32 fortified positions between the Vire River and Port-en-Bessin. Some of the fortifications were at the crest of the bluffs, some were below the crest but still at elevated positions above the beach flats and some were just inshore of the beach flats. The accompanying illustrations (Fig. 32) show a sampling of positions at various locations along the beach and various elevations.

A number of features of the defensive positions appear in the examples. In the case of the concrete casemates such as the one shown near Vierville draw, wing walls were installed to shield the muzzle blast of the gun from observation by the fire support ships standing offshore. While the walls limited the traverse off the guns in the seaward direction, they did not hinder fire delivered against landing craft closing in to shore and about to debark their troops. Generally the gun positions were selected to bring practically the entire extent of the landing beaches under enfilading fire. These wing walls were even more conspicuous in the fortifications at Utah Beach. The open position just east of the St.-Laurent draw had a 76-mm howitzer identified as a Russian weapon. The policy applied during construction of the Atlantic Wall had been one of standardization in regard to concrete works. But when it came to weapons, all captured stocks of weapons and other materiel were put into service.

Figure 32—Hostile Fortification of the Beaches and Bluffs. Upper view shows a concrete gun emplacement on the western end of Omaha, near the draw at Exit D-1. It can be seen that the gun has limited traverse to seaward but has a clear field of fire covering the beach sectors to the east of Vierville. The lower view shows typical trenches on the high ground atop the bluffs, generally located between fortified positions guarding the draws. In the example the trenches overlooked Easy Red Beach. Weapons usually installed in such locations included machine guns.

The diversity of weapons available to defending German troops was extremely broad. Most of the guns were in the group of 76-mm to 88-mm, the latter being the widely used tank, antitank, and antiaircraft design. However, larger caliber guns were also numerous in the defensive positions at Omaha Beach. Heavy coastal batteries were located both west and east of the beach areas. The six guns of 155-mm caliber at Pointe du Hoc had a range estimated to be 25,000 yards and were believed capable of dominating both American beaches. This is about 14 miles to Omaha Beach, while the distance to Utah Beach is just under 10 miles. A concrete observation post and range finding station were part of the installation. The accompanying sketch (Fig. 33) has been extracted from an intelligence summary dated 21 April 1944. This type of gun emplacement afforded considerable cover to the weapon and its crew while at the same time retaining mobility. In the event that the invasion led to a successful beachhead the guns could have been extracted to fight another day.

A variety of additional defensive measures, over and above the weapons, were included in the Omaha sector of the Atlantic Wall. Antitank ditches show up in several photographs of the terrain, particularly in front of the draw on Easy Red beach which is marked on maps as Exit E-1. Intelligence data showed a generous use of similar antitank ditches at the les Moulins draw, marked on maps as Exit D-3. At the Vierville draw, Exit D-1, data sources did not show any ditches but at this location the seawall served as a formidable antitank barrier. Barbed wire in several forms was effectively blended into the total array of obstacles. The pictures of Exit D-3 shown earlier include an example where wire was strung across the front of the beach flat just inshore of the shingle band. In a number of cases the distribution of wire was closely integrated with firing trenches. The firing trenches in turn were an important element in the fortified positions sited at the beach exits. Additionally, firing trenches were placed along the crest of the bluffs. These positions were mainly between beach exits and provided support in protecting the exits from invading troops. Trenches overlooking Easy Red beach can also be seen in the photographs.

The prolific distribution of antitank and antipersonnel mines throughout the defenses at Omaha Beach was a consequence of the experience of Field Marshal Rommel. He had developed an assurance in his earlier campaigns that these weapons were effective. The layout for the important defensive positions at the draws along the beach included areas where patterned fields of mines were planted. An example of the use of mines is the draw at les Moulins. The beach flat on the east side of the exit road had several areas where a dozen or so mines were planted in each. Then, atop the bluffs on the west side of the road much larger patterns were planted. Many of these sections contained five rows and sometimes a dozen mines in each row. In the relatively open areas between defensive positions, mines were extensively used to impede progress of invading forces. The net effect of such widespread mine planting to comply with Rommel's orders was that German mine production actually never caught up with demand. In part the use of captured foreign stocks of mines helped to make up the shortage. A type used frequently was the Mustard Pot, a French antipersonnel mine having four ounces of explosives and a chemical-type igniter with an

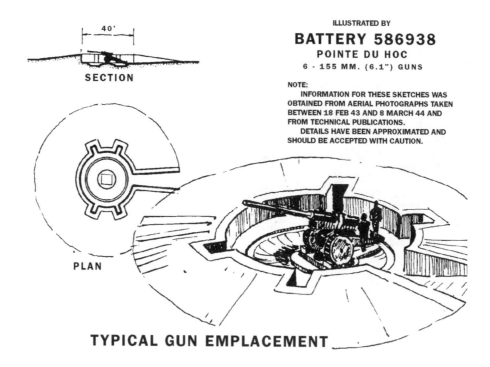

40'

SECTION

ILLUSTRATED BY

BATTERY 586938
POINTE DU HOC
6 - 155 MM. (6.1") GUNS

NOTE:
INFORMATION FOR THESE SKETCHES WAS
OBTAINED FROM AERIAL PHOTOGRAPHS TAKEN
BETWEEN 18 FEB 43 AND 8 MARCH 44 AND
FROM TECHNICAL PUBLICATIONS.
DETAILS HAVE BEEN APPROXIMATED AND
SHOULD BE ACCEPTED WITH CAUTION.

PLAN

TYPICAL GUN EMPLACEMENT

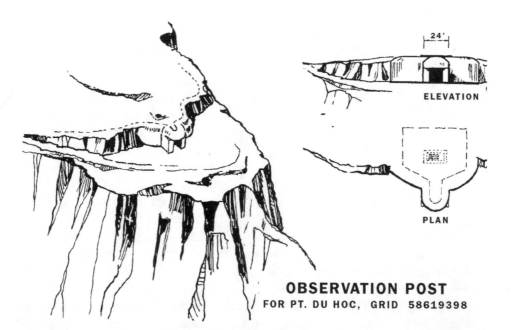

24'

ELEVATION

PLAN

OBSERVATION POST
FOR PT. DU HOC, GRID 58619398

Figure 33—*The Artillery Installation at Pointe du Hoc.* *The sketches are from Bigot intelligence summaries of April, 1944. Open emplacements enabled the rapid repositioning of the gun batteries which was exactly what happened, leaving the Rangers who scaled the cliffs without any hard-earned booty.*

actuation pressure of 25 to 35 pounds. Improvised devices augmented conventional designs of mines. The chemical igniters were used with a sheet metal can about the size of a ration container filled with explosive. Such igniters were also adapted to mortar shells. Of course, the standard "S" mine was the major type of antipersonnel mine and there were non-metallic Schumines interspersed. Appropriate distribution of Tellermines, French and other foreign types of antitank mines and improvised devices were all part of the defense tactics.

Obstacles on the tidal flats were an important element in the defensive measures at Omaha Beach. Hedgehogs were the most numerous, showing up in various photographs taken before and during the landings. These were constructed of steel angles, three sections to each unit. The three primary members were joined by welding or riveting using a gusset plate to achieve a strong joint. Appendices H through I provide details on obstacle construction and placement on the beaches. The accompanying aerial reconnaissance picture (Fig. 34) was taken mid-May, just several weeks prior to the landings, at low tide in front of the draw designated as Exit E-1. Many of the hedgehogs were attached to concrete foundations. Poles are visible in the photograph, distributed in a scattered way ahead of the hedgehogs. No Tellermines were in place on this particular group of poles, but the general situation on Omaha Beach was that many poles were tipped with mines. Also, no ramps nor Element C show up on this stretch of beach but both did appear elsewhere on Omaha. A general assess-

Figure 34—*A Low Tide View of Obstacles in Front of the Draw at Exit E-1.* *This aerial photograph was shot during mid-May of 1944 and probably conveys a lower density of obstacles than existed on D-day.*

ment of the degree to which the tidal zones were guarded by obstacles at Omaha would say that the density was about average. The prime target beaches north and east of Normandy exhibited heavier construction and denser distribution while the Utah sectors were a bit sparser.

Before considering the situation on the ground, brief note should be taken of the defenders' weakness on the seas and in the air. Allied naval and air forces had taken a toll to the point where the German forces were devoid of these important supporting elements. This deficiency was evident in the absence of reconnaissance activity prior to D-day and in the fight for the beachhead.

An attempt to describe the defending troop picture at Omaha Beach opens up utterly perplexing problems. During the period of preparation for the landings, the intelligence services provided the Allied field forces with less than satisfactory information on German troop dispositions. Throughout the spring of 1944 it was believed that the 716th Infantry Division held the entire coast from the Orne River to the Vire Estuary. The earlier descriptions of German forces in this account classified this unit as a static division, which is to say that it was not up to standards maintained by field divisions in regard to mobility equipment, training and qualifications of personnel, and a general capability to accomplish attack missions. Moreover, the division was believed to have as many as 50 percent foreign troops, mostly Russians and Poles. To complete the intelligence evaluation, it was believed that only one reinforced battalion of the division was defending the sector assigned to the U.S. V Corps.

This evaluation of the enemy troop disposition along Omaha Beach was slow to die. In September of 1945 the Historical Service personnel attached to First Army prepared *Omaha Beachhead* for publication by the War Department, upon which the above is based. That source notes that any German counterattack by "local" reserves of the 716th Infantry Division would be unlikely, and that any serious threat to the Allied invasion at Omaha would need the "mobile" reserves of the 352d Infantry Division, based in the St.-Lô vicinity about 20 miles inland. This latter unit was rated as being of good quality with a nucleus of veterans from campaigns on the Russian front and fully capable of launching an offensive against any breakthrough of the Atlantic Wall.

Further intelligence information became available on the eve of embarkation. Gen. Bradley relates in his book, *A Soldier's Story,* that just before boarding the flagship *Augusta* in Plymouth harbor, First Army G-2 Section (Intelligence) learned of the movement of the 352d Division from St.-Lô to the assault beaches for a defense exercise. The information was passed on to headquarters of V Corps and 1st Division, but was not widely disseminated due to the sealing off of many of the troop units on invasion craft.

On several counts the intelligence was incomplete and inaccurate. There had been a major upgrade of defending troops on the sectors comprising Omaha Beach. In mid-March 1944 under the initiative of the German Seventh Army, the 352d Division moved northward from St.-Lô and took over the west end of the Orne-Vire sector, i.e., Omaha. In the process the major part of the 726th Regiment of the 716th

Division was attached to the 352d Division. The net effect of the changes was that defending forces opposing U.S. V Corps landings were substantially improved in quality and approximately doubled in numbers. Additionally, German mobile reserves were positioned in Bayeux, a mere five or so miles from the main line of resistance—the shoreline. In support of the validity of this description, *Cross-Channel Attack* by Gordon Harrison provides meticulous documentation. It is unquestionable that the strengthening of the defenses in the Omaha Beach sectors took place in the early spring of 1944 and that the process was a carefully planned one having a far-reaching impact. These facts thoroughly discredit the notion that some units of the 352d Division, by a great coincidence, just happened to be at defense positions along Omaha during a training exercise. An account of the defense arrangements by Adm. Samuel Eliot Morison in his book *The Invasion of France and Germany* closely matches that of Harrison. Based on careful research, Adm. Morison reaches the conclusion:

> "... The major mistake of Allied Intelligence was the assumption that this (Omaha Beach) and the British sector were defended by only one static German division, the 716th, with no armor or wheeled transport. One of the persistent myths about Omaha is the story that all the trouble was created because a first-line, tough German division 'just happened' to have been sent there for a tactical exercise when our troops landed. This yarn makes a good cover for faulty intelligence, but there is nothing to it. . . ."

PREPARATORY BOMBARDMENT AT OMAHA BEACH

Misfortune continued to plague V Corps as the shore bombardment was about to commence. The weather had an unfavorable influence on air operations to an extent that was directly evident in the progress of the battle to establish the beachhead: the battle for the first one thousand yards. The plan called for R.A.F. heavy bombers to attack targets from the Seine westward to Cherbourg between midnight and dawn. More than 1,300 bombardment aircraft were to deliver some five tons each. This kind of night bombing operation had been fairly regular over a period of several months and was more of a harassing nature than an accurate strike at selected objectives. There was an intent to avoid alerting the defenders that landings were imminent. Then, commencing at 0600 hours, 30 minutes before H-hour, the plan called for heavy bombers of the Eighth Air Force to strike all fortified positions of the beach defenses. The sector assigned to V Corps would be hit by 480 B-24 bombers delivering four tons each. There were 13 targets specifically identified for attack. Ordnance to be dropped was mainly 100-pound bombs of fragmentation and high explosive types with some 500-pound bombs reserved for the most difficult targets. Instantaneous fuses were applied to all bombs so as to minimize cratering which might turn out to impede vehicle traffic across the beaches. A few special targets, including the guns atop Pointe du Hoc, were to get an attack by 18 medium bombers of the Ninth Air Force in the final moments of the air bombardment.

Weather predictions proved to be reasonably accurate in that conditions made the going difficult but not impossible. The concern of air commanders was the ceiling at 10,000 to 12,000 feet with some scattered clouds at 3,000 to 7,000 feet. This meant that the bombing would of necessity be on instruments, through the overcast. In these conditions the specter of losses due to friendly fire haunted the high command and led to an order that there be a delay of several seconds in the time for release of bombs. This of course, would increase the clearance between the area under fire and the approaching assault craft.

The consequence of the delay in bomb release was that the effectiveness of aerial bombardment at Omaha Beach was virtually nil. The account by Harrison in *Cross-Channel Attack* states that coastal defenses were not hit at all and that bombs were scattered as far as three miles inland. Adm. Morison's research concurs that no bombs fell on Omaha Beach. Col. Benjamin Talley had an assignment to observe operations and act as an information gathering agent for V Corps Headquarters with a pair of DUKWs to provide his team with mobility and a radio platform. His observations were made traversing offshore along the beach until about 1100 hours when he was able to land his group on the 1st Division sector. His personal observation was that no evidence of effective bombing against defensive positions could be found nor were there any bomb craters. He did find that Pointe du Hoc had been saturated.

Preparations for naval bombardment appear to have been adequate, thanks to continuing pleas from the Supreme Command for reinforcement of the original allotment of warships. Assault Force "O", also known as Task Force 124, embarking V Corps included in its bombardment group the battleships *Texas* and *Arkansas*, Royal Navy light cruisers *Glasgow* and *Bellona*, French cruisers *Montcalm* and *Georges Leygues*, and 12 destroyers mostly American. Actually there were additional destroyers in the force whose assignments as convoy escorts were not completed early enough to permit them to take a place in the fire support line-up. The larger ships were positioned so as to fire at targets in the range of five to seven miles while the destroyers were closer in, say about three to four miles from shore, but even much closer at times. The fire support areas were on each side of the transport area which was out about 11 miles. *Texas* was on the right, within easy reach of the Pointe du Hoc while *Arkansas* was on the left capable of reaching both flanks of Omaha.

Firing commenced about 20 minutes ahead of schedule when, at about 0530 hours, a shore battery near Port-en-Bessin, with barely enough daylight, spotted the *Arkansas* and opened up. This action served as a trigger and other shore batteries opened up on the destroyers. However, it may be recalled from descriptions of the casemate designs that many batteries were limited in traversing to seaward by the wing walls of their concrete structures. This was the penalty to be paid for the protection from flash observation and from fire which many of the defensive weapons enjoyed. Of course, some of the shore positions were open, as seen in the illustrations including the Pointe du Hoc batteries, and were not limited in their traversing capability.

By and large the naval bombardment was effective even though only a fraction of the shore batteries were completely neutralized. Spotter aircraft were aloft over the target area but smoke and dust limited visibility in locating all targets precisely. Furthermore, intelligence activity prior to D-day, even with extensive aerial photographs, had failed to identify many of the fortified positions on shore defending the draws. Another of the general problems was the limited time for bombardment. This was mainly the result of Army preferences in regard to planning the approach to shore under darkness and fixing H-hour in relation to low tide. Naval planners had hoped for a bombardment period on the order of several hours, as contrasted to the one-half hour actually allotted.

On the western flank of the American area of responsibility Pointe du Hoc was the priority target. The main batteries of the *Texas*, 14-inch naval rifles, dug craters at the site of the 155-mm (6.1-inches) batteries but provoked no counter-battery fire. The German guns, being mounted on wheel carriages, had been repositioned, as the Rangers learned later after scaling the cliffs. The adjacent cliffs also held fortified positions and these had not been evacuated. Two destroyers fired on weapons and on a radar station. Another destroyer struck at targets on Pointe de la Percée, another promontory but closer in to Vierville and having good fields of fire on the western end of Omaha. The *Texas*, while spending considerable ammunition and valuable time on the mostly fruitless effort at Pointe du Hoc, also had its attention on Exit D-1 at Vierville. There were weapons emplaced on both sides of the exit road and the *Texas'* secondary battery was trained on these targets.

Additionally another destroyer and several smaller fire support vessels joined. The next important target area, Exit D-3 at the village of les Moulins, about 2,000 yards eastward from Vierville was struck with intense fire from the *Arkansas* and the cruiser H.M.S. *Glasgow*. A considerable tonnage was allotted here as this group of fortifications was expected to be crucial to progress of the assault. This essentially completes the description of naval fire in support of the 116th Infantry and its assault partners, Sherman tanks, both DD and conventional, and the Navy plus Army engineer teams working on the tidal zone obstacles. The additional component of naval fire support was the launch from LCTs of five-inch rockets, about 1,000 rounds from each modified landing craft. Altogether, Omaha Beach received approximately 10,000 of the naval rockets in the final 10 minutes as the climax of more than one-half hour of intense terror.

The eastern beach sectors, Easy Red and Fox Green, were assigned to the 16th Infantry and required that substantial fire be delivered on its Exits E-1 and E-3. The first exit led to the village of St.-Laurent and the second led to Colleville. Both were well defended. In both cases there were fortified positions on each side of the unimproved road heading up the draw and there were also defenses positioned on the upward slope and on the crest of the bluff between the exits. At Exit E-1 the cruiser *Georges Leygues* directed its six-inch batteries at fortified positions along the bluffs so as to neutralize control of the exit. One of the Royal Navy destroyers added fire from its four-inch guns. This area had a share of naval rockets as 1,000 rounds were fired from an LCT(R), i.e., an LCT fitted for launching rockets. Additionally, LCTs bringing Sherman tanks ashore were outfitted to enable the tanks to fire while still afloat.

Finally, at Exit E-3 on Fox Green, four destroyers and several smaller ships fired at the defenses from close-in positions. In the bombardment period of about 40 minutes these ships each delivered about 250 rounds. Where smoke from the continuous explosions partly obscured the targets there was still no let-up and blind firing was the last resort. The fire support plan had included the *Arkansas* firing on Fox Green but this was superseded when some priority targets appeared just over the boundary between U.S. and British forces. Fox Green was pounded with a generous ration of naval rockets as three LCT(R)s delivered 1,000 rounds each. The French cruiser *Montcalm* was occupied with targets at Port-en-Bessin, on the First Army eastern boundary and several others in that direction which had opened fire at the first sighting of Allied naval forces. Obviously it was a period of torment for the French crews participating in the bombardment of French soil. However, they fully realized that the total cost of the 1940 defeat was an incalculable burden that had to be distributed widely and that all Allied forces were sharing in sacrifice. Extensive joint training with U.S. naval forces also prepared the French ships for a fully integrated contribution to the total invasion effort.

An assessment of the bombardment contribution to the success of the landing operations produces a few clear-cut conclusions and some others which are at best nebulous. First of all, the aerial bombing scattered explosives over an area reaching inland in some places as far as three miles. No evidence was found that open positions or fortifications structures of the main line of resistance had been hit from the air. The most complimentary finding was that large numbers of land mines may have been exploded inland and thereby expedited engineer clearing tasks but this is more speculative than substantive. Attribution of the mistiming of the bomb release to bad weather is not a plausible justification since ideal weather along the English Channel is more exceptional than usual. With regard to naval gunnery the judgement of historian Adm. Morison is that considerable results were achieved and that naval bombardment may have reduced hostile resistance by one-half or more. He suspects that expectations of what could be accomplished from the sea may have been too high. He concluded that more ships could not have produced more benefits due to the limited space for maneuvering. On the other hand, more time allocated to sea bombardment would have been advantageous. On the whole, he believes the compromises and tradeoffs were reasonable. He makes little mention that the defense structures were designed specifically to resist attack from the sea. It should also be realized that naval gunfire was called upon throughout the day after the preparatory bombardment was lifted in order to compensate for the continuing shortage of artillery and armor support. It was in this role that the Navy won accolades from many high level Army commanders.

A Guide To Amphibious Fundamentals

This account now addresses the assault elements of V Corps as the landing craft of the early waves were nearing shore to debark their troops on the sands of France. The 16th Infantry Regiment of the 1st Division was on the left, assigned to land on

Fox Green and Easy Red beaches. The 116th Infantry Regiment was on the right, assigned to land on Easy Green, Dog Red, Dog White, and Dog Green beaches. It is pointless to rehash the question of whether this was a one or two division landing. Initially there would be only one division headquarters ashore, the 1st Division; and technically the 116th Regiment was attached to the 1st Division. Obviously, with the limitations on boat spaces and communication equipment this arrangement appeared logical to the planners. It should not be taken as a sign that there was any lack of equality in responsibilities and contributions between the two divisions. The fact is incontrovertible that the D-day impact on Omaha Beach was at the level of two divisions. Moreover, the assignment of Brig. Gen. Norman Cota served to ease a smooth transition from the attachment status to full independence of the 29th Division. Gen. Cota, the assistant divisional commander of the 29th Division was to come ashore with leading elements of the 116th Infantry and assist Maj. Gen. Clarence Huebner, Commanding General of the 1st Division, until such time as the 29th Division headquarters took control of its own units. A Ranger force of two battalions under command of Lt. Col. James Rudder operated as an attachment to the 116th Regiment, even though its mission was somewhat removed. These two battalions, the 2d and 5th Rangers, were assigned the batteries atop Pointe du Hoc and also the defensive positions at Pointe de la Percee, both locations west of Dog Green beach.

If battlefield actions are frequently clouded by confusion, the situation is compounded by the particular characteristics of amphibious operations. Army commanders surrender control to naval commanders during the seaborne periods. Communications are virtually non-existent at crucial moments. The landing force is vulnerable to the vagaries of the weather. Plans cannot have the flexibility to cope with unforeseen developments. The landing force is dependent on outside agencies for information about the enemy. This listing could be extended to great length but the gist is established by these few items.

As an aid to fathoming the many individual events comprising the D-day landings, an account by (then) Col. Paul Thompson has been extracted and included in the following box. The phased structure overlay on the diversity of actions will assist the reader in integrating much of what has been presented in this fairly comprehensive account and in the following detailed picture of the progress of small units. The presentation by Col. Thompson is especially helpful in visualizing the role of engineer troops. He differentiates between the obstacle clearing units, the divisional engineers, and the engineer special brigades. In this connection he may be more precise than warranted by happenings on the ground throughout the day. An examination of unit histories and after-action reports shows much overlap and even instances of conflicting descriptions of a single event.

The Structure of Landing Operations

Extracts from "D-Day on Omaha Beach"; by Col. Paul W. Thompson published in *Infantry Journal*; June, 1945.

What happened between H-hour and midnight? . . . The details of battle invariably are complicated . . . It will simplify our task if we consider the invasion operation by phases. Selected somewhat arbitrarily. . . .

PHASE I

The Infantry-Tank Assault (H minus 10 minutes to H plus 20 minutes)—. . . the leading wave of assault craft . . . was approximately 2,000 yards offshore. . . . the long ragged line . . . LCVPS (each) carrying one 30-man infantry assault section . . . was the sharp edge of the invasion spearhead . . . just behind it and even a few yards ahead, were a relatively few larger craft, LCT(s)s . . . perhaps a dozen . . . loaded with M4 Sherman tanks. . . . Approximately 600 yards behind . . . LCMS . . . carrying the unique obstacle clearance teams. After 4,000 yards . . . came the second wave of LCVPS. . . . By that time, the fire fight on the beaches would have been joined. . . . This new wave would bring ashore additional infantry. . . . German defenders did not cover sea approaches . . . were not able to engage invasion armada until the craft were within a few hundred yards of the beaches . . . widely spaced and tiny landing craft did not make profitable targets . . . The illusion (of a surprisingly cheap success) exploded about H minus three minutes . . . leading wave within 500 yards of the beaches . . . guns and mortars opened up . . . craft . . . plunged into a belt of fire . . . there were hits; there were many more misses . . . infantrymen . . . saw and heard rounds from 88-mm, 50-mm, 20-mm, and other point target guns . . . casualties mounted . . . here and there a soldier took cover . . . but most of them kept moving . . . the beaches were being carried by mass infiltration . . . But how about the German commander . . . what should he do?. . . . probably delayed too long in deciding to concentrate. The assault tanks, now battered . . . were plugging away at the embrasures . . . the second wave touched down . . . carrying the special obstacle-clearance units . . . tide rising fast—a foot every 20 minutes . . . within a couple of hours, this would . . . prevent landing craft from reaching wading depth . . . men ashore would become hostages. . . . compromise solution to concentrate on clearing lanes. . . marked by

buoys . . . explosive was the chief tool . . . each man carried 40
pounds . . . forms could be fitted quickly to piles, steel frames . . .
by hand. . . . The LCMS made good targets . . . the nature of the work
. . . attach proper charge, coordinate with neighboring teams, . . .
detonate charges . . . working not only against enemy fire, but
against time . . . suffering heavy losses . . . unable to keep lanes
cleared . . . obstacle clearance plan failed . . . coxswains of landing
craft drove ahead . . . many craft were lost; but most got through.

PHASE II
The Assault Continued (to H plus one hour)—another wave composed
chiefly of LCVPS and partly of LCMS . . . marked point assault formations . . . transported into standard combat teams, with supporting
arms and services . . . new phase consisted of . . . platoons from
reserve company . . . heavy weapons companies . . . two platoons of
divisional engineers . . . forward echelons of the engineer special
brigades—the units which had responsibility of organizing the
beaches . . . scarcely H plus 60 minutes . . . three types of engineers: obstacle-clearance . . . divisional engineers . . . beach organizing engineers . . . missions (respectively): clear lanes through belts of
underwater obstacles . . . clear mines and obstacles . . . establish
communications, mark beaches, remove hazards, and establish
routes off the beaches. . . . First bulldozers ashore . . . assault
battalions . . . not fighting as teams . . . early crises passed successfully . . . source of potential danger: the gap opposite St.-Laurent . . .
where German defensive works still remained strong. . . .

PHASE III
Build-up to Regiments (to H plus three hours) . . . building up ashore
of . . . regimental combat teams . . . and supporting services . . . fire
fight was raging . . . defensive works reduced . . . others still in
action . . . beach near St.-Laurent . . . a source of danger . . . enemy
artillery . . . cover the beaches . . . snipers appearing . . . tide continued to rise . . . by H plus two hours incoming craft encountering
obstacles before they grounded . . . howitzers and guns added . . .
offensive and defensive power . . . engineer special brigade units
(arrive) in strength . . . came in LCVPS, LCTS, and rhino ferries . . .
waterproof tractors . . . wade in depths up to six feet . . . assist
debarking vehicles across water gap . . . to the dry beach. ESB DUKWS

. . . preloaded with ammunition . . . launched from LSTs 1,000 yards out . . . Taking stock, . . . H plus three hours—two full regiments, two Ranger battalions, . . . supporting troops . . . exceeded 10,000 men . . . moving up, reinforcing . . . mopping up.

PHASE IV

The Follow-up Regiments Land (to H plus six hours)—. . . two additional regiments (infantry), divisional artillery, tanks, antiair guns, 4.2-inch mortars; engineers . . . came ashore. LCI(L)s (250 men per craft) . . . a floating reserve brought in opposite St.-Laurent . . . (enemy) pocket cleared up . . . Late in Phase IV the tide reached its height . . . scene of devastation . . . underwater obstacles . . . peak of effectiveness . . . dead were everywhere . . . wounded huddled . . . in groups . . . Enemy fire . . . still falling in and out of water . . . Obstacle clearance engineers . . . could do nothing with the tide covering everything . . . beach organization plan behind schedule and getting more so . . . infantry assault sections . . . operating inland . . . 50 yards . . . some of them 1,000 yards . . . only the remotest possibility . . . being driven back into the sea . . . disorganization more troublesome than serious . . .

PHASE V

The Power Play Continued (to midnight of D-day)—. . . there was ashore the headquarters of the assault corps . . . most of the combat echelons of two infantry divisions (the 1st and 29th). H-hour regiments . . . extended along the Vierville-Colleville road . . . gaps plugged by follow-up regiments. By midnight of D-day the situation was basically good . . . units were astride their objectives . . . each commander . . . prepared to hold what he had won. . . . a beachhead . . . had been established, strong forces had been landed, and that inflow of additional forces was going on, hour after hour . . . and behind it other divisions, many others. That was the important thing.

Insight contained in Col. Thompson's sketch cover the mutually supporting capabilities of the units ashore at the time intervals around which he structured phases. Firstly, he points out the characteristics of landing craft bringing the early waves ashore and the predominance of the smallest craft types. There is good coverage of the difficulties faced by the small units as they reach shore and encounter heavy small arms fire. He describes the efforts of small groups to move forward despite the severe casualty rate. Balance prevails on the one hand in the descriptions of the losses and hardships of the invaders and on the other hand their advances and their successes. He accepts that losses are inevitable in warfare when attacking a hardened, entrenched enemy and that the attacker can concentrate forces to overwhelm the defender. There is an absence of despair in his writing. Clearly his views are objective, the limited success of the obstacle clearing engineer teams being a case in point. Col. Thompson was intimately familiar with the intensive measures taken to prepare these teams for their difficult tasks and certainly would have preferred to report a successful accomplishment of that mission.

A further aid to following the evolution of events during the amphibious assault is a typical landing diagram. The example provided in Chapter IV covers the western sectors of Omaha Beach upon which the 116th Infantry Regimental Combat Team landed. It is reproduced from *Omaha Beachhead*, published by the War Department, Historical Division in September 1945. The diagram shows the distribution of troops through the first few phases. The DD Sherman tanks can be seen on Dog Green and Dog White arriving some minutes ahead of the conventionally waterproofed Shermans on Dog Red and Easy Green. Close behind are four rifle companies of the 116th Infantry. Note that the 1st Battalion had only one company forward and that the 2d Battalion had three companies in line in the initial assault. The Special Engineer Task Force, including naval demolition components, were close behind, following which there was a 27-minute gap to provide the engineer teams unobstructed access to the obstacles. Of course, this was not the way things turned out. The leading elements of both the divisional engineer battalions—the organic unit, the 121st Engineers and the attached unit, the 112th Engineers plus the leading element of the shore party, the 149th Engineers, can be spotted in the wave arriving at H plus 40 minutes. The 1st Battalion of the 116th Infantry continued to build on Dog Green, with the arrival of its weapons company. In this same wave there were 4.2-inch mortars arriving to support the 2d Battalion of the 116th Infantry. Generally, it will be seen that the landing schedule conformed to the phase structure. It can be expected that a similar pattern prevailed on Easy Red and Fox Green beaches, the sectors assigned for the assault of the 16th Infantry.

INFANTRY LANDINGS AT OMAHA: INFANTRY-TANK ASSAULT

In returning to the progress of the landing forces heading for Omaha the reader should recognize a momentous episode in U.S. military history. Notwithstanding the ultimate victory, there were periods of high sacrifice and intense suffering. Even though the weather was deemed fit to carry on with the operation it was disagreeable for the troops. The seas were choppy with waves generally about four feet high but with extremes reaching to eight feet high. Such sea conditions can produce great discomfort to troops in small, flat bottom craft. The wind was a steady 20 miles per hour but gusts reached much stronger levels. The easterly flowing tidal current was stronger than expected and contributed to navigation errors, especially where the crews for the small boats were relatively inexperienced. However, the mislandings were variable throughout the Omaha fleet with the result that troop units became intermixed and confusion prevailed during landings and after reaching shore. By contrast the situation at Utah Beach produced a far greater navigation error, for reasons to be explained later, but the constant nature of the error did not lead to intermixture of troop units. It should be realized that weather descriptions vary widely in reports by veterans of the operations and by historians as well. The above remarks are based mainly on the records preserved by Col. Gara of the 1st ECB. The spread ranges from "not too bad" to somewhere more severe than the descriptions above, based on a sampling of opinions among veterans, as available at the Ryan (*The Longest Day*) archives.

The transport area for Omaha Beach stood approximately 12 miles offshore and the APA-type ships arrived without mishap. The transports assigned to the left beaches, Easy Red and Fox Green, bringing in units of the 1st Division were the *Samuel Chase*, the *Henrico*, and the British ship *Empire Anvil*. For the right-side beaches Dog and Easy Green there were the *Thomas Jefferson*, the *Charles Carroll*, and the British ship *Empire Javelin* bringing in troops of the 29th Division. Among the military historians who have analyzed D-day events in minute detail there is a school of thought that says U.S. forces would have had a less difficult time reaching shore if the transport area had not been so far out, 11 to 12 miles, as designed. The comparison is made to the offshore distance of about seven miles as was the case at the British landing beaches. It must be noted, however, that the enemy guns on Pointe du Hoc, 155-mm weapons, captured French artillery, had an estimated range of 25,000 yards (14 miles) and could have made things very uncomfortable at a close-in transport area.

Shortly after troops debarked attack transports by rope nets and hopped into landing craft the first batch of problems cropped up. The standard procedure for sorting craft into their assigned waves involves a rendezvous in which earliest craft loaded move to designated locations and commence circling. All craft loaded subsequently search out their wave and join the circle. Sufficient time is allowed to collect the entire wave, during which period a heavy cloud of diesel exhaust builds, despite the prevalence of sea breezes. Thus, a high rate of sea sickness was inevitable, and definitely sapped the physical condition and fighting spirit of troops.

As landing waves became complete and headed for the line of departure, another problem turned up. The small craft took on water due to plowing through rough seas. Many of the craft reached a point where the installed pumps were unable to keep up with the work load of discharging this water overboard. The troops helped by bailing with their helmets. In spite of strenuous efforts to control this difficulty a number of landing craft were unable to maintain speed and keep their position in the formation. The attempts to speed up and recover position usually resulted in taking on more water and aggravated the problem. Disorder in the boat wave formation did not bode well for troop effectiveness upon reaching the beach. Authoritative estimates put the number of boats swamped and sunk at more than ten.

Some experiences during transfer to landing craft in the transport area and on the last leg of a long journey to a hostile shore are contained in the remarks of Col. O'Neill (see the following box). These emergency events further illustrate how even a finely tuned plan can be upset by the misfortunes of war.

Notwithstanding the weather-induced problems, and related difficulties of which a few examples were just noted, the early waves made their way to the line of departure and were dispatched to shore. This line was established by small control vessels at about 4,000 yards offshore, just over two miles. Reckoning from the transport area,

---

Extract from files of Cornelius Ryan

Author of *The Longest Day*, published by Simon and Shuster, New York, NY; 1959

From an interview with Lt. Col. John O'Neill, Commander of the Special Engineer Task Force

. . . We had gone over our plans on board ship with all personnel prior to sailing. I had considerable discussions with the . . . Ship's Captain (the ship was an Irish Sea Packet) concerning the method of debarking the troops. The ship had sally ports along the main deck which the Captain said had been successfully used in the North African invasion. I told him they would not work in a rough sea, and signalled the headquarters ship *Ancon* and requested landing nets which we hung from the upper deck. . . .

During the debarkation operations an LCP craft from a close-by APA ship (U.S.N. attack transport) was apparently badly damaged in loading and made its way in a sinking condition to the side of our ship. They unloaded on our ship and since I had three reserve LCMs, I gave them an LCM and they took off for the beach. They were a mortar section out of the 16th Infantry Regiment.

During the run in from the rendezvous area to the beach we observed a soldier floating in the water in his life belt. He appeared to be unconscious. We snagged him with the boat hook without stopping completely, and hauled him aboard the LCM. He was revived during the rest of the trip in and although very weak, landed and stayed with us until the evening of D-day when he gained his strength and made off to find his artillery unit.

the small craft had already completed about 10 miles of the run into shore. Up to that time there were two redeeming qualities to the run in.

The defending German troops had not opened fire, and in fact may not have yet detected the presence of the initial waves. It may be recalled that their casemates were designed with wing-walls affording some protection from seaward—and thus having limited visibility in that direction—while there was no sacrifice in their ability to take the inshore areas in enfilade. The second favorable turn of events was that sea mines had not been encountered. This was in sharp contrast to the situation at Utah Beach where significant numbers of ships and craft were lost to sea mines.

In the close-in reaches things turned decidedly for the worse. At about 1,000 yards offshore, landing craft came under effective fire from artillery pieces in casemates and various other protected positions of the defenders. By all accounts the intensity of defensive fire confirms that the preliminary bombardment had not produced the intended effect. The apologia regarding aerial bombardment have been rehashed to excess but it became increasing clear that naval fire also had its own limitations. Possibly Adm. Morison's conclusion that the time allowed was simply too brief to silence the defensive positions is a better explanation.

An attempt to describe the actual events of the landings of the initial waves faces the problem of valid information. Some researchers focused on interviews with individual veterans of the campaigns. The shortcomings of this approach are well known: individuals have limited scope and are often not positioned to view even small unit actions in their entirety, and may also report errors of fact. Many historians tend to rely on documentary materials such as after-action reports and unit histories, which in many cases are sketchy and prepared to meet only minimum reporting requirements. Col. Samuel L.A. Marshall pioneered a technique which offset some of these deficiencies, this being a group interview. Following this approach, at the first opportunity after an action a small unit would be assembled, often company-sized. A senior interviewer would address questions to the group and probe for answers until all inconsistencies were resolved, which sometimes was a very extended and argumentative process.

Among the many actions investigated in detail by Col. Marshall was the landing at Dog Green beach, on the extreme right flank of Omaha. His article covering this landing has been rated as one of the epics of military history and has been abstracted here (in the accompanying box). The account notes that two LCA craft (British equivalent to U.S. LCVP-type) of the six bringing in Company A of the 116th Infantry were hit by artillery fire and that the immediate death toll was 20 soldiers. This was even before the troops debarked the landing craft and headed for shore on foot. Col. Marshall's description is in sharp contrast to that appearing in *Omaha Beachhead*, an official War Department historical document, an extract from which states:

". . . Enemy guns had been sited to cover every part of the beach; nevertheless there were sections where units landed without meeting any artillery fire whatever. Furthermore, of the nearly 200 craft carrying the assault infantry to shore in the first two hours, only about 10 are known to have been hit by artillery before debarking their troops, none was sunk by this fire, and in only a few cases were the casualties serious. Larger craft, particularly LCIs, may have been a favored target for both shore and inland guns, and may have suffered relatively more."

A Grim View From The Right Flank

Extracts from "First Wave at Omaha Beach", an article appearing in *Atlantic Monthly*, November, 1960 authored by Brig. Gen. Samuel L.A. Marshall.

Unlike what happens to other great battles, the passing of the years . . . have softened the horror of Omaha Beach on D-day. On this two-division front landing, only six rifle companies were relatively effective as units. Three times that number were shattered. . . . Let's follow along with Able and Baker companies, 116th Infantry. . . . Their story is lifted from my fading Normandy notebook. . . .

Able Company is still 5,000 yards from the beach (Editor's Note: Dog Green) when first taken under fire. The shells fall short. At 1,000 yards Boat No. 5 is hit dead on . . . six men drown before help came . . . within 100 yards . . . a shell into Boat No. 3 kills two men. Another dozen drown, taking to the water as the boat sinks. At exactly 0636 hours ramps are dropped along the boat line and men jump off in water . . . waist deep to higher than a man's head . . . the line is instantly swept by crossing machine-gun fires from both ends of the beach. . . . Even the lightly wounded die by drowning, doomed by . . . overloaded packs. . . . All order has vanished from Able Company before it has fired a shot. A few move safely through the bullet swarm to the beach, . . . they return to the water to use it for body cover . . . they creep toward the land at the same rate as the tide. That is how most of the survivors make it. . . . Within seven minutes after the ramps drop, Able company is inert and leaderless. . . . Capt. Fellers and Lt. Kearfoot never make it. . . . No one saw the craft go down. . . . Half the drowned bodies were later found. . . . By the end of 15 minutes, Able Company has still not fired a shot. . . . By the end of one-half hour approximately two-thirds of the company is forever gone. . . .

Baker Company . . . land 26 minutes after . . . full load of trouble on way in . . . bail furiously with helmets to keep the six boats from swamping . . . Capt. Ettore Zappacosta pulls 45 and says "by God, you'll take this boat straight in." His display of courage wins obedience. . . . Frightened coxswains . . . veer right and left away from the Able Company shambles . . . Not seeing the Captain die, Williams doesn't know that command has now passed to him. . . . By the end of 20 minutes, Williams and 10 men are over the sand . . . in lee of the seawall. Five others are hit by machine gun fire . . . six men are never heard from again . . . When the shelling lifts, three of them do not return . . . seven survivors . . . toward the fortified village of les Moulins . . . Without being detected, he gets within 20 yards of the gun . . . heaves a grenade . . . he starts crawling back . . . three bullets rip his rump and leg . . . hands his map and compass to S/Sgt. Price . . . behind a hedgerow . . . seven Germans on even terms T/Sgt. Pearce settles fight . . . kills the seven Germans with a Browning automatic rifle . . . village already in hands of Lt. Walter Taylor and 20 men.

Inland from Vierville about 500 yards lies the Chateau de Vaumicel. . . . To everyone but Taylor the target looks prohibitive. Still they follow him . . . open fire with rifles and toss a few grenades . . . 24 of the enemy . . . with their hands in the air. . . . They make it to the chateau . . . The question is whether the ammunition will outlast the Germans . . . at sundown just as the supply runs out . . . the arrival of 15 Rangers who join their fire with Taylor's and the Germans fade back . . . Price paid the perfect tribute to Taylor. . . . "We saw no sign of fear in him . . . Marching or fighting, he was leading. . . ."

In some important aspects of the right flank Dog Green beach landings, there is reasonable concurrence among the more prominent accounts. *Omaha Beachhead* describes the events as perhaps the worst of those at all sectors. The fortified positions at Exit D-1, the Vierville draw, survived the bombardment and fired accurately at the incoming landing craft. Additionally, these craft took fire from the more westward positions at Pointe de la Percée. In this account one of the LCA craft foundered at about 1,000 yards out and the men jumped into the sea only to be taken down by their heavy loads. There is a description of another LCA being hit by four mortar rounds and disintegrating. The assault teams leaving the landing craft which ground to a stop in water four to six feet deep were immediately swept by accurate fire from automatic weapons. Losses continued as troops became disorganized in the attempt to safely reach shore. One boat team had enough survivors to attempt a firing line but the leaders became casualties and the effort to organize came apart. Within Company A of the 116th Infantry all officers and most sergeants were either killed or seriously wounded. Estimates of total casualties range as high as two-thirds. The objective of all remaining troops became survival. One technique was to return to the water and to crawl back only at the rate of the advancing tide. Another was to huddle behind the doubtful cover of the tidal obstacles. Comparatively, the ultimate degree of safety during the early hours on Dog Green beach was to gain the shelter of the seawall. There seems to be widespread agreement that 15 minutes after landing, Company A was out of action for the day. Thus it can be seen that the tenor of the descriptions in *Omaha Beachhead* begins to converge on those of Col. Marshall despite the disparity pointed up by the above quotations. The account of events conveyed in *Cross-Channel Attack*, published five years after *Omaha Beachhead*, though brief in detail, does not differ substantially from the composite picture.

Some progress was made in improving armor support, intended to be an influential factor for the first time in U.S. amphibious operations. The plan called for Sherman DD-tanks (dual drives, capable of swimming ashore) of Companies B and C of the 743d Tank Battalion to be launched 6,000 yards offshore of Dog Green and Dog White beaches respectively. The tanks had been transported across the channel by LCT. The third company of tanks were conventionally waterproofed and scheduled for discharge upon beaching at Dog Red and Easy Green. The plan was sacrificed to the good judgement of the commanders of the LCTs bearing the Sherman DDs. The offshore launching was scrapped and the DDs were brought in until they grounded to a halt. This precaution was not taken on the left-side beach sectors and the result was a catastrophe of the worst kind. Thus the tank support did arrive on the beach sectors of the 116th Infantry.

Losses immediately began to accumulate. In front of the Vierville draw accurate artillery fire sank an LCT and Company B of the 743d Tank Battalion lost its commander. Only one officer escaped death or serious wounds. Eight of the sixteen tanks of the company actually landed and returned fire. The other two tank companies landed to the left of Dog Green beach and got all their tanks safely onshore. But, an answer to the question of whether the infantry on Dog Green, Company A of the 116th, had any fire support remains elusive. The speed with which eight main battle tanks were lost indicates that the enemy's lethal 88-mm guns were all located and manned by proficient crews.

Before leaving the sectors of the 116th Infantry, the situation of the 2d Battalion assault should be noted. The landing diagram put three companies in line just east of Dog Green. Generally the beach sectors between exits were not so strongly fortified as were the exits themselves. Thus Dog White sector, the attack target of Company

G, was a less difficult assignment than Dog Green, in front of the Vierville draw. Also, some of the bluff areas in the vicinity of les Moulins were shrouded in heavy smoke due to grass fires ignited by the naval bombardment. As a consequence the accuracy of fire from defensive positions on Dog Red and Easy Green was significantly reduced. Companies E and F both benefited from the concealment and their losses in the assault were at a lesser level than suffered by Company A. A further problem affected the assault sections of the 2d Battalion. Mislandings were multiplying and the companies lost unit integrity. Much of Company E was swept about one mile to the east and became intermixed with elements of the 16th Infantry. Overall, the picture of the 2d Battalion was one of disorganization, heavy losses among officers, and reduced assault capability, even though the situation was not so severe as that in front of Vierville.

A similar set of misfortunes beset the troops of the 16th Infantry on Easy Red and Fox Green beach sectors. The plan for these eastern beach sectors called for a balanced distribution of two battalions, the 2d and 3d with Companies E and F abreast on Easy Red and Companies I and L abreast on Fox Green. These troops came off the attack transport *Henrico* and the British ship *Empire Anvil*. Compared to the other Omaha Beach sectors Easy Red, more than a mile long, was a bit more hospitable. Of the 12 assault teams assigned to this sector, only two landed there but they were joined by two teams of the 116th Infantry who were far off course. Actually they hit the eastern end of the sector where fortifications were sparse. After debarking from landing craft they waded toward shore although swimming was necessary in deep water spots. This constituted a struggle and many weapons were jettisoned including mortars, bazookas and flamethrowers. All told, losses were relatively light on Easy Red. The disappointment there was that so few assault troops found this favorable location for scaling the bluffs.

The situation at Fox Green was comparable to the worst of what was happening on the western sectors. Characteristically the losses in some assault teams were at the level of one-half, the leadership ranks were especially hard hit, and disorder prevailed in the location and timing of boat landings. There were 14 boat loads of assault infantry that did not belong there. Of the 12 teams that should have landed on Easy Red, 10 were swept eastward to Fox Green. These 10 teams were equally from Companies E and F of the 16th Infantry. The other four teams were from Company E of the 116th Infantry, swept off course from Easy Green sector, about 2,900 yards to the west. Troops of the 16th Infantry, 3d Battalion which were slated for Fox Green beach were similarly swept eastward, with many of Company L arriving on Fox Red which was not intended to be a landing site. Two landing craft of the six went down due to swamping in the rough seas. Company I was taken as far east as Port-en-Bessin before the navigation error was discovered and then brought back to Fox Green 90 minutes late.

The resistance put up by the defenders of Fox Green was ferocious. At the Colleville draw, Exit E-3, a 75-mm gun was positioned on the bluff with a field of fire to enfilade the assault teams coming ashore. Additionally, a casemated 88-mm gun was well located. Automatic weapons fire sprayed the landing craft as ramps were lowered. Many of the troops were killed or wounded during the struggle to make shore. Those who closed in then came under machine gun and mortar fire. There was no seawall to aim for and the shingle bank afforded only a slight defilade. The general situation at Fox Green during the initial phase was an attempt to survive by burrowing into the shingle. Little if any thought was given to an advance beyond the beach.

Armor support on the eastern sectors was patterned similarly to what was described for the landings of the 116th Infantry on the sectors to the west. The 741st Tank Battalion was equipped with two companies of the dual-drive, swimming tanks and one company of conventionally waterproofed Sherman M4s. However, one drastic difference prevailed in the manner of landing the 741st as compared to the 743d. Recall that the commanders of the LCTs and of tank companies of the 743d determined that sea conditions would not permit a safe launching of the DD-Shermans at a distance of 6,000 yards offshore and that the best solution to the problem was to beach the landing craft. For whatever reason this technique was not followed with the DDs of the 741st Tank. The launching off LCTs took place as planned at about 6,000 yards from shore. Under the pounding of the sea, flotation gear suffered canvas rips, the supporting struts collapsed, and engines became flooded. One by one 27 of the DDs sank leaving only five to make their way to shore. Some of the tank crews escaped through their tank hatches and got their life belts inflated, or may even have launched rafts. Unfortunately the infantry craft passing by were under strict instructions to push ahead and leave rescue operations to others. The casualty rate was appalling. Company A of the 741st Tank was the unit with conventional waterproofing and fared somewhat better than its fellow companies. An explosion far at sea disabled two tanks and enemy fire shortly after landing knocked out three more.

Altogether about one-third of the tanks of the 741st survived to engage in some action. Most were on Easy Red where they found some targets between the St.-Laurent and Colleville draws. On Fox Green where the need was greatest only one lonely Sherman DD and several conventionally waterproofed Shermans survived as effective fighting units. It appeared that enemy gunners tracked all tanks as they made their way to shore and had a high rate of hits to reduce the fire support so desperately needed by the assault forces.

The Special Engineer Task Force was the third vital component of the initial assault along with the infantry teams and their armor fire support. The typical landing diagrams show engineer teams arriving ashore at H plus three minutes. Obviously, landing waves could not and did not operate with such precision as to maintain accurate spacing between the closely bunched initial waves. Suffice it to say that the engineer demolition teams were an integral part of the assault. The necessity for the early attack on the problem of tidal zone obstacles derived from the timing of initial landings with respect to the state of the tide and has already been covered rather thoroughly.

Many of the military histories of the Normandy invasion carry conflicting de-

scriptions of the role and structure of the demolition teams so a brief review is warranted. The assignment called for creation of clear lanes through the obstacles on the
tidal flat, frequently referred to as underwater obstacles which they were at high tide—
but only then. The lanes were to be 50 yards wide with eight lanes allotted to each of
the three infantry regiments in the initial assault, namely the 116th Infantry on the
western sectors and the 16th Infantry on the eastern sectors of Omaha, and the 8th
Infantry on Utah. The demolition teams were comprised of two parts, one Navy but
with an Army component and the second and larger part being an all-Army group.
The Navy group was composed of five trained personnel of their Naval Combat Demolition Units, three seamen for non-specialized duties, and five Army personnel from a
combat engineer battalion, for a total of 13. The all-Army group was a 26-man team
with a lieutenant in charge. On Omaha these teams came from the 146th and 299th
Engineer Combat Battalions. Overall control was assigned to an ad hoc organization,
the Special Engineer Task Force under command of Col. John O'Neill. Additional
capability was provided to the teams by adding tank dozers.

Techniques employed in neutralizing the obstacles were developed over many
months. Initially, development work was centered at Fort Pierce, Florida, a Navy
facility, but made available to Army use after the Engineer Amphibian Command
was phased out. Most of the personnel of the Omaha Beach Engineer Special Brigades had some training at Fort Pierce, and the Engineer Board conducted experimentation there. In early February of 1944, Col. O'Neill was among a group sent
back by Gen. Eisenhower to witness demonstrations there. Development work continued in the European Theater, practically up to the time of embarkation for
Normandy. The central problem was a determination of efficient means to sever the
steel obstacle structures with explosives so as to minimize the amount of material
required and to prevent unnecessary fragmentation which could be a hazard to demolition personnel. A device evolved from this effort which consisted of a small canvas
pack of explosive with fittings for rapid attachment to the structure and for connecting to a primacord ring which would fire the multiple packs simultaneously. These
came to be called Hagensen Packs in recognition of the naval officer who originated
the concept.

Numerous operational details were refined for adaptation to the cross-Channel
environment. The crossing to the transport area was planned by LCT each of which
would tow an LCM. The latter craft, with length in excess of 50 feet, had an adequate
capacity to cope with the composite demolition team which came to 40 including an
officer and a medic in each Army component and 13 in the Navy component. The
transfer to LCMs was planned for the final run into the beach. Each of the craft were
loaded with 1,000 pounds of explosive, demolition accessories, mine detectors, and
related engineer impedimenta. The several craft allotted to the command group were
to carry a ton of extra explosive. There was a possibility that land mines might be
encountered on the tidal flats. That turned out not to be the case although Tellermines
attached to the obstacles were found in abundant quantities. Working arrangements

were formulated for sharing the work load in each lane, with the Navy component of the team concentrating on the seaward area and the Army party working the inshore area. A final test of the readiness of the demolition teams was available at the Assault Training Center—Woolacombe in late April and early May, 1944. Tank dozers were ordered to the Center for combined training.

The Channel crossing was exceptionally difficult for the gap clearing-demolition teams. As was the case for other engineer troops making the crossing in LCT craft they spent at least four days exposed to miserable weather, cramped quarters, and hardly adequate sanitary conditions. All this was on top of the problem of motions of a flat-bottomed boat plowing rough seas. A number of the LCMs under tow broke loose and had to be recovered, a rather difficult task in the circumstances. Three of the LCTs broke down and became total losses forcing a transfer to the LCMs in order to complete the voyage, under conditions even more cramped. Upon arrival in the transport area, about 0200 hours on the morning of D-day, the transfer to the LCM craft was completed but not quite within the limited time allotted by the schedule. Finally, the wave of demolition teams found their way to the line of departure and were sent off to the beach, with only a few stragglers.

The demolition teams arrived ashore, nearly in line, with an interval of roughly 300 yards separating the craft. Those who had to come much of the way in LCMs were still later. The easterly flowing tidal current swept this wave off their targets but the disruption was not so marked as occurred in getting the infantry assault teams landed. Nevertheless, several stragglers were late by as much as 10 minutes, due to delays during the transfer to LCM craft. During this final run-in there were encounters with struggling tank crews in the water who had escaped from sinking DD-Shermans. But, orders had been explicit that no rescue effort be allowed to divert the teams from their mission since other naval craft were assigned to rescue.

Planning put Team No. 1 on the westernmost beach sector, Dog Green, but their actual landing was at least one beach sector off placing them near the boundary of Dog White and Dog Red. As the ramp dropped, accurate small arms fire covered the craft but the team scrambled into the water and headed for the seaward row of obstacles. Explosives were distributed between individual 40-pound packs which each man carried and a reserve supply on a rubber boat which was to be floated in from the grounded LCM. The Army and Navy team leaders made an adjustment in division of work so that both components of the team would immediately set to work on the seaward row of obstacles. Obviously they were concerned about the incoming tide reducing access to the seaward rows, which in this case included Element C, the sturdiest and largest of the obstacles on the tidal flats. The Army engineer group promptly fixed charges to the gates, set off the purple smoke warning signal and then fired the detonators. They next worked in the direction of the Navy men who were loading ramps, posts, and hedgehogs. The placement of Tellermines fixed to posts and ramps posed a particular hazard since the danger existed that the timber members could be cut while leaving the mines still functional, thus creating a floating bomb. Therefore one of the Hagenson packs was attached, with great care, to each of the mines.

The demolition task proceeded in a satisfactory way while enemy reaction, and related problems, were building at an alarming rate. Sherman DD-tanks operating on the 116th Infantry beach sectors moved about seaward of the obstacles while searching for targets ashore. The tank fire barely cleared the demolition working parties while at the same time attracting fire from shore. Fire was also directed at the demolition personnel themselves. Casualties mounted. Two seamen who attempted to launch the rubber boat with reserve explosives were hit by snipers onshore. The Army medic attempting to render first aid and assist the wounded to shore was himself hit and instantly killed. The reserve explosives were lost. In the midst of these problems the assault teams of the 2d Battalion, 116th Infantry reached this beach sector, somewhat behind schedule, and drew more intense fire from defensive positions. To compound the lane clearing task the infantrymen used the obstacles as cover in their attempt to move forward. They made little progress and in fact became pinned down.

As the remainder of charged obstacles were readied for detonation, leaders applied strong pressure to clear all troops out of the lane. The example of strong leadership worked beyond expectation. Not only did the infantrymen move forward they also helped wounded demolition men vacate the danger area. Then, according to plan, a purple smoke signal was sent off followed by the roar of the detonation. After the smoke, water spouts, and debris settled down Team No. 1 was pleased to see the results of many months of intense training—the gap was blown clean and the 50-yard wide lane was ready for high tide. Green marker buoys were attached to obstacles on each side of the clear lane to guide coxswains of later waves. The task was completed in 20 minutes, a superb performance under terrible difficulties. With additional waves due ashore from H plus 30 minutes onwards there was no interference between incoming traffic and gap clearing teams. One further hurdle faced Team No. 1—the survivors and the casualties had to move forward, at least to the meager safety at the shingle line. In the process two Army and one Navy members of the team took fatal hits. Upon reaching the shingle embankment trenches were dug and lined with inflated life belts so the wounded could have a small bit of relief.

Teams No. 2 through 5 had essentially no success. The first of this group was a late arrival and the incoming tide made work virtually impossible. Team No. 3 took a salvo of artillery as its boat ramp lowered, its explosives detonated, and only one man survived alive and unwounded. The next team took heavy casualties while attempting to charge individual obstacles and never succeeded in clearing a gap. Team No. 5 was first ashore on its assigned beach and rapidly managed to get charges attached to obstacles. However, when the time to detonate arrived the area was overrun by infantry seeking some cover among the obstacles and who were nudged forward only by the threat of the advancing tide. An attempt to detonate the charges met with partial results and a partly clear gap.

Team No. 6 landed on Easy Green beach, east of the les Moulins draw, where their results were quite satisfactory. The obstacles here were sparsely distributed, only two rows of ramps and one of hedgehogs. The problem of infantrymen taking cover recurred here. In this case though the team leaders devised a simple solution consisting of detonating the charges individually rather than connecting a large field with primacord for simultaneous firing. It then became necessary to move only small groups of the troops at one time. A gap was created in excess of 50 yards wide. Later as the day wore on and the tide rose, two LCT craft missed the markers of the clear lanes, struck mined obstacles and went to the bottom. However, the sinking obstructed only about half the lane and it continued to be a useful channel. Teams 7 and 8 were not successful in clearing useful lanes. Troops obstructed progress as they hesitantly moved through the lines of obstacles. The inshore teams of engineers took heavy losses and were not able to demolish the lines of hedgehogs.

At this point the reader is again requested to focus on the matter of accuracy in information. The critical issue is the situation on the Easy Red beach sector. At the risk of excessive repetition consider a brief recapitulation. As the infantry assault teams went ashore, Companies E and F of the 2d Battalion of the 16th Infantry, with the exception of one boat team of each company, were swept eastward onto Fox Green. Additionally, Company E of the 116th Infantry was swept eastward more than a mile and landed mostly on Fox Green except for two assault teams on Easy Red. The status is summarized in *Omaha Beachhead* this way: ". . . Except for these four sections—about a hundred men—the only assault elements on Easy Red beach for the first half hour were four DD-tanks, one already disabled."

In tracking the progress of the demolition teams on the eastern sectors of Omaha there are complications. Several historical accounts contain details of the operations of the demolition teams and appear to be well researched and carefully documented. The Army series on World War II (often described as the "green books") includes *The Corps of Engineers: The War Against Germany* which emphasizes the engineer contribution to the obstacle clearing mission. Navy participation is stressed in *The Naked Warriors* which deals with underwater demolitions in a broad way. Both of these accounts report in detail the attempts to clear lanes through the obstacles on Easy Red early in the landings.

Several of the demolition teams managed to reach Easy Red early in the landings, as we rely on the principal sources for a valid picture. The "green book" on the Corps of Engineers reports Team No. 9 in the center of Easy Red, ahead of any infantry, where they succeeded in clearing a lane. The naval story concurs in the absence of other assault troops but notes that the landing craft took an artillery hit before the ramp could be lowered and that one death and three wound casualties resulted. After attachment of charges to obstacles it was necessary to fire two detonations to complete the task.

Team No. 10 produced a lane wider than the others, extending to near 100 yards. They encountered difficulties due to the arrival of assault infantry. Casualties during the work slowed progress. A possible explanation of the interference of infantry troops may be that work was delayed to the extent that waves due ashore at H plus 30 minutes arrived before detonation could be completed. In any case, the obstacles farthest offshore were ramps and were charged by the Navy contingent. The Army troops worked on posts and ramps comprising the obstacle rows positioned inshore. Here again, as was the case at the neighboring team, a number of detonations was necessary before the lane was completely clear.

Team No. 12, also landed on Easy Red then cleared a minimum-width gap. This team suffered severe losses as six Army and four Navy deaths along with nine wounded resulted from enemy mortar fire. It appeared that a premature detonation of charges was initiated by the incoming rounds. Survivors evacuated their wounded to shore, then marked the lane. The balance of the team checked the lane to assure that all obstacles were neutralized and that boat traffic could pass safely.

Of the eight teams assigned to the eastern sectors, three were relatively successful on the gapping mission. The other five encountered misfortunes of a magnitude such as to ruin their chances of clearing a useable lane. Team No. 11 landed on the far left of Easy Red which put them within the range of the defenders at the Colleville draw, Exit E-3. Apparently none of the assault infantry teams landed in this location and thus no force had a suppressing effect on the fortifications at the draw. More than half of the gapping team became casualties. The survivors attempted to carry on and managed to attach charges to obstacles but a failure occurred during the detonation procedure and time ran out. Team No. 13 was hit by artillery during unloading of materials from their craft and suffered heavy losses. The Army group of this team had sufficient able bodied personnel to carry on but then met the problem of nearby troops seeking cover among the obstacles. This team was not able to detonate any charges. Team No. 14 arrived early at Easy Red and had no interference from other troops. Unfortunately their LCM was hit by artillery just after they had floated off a rubber boat with the explosives reserve. In due course they were able to attach charges to obstacles and prepare for detonation. Then the problem of troop interference cropped up, eventually forcing the demolition team to abandon their effort and join the group seeking cover at the shingle bank.

On Fox Green sector Teams No. 15 and 16 had experiences paralleling the worst of their neighbors. They had losses to small arms fire while debarking their landing craft. After launching their explosives-laden rubber boats they attracted artillery. Personnel losses mounted while the teams exerted maximum effort to attach explosive charges to obstacles. Finally, detonation was foiled when shell fragments destroyed the firing hookup. Both these two teams had been late getting ashore, Team No. 15 by more than 10 minutes, so they had reached the point where there was no time to make repairs and try again for detonation. Team No. 15 was reduced to four effective members when it gave up the effort and headed for the shingle bank. Team No. 16 similarly drew fire from shore when launching the rubber boats. However, its main problem was the presence of friendly troops using the obstacles for cover. Unable to clear the troops out this team was also forced to abandon the task and move ashore.

A summary of the initial assault, arbitrarily using our Phase I designation, yields a discouraging picture (Figs. 35 and 36). There was much more failure than success. The infantry component had not moved forward to attack objectives but was hanging on in a fight merely for survival. Heavy losses were taken all along Omaha but at some positions units were so decimated, leaderless and shaken that they could not function at all. The only bright side was the fact that troops were ashore and might yet rally as reinforcements arrived. Fire support was also fraught with failure when the DD-Shermans launched offshore went mostly to the bottom as flotation gear tore apart. Where DDs were brought in close so as to crawl ashore on the tidal bottom loss rates were also high, mainly to 88-mm guns. The tank companies using conventional waterproofing did not fare much better. Finally, the third component of the initial assault, the joint Army-Navy gap clearing teams had a comparable lack of success, not withstanding their valiant effort and terrible losses as counted by their dead and wounded. They managed to detonate hand-placed charges on the tidal zone obstacles to create five seemingly clear lanes. Marker buoys for the lanes were mostly lost or swept away which limited the usefulness of the lanes when high tide prevailed later in the morning. Only six of the 16 tank dozers which were intended to support the gapping teams reached shore due to drowning losses and hits by enemy artillery. Of the six there were three more losses to enemy artillery shortly afterward. A frequent criticism is leveled at American planners and commanders by a considerable number of military historians to the effect that if only they had made greater use of specialized armor, then performance of the Omaha landing force would have benefited correspondingly. Clearly, the record of the Sherman DD-tanks does not support such critics.

Figure 35—*Troops Under Fire During Trek Through Tidal Zone Seek Cover.* *Note bunching behind conventionally waterproofed tank on left, also use of hedgehogs. Closer inshore a DD-tank is visible. This shot is a widely used classic taken by Robert Capa for* Life *Magazine. Based on tide this is one of the earliest views of Omaha.*

Figure 36—*Troops Mislanded Move Laterally Along Beach to Join Units.* *Photograph conveys sense of confusion due to scattering of units along Omaha which compounded casualty rate before moving forward to engage enemy. Stranded landing craft indicates tide has commenced to recede. Though not actually a Phase I view, a continuing problem is graphically illustrated.*

ENGINEER RECONNAISSANCE OPERATIONS

In the phased structure of the landings proposed by Col. Thompson in his *Infantry Journal* paper Phase II is a period titled "The Assault Continued", extending from "The Infantry-Tank Assault" to about H plus 60 minutes. As noted in the landing diagram, the tempo of build-up ashore grows. Scheduled waves were 10 minutes apart. A gap was built into the schedule from about H plus five minutes to H plus 30 minutes to allow the demolition teams to clear lanes through the tidal obstacles. From this point onward the intensified build-up needed to compensate for the lost time.

Engineer troops were very conspicuous in this phase. Previously, the bulk of two engineer combat battalions, the 146th and 299th, were integrated into the teams assigned to gap-clearance on the tidal flats. During the continuation of the build-up the infantry battalions of the initial assault were augmented by their reserve companies and their weapons companies. They began to take the normal form of infantry units— as contrasted to the light, specialized organization of the 30-man teams created for the conditions of initial assault. But, more to the point is the landing of engineer reconnaissance teams and command groups. Divisional engineers amounted to four combat battalions. On the western sectors were the 121st and 112th Engineers, the organic and attached battalions of the 29th Division respectively. On the eastern sectors were the 1st and 20th Engineers, the organic and attached battalions of the 1st Division respectively.

The engineer special brigades also had their early elements ashore during this phase. While the primary role of these units centered around beach organization and development over a period of time, they also contributed notably to opening beach exits and facilitating the movement of troops off the beaches. An examination of the records of these units shows a considerable overlap with the divisional engineers on Omaha Beach. This is in contrast to the situation on Utah Beach where the mission of divisional engineers centered on the movement inland and did not call for early arrival of their troops on the beach. The 6th Brigade operating on the western sectors of Omaha included the 147th and 149th Engineers assigned to support of the 116th Infantry. The other battalion of the brigade was the 203d Engineers. The 5th Brigade operating on the eastern sectors of Omaha included the 37th Engineers assigned to support of the 16th Infantry, and the 348th Engineers assigned to the follow-on 18th Infantry. The other battalion of the 5th Brigade, the 336th, was due later to organize the Fox Red sector.

Resuming the description of operations ashore, the expectations built into the plan were not realized. Enemy fire did not abate as new waves landed. Troops clustered along the shingle line remained pinned down. No friendly weapons firings covered the new landings, which naturally were closer inshore as the tide advanced. Mislandings continued to be a problem, particularly for the engineer units whose task assignments were keyed to particular sections of the terrain and whose effectiveness was most dependent on the presence of active leadership.

The situation on the western, or right flank, sector did not improve noticeably. Company B of the 116th Infantry, with a mission of reinforcing the devastated Company A, was widely dispersed during the landings and had only several of its boat teams on Dog Green. These troops joined the survivors of Company A at the waters' edge in the fight to stay alive. The companies of the 2d Battalion were on adjacent beaches to the east attempting to rectify the problem of scattered units. This required lateral movement along the beach which produced additional casualties. Next came the landings of the 3d Battalion of the 116th Infantry, following up on the 2d. The bulk of these troops hit shore on Easy Green, a beach sector that had been missed for the most part during the prior landings, but which became crowded. Hostile fire was less intense than what had been encountered earlier except that the boat teams which spilled over onto Easy Red found that the fortifications at Exit E-1 were still deadly.

A fortuitous development came during this phase which had a profound impact on progress of the invasion. This was the arrival of new effective leaders for the decimated units. As noted earlier, among the early assault teams the casualty rate for company grade officers, and senior non-coms as well, was horrible. As a result disorganized and leaderless groups were numerous. The commander of the 2d Battalion, 116th Infantry, Maj. Sidney Bingham reached shore and was followed in due course by other key leaders. Toward the end of this phase the command group of the 116th Infantry came ashore bringing not only the regimental commander, Col. Charles Canham, but also the assistant division commander, Brig. Gen. Norman Cota. The inspirational leadership of Gen. Cota was a critical contribution to forward progress from this point onward.

Maj. Bingham found the remnants of his Company F to be scattered and leaderless, but managed to assemble a group of about 50. He led this force in an assault up the draw at les Moulins, Exit D-3 at the junction of Dog Red and Easy Green. They were unable to subdue the machine gun position on the top of the bluff and withdrew to the cover of structures at the base of the draw. But, the attempt to advance was a noteworthy achievement in the circumstances. Also during this period the 3d Battalion of the 116th Infantry arrived ashore. The landing schedule called for the 3d to land behind the 2d in a follow-on role. As it actually happened the new landing was east of the les Moulins draw, where fortunately the hostile fire was comparatively light. By this time, the standard for such ratings was the intense resistance in front of Vierville on the west and on Fox Green sector on the east flank. In reaching the shingle embankment Company K had no losses while Company I had only a few casualties. Company L came in against light resistance, to the left of the other two companies, and Company M came in farther to the left, even having some of its boat teams arriving at Exit E-1, on a sector of the 16th Infantry. One of their landing craft struck a mine and was on the verge of sinking. Overall, the western sector follow-on infantry units were not mauled to the extent that befell the initial assault.

Engineer activity ashore on the western beach sectors did not get off to an auspicious start. Advance personnel of the 121st Engineer Combat Battalion were scheduled to land on Dog Green and Dog White, the far right sectors, at 0710 hours. They numbered approximately 100 and came in from the transport area aboard two LCM craft. Mislandings put the teams somewhat more than one mile to the east.

As noted in Chapter V, Col. Ploger, commanding the 121st, made his way to shore despite deep water and a shrapnel wound in the leg. He found himself totally alone when he reached the shingle. His immediate task was to assemble sufficient force to reduce the obstacle blocking Exit D-1. This was an eight-foot high concrete wall which extended from the bluffs on the west to a concrete pillbox so that the exit was totally inaccessible. Successful accomplishment of this mission was critically important to the movement of the 29th Division through Vierville to Isigny (about seven miles west by southwest of Vierville) for linkup with the 4th Division and Utah Beach. Thus, the reconnaissance function in Phase II concentrated on locating individuals and clusters so as to create functional units. Col. Ploger looked for engineers, infantry, tankers, or any able-bodied troops. He was also concerned with the location of tactical supplies and equipment, particularly explosives which most of his men should have brought ashore in 10-pound lots. During preembarkation planning he had determined that 1,100 pounds of TNT would be required for this demolition task.

A summary of the early period experiences of the 121st Engineers is dominated by the heavy losses of units reaching shore. Both Companies B and C arrived early. The commander of Company C was killed by a hit on the head before he could step off the ramp of his LCM. Before the first 24 hours passed, all three line company commanders were casualties in addition to six other officers killed or wounded. The battalion commander, Col. Ploger having reached shore at 0730 hours, ignored his leg wound until it finally incapacitated him after the capture of St.-Lô, more than seven weeks later. Most of the 62 D-day casualties of the battalion resulted from incoming fire during the early period of the assault. Progress on the primary mission at Exit D-1 was virtually nil. However, isolated detachments did get involved as infantry in an attempt to clear the enemy mines, and wire from positions threatening their objective area.

The 112th Engineer Combat Battalion operated in parallel with the 121st, being assigned to sectors Dog Red and Easy Green. Their mission was to open Exit D-3, through the draw at les Moulins. The early contingent of the unit arrived ashore also in the H plus 40 minute wave by LCM. Losses were heavy in this battalion and in fact the commander was killed early. Frustrations and difficulties surrounded their effort to make progress at the well-defended draw. The troops were pinned down by accurate, observed enemy fire. Small groups joined infantry in attempting to advance beyond the seawall. It was much later in the day before significant progress could be made in neutralizing the land mines and other obstacles blocking the draw.

The wave of landing craft scheduled for H plus 40 minutes also brought in advance elements of the 6th Engineer Special Brigade. On the right-hand beach sectors the 147th Engineers had assignments similar to the those of the 121st Engineers. Examination of historical records shows that some overlap prevailed in the missions of the two units, both units deployed on Dog Green and Dog White and both arriving ashore about the same time. Survivors of the struggle through the tidal flats were scattered and in no condition to concentrate on engineer tasks. For the most part they ultimately linked up with infantrymen in the vicinity of Vierville.

A few notes on the other early landing elements of the 6th Brigade completes the picture of engineer activity on the western beach sectors. The 149th Engineers, sort of a sister unit to the 147th, was scheduled to have an advance party ashore on its assigned sectors, Dog Red and Easy Green. The mission of this battalion was centered on the tasks at Exit D-3, the route through the draw at les Moulins. Here again the historical records are not clear and the distinction between the mission of the 149th and that of the 112th is difficult to ascertain. The first group of the battalion reached the shingle of Easy Green. They set to work there on clearing a path through the dune area to reach the road parallel to the shoreline. A second detail moved forward cutting gaps in barbed wire but was stopped by an antitank ditch and under enemy fire was forced back to the shingle line.

The eastern beach sectors produced an anomalous distribution of troops during the initial assault. Easy Red sector was missed by most of the boat teams of the 2d Battalion, 16th Infantry. Only two of the 12 craft landing these troops landed correctly which was doubly unfortunate since Easy Red along several stretches was not strongly defended. The boat teams of the 3d Battalion partly were swept to Fox Red sector which was not intended as a landing site and some landed even farther to the east to the vicinity of Port-en-Bessin, which led to a retracement back to Fox Green where they were 90 minutes late.

In the follow-on landings Company G of the 2d Battalion landed correctly except that one of the craft took on water and was late. There were no casualties prior to ramps down but during movement across the tidal zone until the shingle was reached 63 men were hit by a combination of small arms and mortar fire. Company H, with the heavy weapons of the 2d Battalion, arrived late by 20 minutes and off course enough to be close to Exit E-3. At this location enemy fire was heavy, substantial equipment and weapons were lost and the company became pinned down.

The 3d Battalion fared no better. Company K landed in disorder and took heavy casualties, nearly 50, while making no contribution to unit integrity on Fox Green. The heavy weapons unit of the battalion, Company M, also was scattered during the landing and had lost one of its craft due to capsizing. Despite its problems Company M was prepared to deliver supporting fire shortly after landing. Company I was also scheduled for landing in this period on Fox Green but ran into severe problems. Their craft were mislanded to an easterly position. Two were swamped before reaching shore, two others took artillery hits while attempting to land, one struck a mine and one impacted an obstacle. The battalion command party was mislanded to the west, a strange occurrence, and was late in arriving to sort out the problems.

Engineer support on the eastern sectors was provided by an array of troops comparable to that on the western sectors. Divisional battalions, the 1st and 20th Engineers were both experienced units. The 1st Engineers, integral to the 1st Division, had served in the campaigns through Tunisia and Sicily. The 20th similarly had participated in the Mediterranean campaigns, although at that time it was structured as an engineer combat regiment. In addition to these two battalions there were three battalions of shore party engineers, structured and trained as combat battalions, providing similar engineer support during the early phases even though their roles would differ as time wore on and the shore parties concentrated on beach development.

In their broad mission statements the two sets of engineer battalions had much in common. Overlapping roles, as noted in describing engineer activities on the western beach sectors, were encountered on the eastern sectors as well. Information sources for reconstructing events on the eastern side were no better for the western side. The sparse historical documents which exist differ one from another when relating particular events. Perhaps this outcome was inevitable because the advance parties of all the engineer battalions were scheduled for landing at approximately the same time.

An advance party of the 1st Engineers reached shore about H plus 30 minutes after a stormy transfer to LCVPs off the *Samuel Chase*. The mission of the battalion was to clear Exit E-1 to the vicinity of St.-Laurent by providing four lanes, each eight yards wide. During landing, troops became scattered and this resulted in a major effort to collect personnel and commence work. This problem persisted throughout the morning and was equally evident as the main body of troops reached shore. Fortunately the losses to the landing team were quite light. After orientation to the terrain features the landing party determined they were well to the east of their destination, and set off to their assigned draw.

A team of Company A of the 20th Engineers had a similar mission at Exit E-3 on the Fox Green sector. They reached shore at H plus 40 minutes but resistance was much more resolute there than on the neighboring sector. Troops who struggled ashore were pinned down on the beach and could not advance beyond the shingle. Their following boat teams in LCTs were hit, craft were sunk, and the strength of the company was down to 27 of whom nine were wounded. The other two companies arrived later but mission accomplishment was terribly behind schedule and was destined to remain so.

The 37th Engineers of the 5th Brigade had assignments at Exits E-1 and E-3 of Easy Red and Fox Green respectively. A command group of the battalion came ashore early by LCVP off the attack transport *Samuel Chase*. Heavy sea swells made the transfer to landing craft perilous and the run in to shore soaking wet and uncomfortable. The landing craft of the advance party came under fire from machine guns and mortars before debarking troops and the fire persisted but no casualties were experienced in reaching the shingle embankment. However, while hanging on in a pinned-down condition the number of wounded grew among both engineers and infantry along the shingle. Eventually, Col. Smith, the battalion commander was hit fatally by a mortar round. Signs of organization were beginning to emerge slowly during this period as infantry troops began to put their machine guns into operation.

A brief summary of the situation before proceeding into the next phase is that the infantry-tank assault did not conform to plan. Most all the troops were taking cover, such as it was, at the shingle line. Due to mislandings many units were scattered. Heavy officer casualties left many units leaderless. No organized offensive action had taken place. Examples of assault teams moving forward to attack defensive positions were not numerous. The attempt to use Sherman M4 tanks as close fire support was not successful—those of the DD version were mostly sunk when launched, those launched close in were mostly put out of action by 88-mm hits, and the conventionally waterproofed Shermans were also contending with a high loss rate. The attempt to clear lanes through the tidal obstacles went poorly despite the valiant efforts of the joint Army-Navy demolition teams. Of the six gaps created only one was marked so as to be useable. The advance parties of divisional and shore party engineers were scattered and had lost much equipment and supplies, mainly explosives. The most positive sign was that the numbers of troops ashore was steadily building and as key commanders arrived there was promise that reorganization and forward advances could be achieved.

ENGINEER MAIN BODIES REACH SHORE

This next phase described in the referenced structuring of landing force operations is "Build-up to Regiments", and extends from approximately H plus 60 to H plus 180 minutes. Thus far, each of the assault infantry regiments has landed with two battalions in line, or more accurately, four companies in line. These were followed by most of the remainder of the battalions, as for example the reserve rifle company and the heavy weapons company. In the following Phase III the reserve battalions, some of which may have already been ashore, were filled out. Supporting weapons under regimental control came ashore in this phase along with supplemental support which provided the regiment the character of a combat team.

A prime source of eye-witness accounts of these actions and those described later is available in the form of reports and recollections of the newsmen who covered the landings. Of the 530 who were accredited to SHAEF, 28 were selected to accompany the assault forces. The Eisenhower Foundation book of 1971 includes papers by two of the more experienced members of the group who had covered campaigns in the Mediterranean Theater. The extracts in the following box are generally applicable to the time period of this section of the account.

During this period naval gunfire support contributed to a solution of a troublesome problem on Omaha Beach. The preparatory bombardment by the Navy produced less than expected results. The loss rate of tanks and artillery deprived the ground forces of locally controlled gunfire support, certainly at the required quantities. As the day wore on, the battleships and cruisers, with their Spitfire-spotters, proved most useful against inland targets. It remained for the destroyers to fill the artillery gap. Their shore fire control parties came ashore with the engineer shore parties and incurred losses of personnel and radio equipment, but operated effectively despite the handicaps. The initial positions of the nine U.S. and three British destroyers was about 6,000 yards off the beach. Between 0800 and 1000 hours a strong forward displacement put the destroyers on the verge of grounding. At a distance of about 1,300 yards offshore, just west of Vierville, the *McCook* demolished gun positions on the cliffs which had been firing on the beach. These emplacements interfered with troops attempting to gain control at Exit D-1. The *Carmick* moved to a position 900 yards offshore, having lost contact with its shore controller, and found targets by observing fire from some tanks near Vierville. On the eastern sectors of the beach, the *Frankford* moved to near 800 yards from shore and struck at targets holding up the advance of troops. Both *Emmons* and *Doyle* spent considerable time off of Easy Red sector and scored hits on targets where requested by the shore fire control party. *Harding* was active off the center beach sectors and contributed to breaking the deadlock at les Moulins. Later in the day, she moved to the west to relieve the *Satterlee* off Pointe du Hoc. The *Baldwin* operated off the Easy beach sectors after taking two hits from shore batteries early in the day. The delivery of 5-inch rounds in quantities between 500 and 1,000 from each of the destroyers clearly had an influence on the direction of the battle.

Some Observations by the Attached Press Corps

Extracts from *D-Day, The Normandy Invasion in Retrospect;*
Eisenhower Foundation; University Press of Kansas; 1971.

A Correspondent's View of D-Day by Don Whitehead

. . . We boarded the Coast Guard Transport *Samuel Chase* on Sunday, June 4 . . . But the storm that swept the Channel forced the postponement of D-day . . . When dawn came, there was the breathtaking sight of that vast array of ships standing off the coast of France. . . .

The Channel was still rough, the waves running as high as six feet. Landing craft were bobbing in the water receiving their loads . . . We saw the DD tanks . . . Only two of the 32 made it to shore . . . they were swamped, often along with their entire crews. . . . The tide was rising fast as we approached the long line of beach barriers . . . We could see the flat mines attached to the wooden posts. . . . It did not take a military man to realize we were heading into chaos. Nothing was moving from the beach. Boats . . . were circling aimlessly. The Navy men could not find the gaps which they had been told would be blown in the barriers.

Gen. Wyman ordered our boat to move along the obstacles . . . He wanted to see for himself the cause of this mess. . . . the German guns were pouring deadly fire onto the beach . . . there was only limited access to the beach . . . Boats swung from their courses and drove through the gaps wherever they could find them. . . . units landed far from their troops. . . . And those who landed were pinned to the beach by heavy machine gun, artillery, and mortar fire.

We rode the rising tide through one of the gaps and waded ashore at 0800 hours. As far as I could see through the smoke of battle, troops were lying along a shelf of shale. Ahead of us stretched mined sand dunes to the bluffs where the Germans were sheltered in their trenches, bunkers, and blockhouses. There was no cover for the men on the beach. The Germans were looking down on them and it was a shooting gallery.

There were many brave men on Omaha that day . . . scores of men whose names were never imprinted on the honor roll . . . they organized small units and established islands of order in the chaos . . . units . . . were working their way through the minefields and up the bluff. . . . I remember vividly Pvt. Vinton Dove . . . He drove a bulldozer from a landing craft and then he began bulldozing a road from the beach as calmly as though he were grading a driveway at home.

The firepower of the Navy was one of our salvations in those first few hours. . . . A radio call for help went from an Army-Navy beach team to a destroyer. We saw the destroyer come racing toward the beach and swing broadside, exposing itself to the fire of the batteries on the bluff. One shell . . . tore a chunk of concrete from the side of the blockhouse . . . the fourth shell smashed into the gunport to silence the weapon . . . a major turning point in the battle for our sector. At 1330 hours Gen. Wyman . . . set up his first sheltered command post in the knocked-out blockhouse . . . as I saw it . . . the battle of the beach was won . . . seven hours after the first wave hit the beach . . .

From the engineer point of view there was a drastic change of emphasis in Phase III. The demolition teams working to clear lanes in the tidal zone ceased work when the tide covered the obstacles. Recall that low tide was one hour ahead of H-hour so that by 0830 hours the incoming tide was more than half way to the high water mark and that the seaward rows of obstacles were to be immersed shortly. The teams working on the tidal flats began to remove mines from those obstacles which were fitted with mines. This was done where troops could not be dislodged from the cover of the obstacles. Also, the removal of mines was a positive measure in helping tank dozers force the obstacles aside or toward shore.

As the build-up progressed during this period the results were mixed. The increasing troop strength provided the means to advance. Col. Charles Canham commanding the 116th Infantry and Brig. Gen. Norman Cota, Assistant Commander of the 29th Division, reached shore about 0730 hours and generated some leadership in the areas where scattered and disorganized small groups had clustered. Nevertheless, by 0800 hours essentially no movement beyond the beach was achieved. The number of lucrative targets on the beach for German gunners grew. In these circumstances, the Navy beachmaster signaled to all control vessels offshore that landing of vehicles would be suspended. This crucial event occurred about 0830 hours. At that time there were approximately 50 of the larger landing craft, LCTs and LCIs, milling about offshore searching for a safe gap through the tidal obstacles so their cargos could be put ashore.

The delay in beaching of LCTs had an adverse impact on the capability of the 121st Engineers to meet their mission requirements, probably moreso than the other engineer units on Omaha Beach. The landing plan of the western beach sectors called for the arrival of three bulldozers towing trailers at H plus 60 minutes. Another was scheduled for ten minutes later. Obviously the landing craft transporting these divisional engineer dozers was caught in the boat traffic which could not get to shore safely, and subsequently was prevented from landing by the temporary suspension. The consequence was that tool sets and explosive supply which were essential to the task at Exit D-1 were not available to the 121st. This in turn led to the necessity to scour the beaches for the materials to make a start on the assigned task. It was only after the later arrival of a Company C bulldozer that significant progress was made at Exit D-1.

Despite the disappointment in clearing and marking lanes through the tidal obstacles, a solution to the problem evolved. With the mines out of the way the groundwork was laid for ramming of the obstacles. The main result of this technique was just after 1000 hours off Fox Green beach sector. An LCT and an LCI(L) charged through the obstacles at full speed, and with all their weapons firing, beached successfully. This event points up another characteristic of the new phase of operations in that larger landing craft appear in significant numbers. A typical debarkation from these landing craft is shown in Fig. 37.

The pace of engineer operations picked up with the arrival of main body forces. The larger craft enabled the manpower buildup to accelerate. Of equal or greater importance was the arrival of engineer bulldozers. These machines were much more productive than tank dozers and were essential for many tasks, particularly the filling of antitank ditches, preparation of vehicular lanes on shore, and the extraction of vehicles stranded or drowned in the surf. Obviously the numbers of all combat vehicles coming ashore in this phase increased.

Engineer troops continued to join with infantry when infantry tasks had the highest priority. There are numerous recorded examples of engineers contributing to firing lines at the shingle embankment and moving forward to scale the bluffs and reduce enemy positions which were keeping the invasion pinned down.

The first significant forward movement in the western sector came between 0730 and 0800 hours, in the areas between the draws. Resistance at these locations was lower than at the beach exits. On the west side of the les Moulins draw Company C of the 116th Infantry crossed the grassy beach and headed for the bluffs following the detonation of explosives in the concertina wire along the beach road. Col. Canham, the regimental commander, and Gen. Cota were influential in getting these troops to move from the apparent, but only partial, protection of the shingle. Some casualties were taken in going across the flat but on the bluff there was smoke concealment and cover from the irregular terrain. The 5th Ranger Battalion had a mission to head westward and linkup with other Rangers on the heights beyond Vierville but mislanded, then joined this advancing group. There was also movement on the east side of the

Figure 37—Upper shot: Main Body of Engineer Shore Party Debarks from LCT. *Note that troops are heavily loaded with equipment and supplies for use prior to arrival of vehicles and dozers. Obstacles may have been sparse at this location or possibly reduced by demolition teams.*
Lower shot: Engineer Main Body Troops Debark from LCI. *Troops coming off personnel ramps on either side of craft encounter deep water indicating that beaching has occurred prior to high tide. Again, troops appear to be heavily loaded.*

draw as small scattered teams of the 3d Battalion, 116th Infantry began to advance up the bluffs. Finding no resistance on the summit these troops then together headed toward St.-Laurent.

Among the engineers, the 121st continued to search for its personnel and converge on the Vierville draw. Individuals and small detachments continued to participate with infantry and were among the group which reached the crest of the bluffs. Others who were becoming oriented to the ground headed for Exit D-1 at the Vierville draw. *Omaha Beachhead* contains remarks about two fatigued engineer troopers halting their trudge to the west with a heavy box of explosives. Later in the morning an assembly point was set up at the base of the bluff to conduct search and reconnaissance, reaching almost to the draw. The crux of the problem during this period was the collection of an adequate supply of explosives for demolition of the roadblock at the mouth of the exit. A concerted effort could not be made on this task until just after the noon hour.

The 112th engineers, operating parallel to the 121st but at the more easterly Exit D-3, encountered similar difficulties. The advance element had been hit hard in its initial landings. However, progress was made during this period by infantry and mixed groups on each flank of the les Moulins draw. The situation on the right side was covered above. On the left side the 3d Battalion of the 116th Infantry landed as a follow-on behind the 2d. The landings were fairly well ordered, compared to what happened on most of Omaha, and by 0900 hours elements of all rifle companies of the battalion were atop the bluff. This was the area nearest to the les Moulins draw. After being immobilized at the shingle the 112th Engineers joined with the infantry. This action may have contributed to the eventual commencement of engineer work in the draw and opening the exit to vehicular traffic. But, it has been noted earlier that this exit remained far behind schedule, and was in fact the last exit to be useable. In the meantime, the high density of land mines in the area provided a challenge to the 112th.

The main body of the units of the 6th Engineer Special Brigade came ashore on the western sectors from Dog Green through Easy Green. The landing diagram shows several LCIs assigned to the 147th and 149th Engineers early in this phase. The brigade commander, Col. Thompson, also landed about this time as related in his earlier remarks in Chapter V. After traversing the beach flats he encountered troops attempting, without success, to detonate bangalore torpedoes at a wire barrier at the seawall, nearby an enemy blockhouse. While in the process of lending a hand to position and detonate the bangalores he was struck in the head by two rounds of sniper fire. When he regained consciousness he was getting first aid inside the blockhouse. This cutting of the concertina wire may be the same operation that sprung Company C of the 116th Infantry to advance up the bluff west of the les Moulins draw!

Some Observations by the Attached Press Corps

Extracts from *D-Day, The Normandy Invasion in Retrospect;*
Eisenhower Foundation; University Press of Kansas; 1971.

Slightly Out of Focus by Robert Capa

. . . I used to know Company E (16th Infantry) very well and the story
I had got with them in Sicily was one of my best during the war. . . .
Col. Taylor . . . tipped me off that regimental headquarters would
follow close behind the first waves of infantry. If I went with him I
wouldn't miss the action . . . At 0400 hours we were assembled on
the open deck. The invasion barges were swinging on the cranes . . .
The sea was rough and we were wet before our barge pushed away
from the mother ship.

. . . the first unmistakable popping reached our listening ears. The
first empty barge, which had already unloaded its troops on the
beach, passed us on the way back to the *Chase.* . . . It was now light
enough to start taking pictures, and I brought my first Contax camera
out of its waterproof oilskin . . . The boatswain lowered the steel
covered barge front, and there, between the grotesque designs of
steel obstacles sticking out of the water, was a thin line of land
covered with smoke . . . Easy Red beach.

. . . The men from my barge waded in the water. Waist-deep, with
rifles ready to shoot, with the invasion obstacles and the smoking
beach in the background—this was good enough for the photogra-
pher. I paused for a moment on the gangplank (Editor: probably
referring to the ramp of the landing craft) to take my first real picture
of the invasion. The boatswain who was in an understandable hurry
to get the hell out of there, mistook my picture—taking attitude for
explicable hesitation, and helped me make up my mind with a well-
aimed kick in the rear. The water was cold, and the beach still more
than a hundred yards away. The bullets tore holes in the water
around me, and I made for the nearest steel obstacle. A soldier got
there at the same time, and for a few minutes we shared its cover.
He took the waterproofing off his rifle and began to shoot . . . rifle
gave him enough courage to move forward and he left the obstacle
to me. . . . I felt safe enough to take pictures of the other guys hiding
just like I was.

. . . I finished my pictures, and the sea was cold in my trousers. Reluctantly, I tried to move away from my steel pole, but the bullets chased me back every time. Fifty yards ahead of me, one of our half-burnt amphibious tanks stuck out of the water and offered me my next cover. . . . Between floating bodies I reached it, paused for a few more pictures, and gathered my guts for the last jump to the beach. . . . The tide was coming in . . . Behind the last two guys, I reached the beach . . . Exhausted from the water and the fear, we lay on a small strip of wet sand between the sea and the barbed wire. The slant of the beach gave us some protection, so long as we lay flat, from the machine gun and rifle bullets, but the tide pushed us against the barbed wire. . . .

The next mortar shell fell between the barbed wire and the sea, and every piece of shrapnel found a man's body. . . . I didn't dare to take my eyes off the finder of my Contax and frantically shot frame after frame. . . . my camera jammed—my roll was finished . . . my wet shaking hands ruined the (new) roll before I could insert it in my camera. . . . The empty camera trembled . . . It was a new kind of fear . . . Only the dead on the waterline rolled with the waves. An LCI braved the fire . . . I stepped into the sea between two bodies and the water reached to my neck.

I held my cameras high above my head . . . I reached the boat. . . . I went down to the engine room and put fresh films in both cameras. . . . I got up on deck again in time to take one last picture of the smoke-covered beach. Then I took some shots of the crew giving transfusions on the open deck . . . brought us to the *Chase*, the very boat I had left only six hours before . . . the last wave of the 16th Infantry was just being lowered, but the decks were already full with returning wounded and dead.

. . . the pictures I had taken on Easy Red were the best of the invasion . . . while drying the negatives, . . . too much heat and the emulsions had melted . . . Out of 106 pictures in all, only eight were salvaged. . . .

Of the two lead battalions of the 6th Brigade, the 147th Engineers were assigned to the most westerly sectors of beach, Dog Green and Dog White. This area had already been witness to the terrible losses within Company A of the 116th Infantry and also the 121st Engineers. With the arrival of the 147th main body on two LCIs the heavy losses continued. Groups of the 147th and the 116th Infantry regimental headquarters were aboard LCI(L)91 when the vessel headed for a landing at Dog White at about 0740 hours. After taking an artillery hit the LCI attempted to retract and reposition for another landing. When encountering tidal obstacles the vessel lowered its ramps and commenced debarking troops into water six feet deep. Another hit ignited a fire which forced troops on the open decks to jump overboard. Shortly afterward LCI(L) 92 arrived at the same beach sector and also came under artillery fire, in this case suffering ignition of its fuel tanks. Both these craft burned for hours. Survivors of the 147th sought cover but also began to join with infantrymen and head toward Vierville. The 149th Engineers are difficult to track through this phase because the historical records show them in scattered locations. Probably they had losses in the sinking of LCIs. The main part of the battalion was scheduled for landing at Dog Red but instead reached Easy Green, just to the left of Exit D-3. They were able to cut gaps in the wire along the shore road but could not cope with an antitank ditch. Enemy fire forced them back to the shingle line.

WILLIAM RUSSELL CALLAHAN—CAPTAIN
116TH INFANTRY REGIMENT
29TH DIVISION, COMPANY F
DOG RED, OMAHA BEACH

"Throughout the day, I saw an Engineer sergeant who had been hit squarely in the face. It looked like one eye and part of the bone over the eye were gone. This NCO was constantly exposed [to emeny fire], directing the other engineer troops, replacing drivers on the bulldozers when they became casualties, helping the wounded—some far less hurt than he. Finally in the afternoon, he stopped long enough for someone to put a clumsy field dressing on his terrible wound. I recall several men dying of shock with far less wounds than he, yet he continued to function and be an inspiration to me and all who saw him."

On the eastern sectors progress was slightly more noticeable. The last description of activity on Easy Red had found only a few boat teams of assault infantry ashore, one each of Companies E and F of the 16th Infantry and two of Company E of the 116th displaced afar from their target beach. They began to advance as additional troops reached shore. Troops of the 16th cut the wire just above the shingle and were able to pass through mined areas on the marshy ground. Enemy rifle and machine gun fire was not heavy as they proceeded next to advance up the bluffs. However, the antipersonnel mine problem was nearly insurmountable, and the advance was temporarily halted. Among the follow-on contingent, Company G of the 16th landed in this area and added to the fire base. In the interval from 0730 to 0830 hours detachments of Company G made their way through the minefield and reached the crest of the bluffs, under cover of their own mortars and machine guns. Losses were very light during this advance. The company commander, Capt. Joseph Dawson outflanked an enemy machine gun trench and threw a grenade to kill the crew. The original occupants of this beach sector, the boat team of Company E under command of Lt. John Spalding, reduced to a strength of 23 by that time, also made their way to the crest of the bluffs. They turned toward the west and approached a fortified position from its rear. The position consisted of pillboxes and connecting trenches and had been pounded by close-in destroyers. A fire fight extended over several hours leading finally to the surrender of a group of approximately 20 enemy.

The second of two regimental command groups reached shore about 0815 hours bringing in Col. George Taylor, the commander. His inspirational accomplishments on the eastern sectors were comparable to those of Gen. Cota and Col. Canham on the western sectors. His often repeated words deserve repeating here. The exhortation he used to troops seeking safety at the shingle line was brief: "Two kinds of people are staying on this beach, the dead and those who are going to die—now let's get the hell out of here". The small, scattered groups at the shingle were organized into operational troops. The display of leadership that had produced the first advances up the bluffs appeared to be contagious. Forward movement along both Easy Red and Fox Green began to accelerate. A significant turn in the fortunes of battle occured as groups of the enemy began surrendering. The darkest cloud in this phase was the difficulty experienced by landing craft in beaching due to the increasing lethality of the tidal obstacles as they were covered by the incoming tide. Earlier it was mentioned that several of the larger craft had neutralized the obstacles by ramming but the main benefits coming from this technique accrued in the next phase and later. The beaches above the high water mark remained under artillery fire. However, as the follow-on troops steadily came ashore, the 16th Infantry was transformed into a full-scale regimental combat team.

Engineers on the eastern sectors moved ahead on their mission tasks at a rate comparable to their infantry counterparts. The advance parties of the 1st Engineer Combat Battalion landed on Easy Red more than 1,000 yards to the east and in a badly scattered condition. There was no progress on the mission of opening Exit E-1 for a period of hours. A team of Company A landed about 0700 hours. The battalion command group reached shore somewhat later, about 0750 hours, in LCVP craft which were able to debark troops only after ramming obstacles. An immediate assessment indicated that collection of personnel into their units and organization for work were the priority matters. Reconnaissance by the battalion commander, Col. William Gara, found a way up the bluffs through mined areas. The team then made its way westward toward the draw. Defensive positions continued to deliver accurate fire against 16th Infantry elements and their engineer support. Following the severe losses of Sherman tanks, naval destroyers were the primary sources of supporting fire. With naval shore fire control parties on the spot in proximity to the defenses guarding the draw, destroyers were brought within 1,000 yards of shore.

The building of the engineer units was the main thrust of the accomplishments in this phase, in contrast to the clearing of the ground. It was determined that the antitank ditch at the exit would be a major task. One of the other engineer units had an operable engineer bulldozer ashore which was preempted for use in filling the Exit E-1 ditch (typical ditch shown in Fig. 38). Collection of materials for working up the draw was essential. Application of bangalore torpedoes was a means of expediting the work of clearing multiple lanes, each eight yards wide.

On the adjacent beach sector, Fox Green to the east, the 20th Engineers had a comparable mission in support of the 3d Battalion, 16th Infantry. The engineer tasks on this sector were directed to the clearing of Exit E-3 in the direction of Colleville. First ashore of the 20th was their Company A, with an advance party scheduled to land at H plus 40 minutes. The main body, due later aboard LCTs, met catastrophe when their craft were hit by accurate artillery fire and none reached shore. That left the company with a strength of only 27 of which number nine were wounded at the shoreline. This understrength detachment got to work clearing a lane several hun-

Figure 38—Antitank Ditch Used Effectively by Enemy Defenders. *Such defensive measures slowed the egress of traffic off the beaches, as for example in the opening of Exit E-1.*

dred yards distant from the main exit with the objective of moving four operational tanks off the beach at the earliest possible moment. The lane was cleared successfully but when the tanks moved they drew fire from enemy antitank guns and were immobilized. The follow-on companies of the 20th came ashore later on both sides of Exit E-3 including some locations off the mark on Easy Red sector. In the circumstances their highest priority was fighting snipers and scattered enemy still operating out of fortified positions.

The 37th Engineers, one of the combat battalions of the 5th Engineer Special Brigade, had assignments on both Easy Red and Fox Green. The historical records of the battalion are much more complete than those of the other engineer units on Omaha Beach, but nevertheless convey an ambiguous picture of coordination between the 37th and the 1st Engineers at Exit E-1 and the 20th Engineers at E-3. A mission statement in the field order of the 37th Engineers directs that support be provided to the 2d and 3d Battalions of the 16th Infantry in crossing the beach and in operating the vehicle and personnel transit areas. Each of the companies of the 37th had a reconnaissance element ashore at about H plus 30 minutes. The main bodies followed at about two and one-half hours later.

The advance party of Company A, led by Capt. Louis Drnovich, landed well off target in the vicinity of Exit E-1. From this location they headed for Exit E-3. The main body, landing off LCTs, went through a similar experience. They were able to get their bulldozer and a tractor ashore after some losses of wheeled vehicles. In the area of the assigned exit they found a mass of disabled and abandoned vehicles littering the dirt road parallel to the shoreline. These were removed from the road either by starting their engines or dozing them to the side. Mine clearing teams went to work on the road with their mine detectors. Progress was labored due to incoming artillery and mortar fire on the working parties, to the extent that the company was pinned down. Patrols were dispatched to eliminate the weapons, or at the very least to locate their forward spotter. These efforts produced no beneficial results. Four tanks found in the vicinity were operational and sent up the draw. Undoubtedly these were the same tanks that the 20th Engineers reported in need of a safe lane to exit off the beach in the Fox Green sector. The 37th Engineers personnel were amazed at the accuracy of fire brought against the tanks. Additional hits were made against attempted landings of LCTs destined for Fox Green. All continuing efforts to locate the defensive weapons produced no results and engineer operations reached a standstill.

The main body of Company B of the 37th reached shore in the vicinity of Exit E-1 where they had an assignment to assist in clearing a lane. Arriving about H plus 60 minutes off an LCI they found infantry pinned down at the shingle by a combination of artillery, mortar, and small arms fire. A squad leader of the 37th, Sgt. Zolton Simon, saw the possibility of moving up the bluffs through a narrow defile and attacking the fortified enemy positions from their rear. He seized the initiative, cut the barbed wire along the beach road, and moved his mine detector crew through the gap. The mine clearing operation was carried forward against enemy fire, which eventually wounded

Sgt. Simon. It took a second wound to put the sergeant out of action, but the team did clear a personnel trail to the crest. Meanwhile one of the engineer officers was collecting immobile infantry remnants and urging them up the trail, all the while exposed to enemy fire. In due course this operation did succeed and the defensive positions were overwhelmed. To cap the turnaround at this location the Company B group was able to borrow a bulldozer from Company C and commence filling in the antitank ditch which blocked access to Exit E-1. This probably was the bulldozer which the 1st Engineers used in their efforts to open the draw to St.-Laurent.

An advance party of Company C of the 37th landed about the same time as the early contingents of the other companies. The mission of the company was the preparation of transit areas on the eastern beach sectors for use by the 16th Infantry and its support units. The main body of the company reached shore on the same beach where Company B had landed but suffered severe losses, both wounded and killed, when its LCI took a direct hit. Meanwhile, Lt. Robert Ross, aware that the primary mission would need to wait, assembled his platoon, added most of an infantry company that had lost its officers, and advanced against enemy troops positioned on the slopes and atop the crest of the bluffs. They passed through mined areas and succeeded in taking two machine gun emplacements and killing 40 enemy troops. Lt. Ross was awarded a Distinguished Service Cross (DSC) for his achievement. The two bulldozer operators of Company C who had worked on the antitank ditch at Exit E-1 were similarly decorated.

JOHN CORNELIUS BUTLER, JR.—CAPTAIN
37TH ENGINEER COMBAT BATTALION
5TH ENGINEER SPECIAL BRIGADE
EASY RED, OMAHA BEACH

"As we landed on the beach, it looked like the whole American army had not moved an inch. We were only gaining ground when the tide went out and losing it when the tide came in."

A summary of the situation on Omaha Beach during the period designated as Phase III is painfully negative but there are some scattered indications of a turn for the better. Losses of personnel were devastating throughout the period as the larger landing craft made their way to shore. Losses of LCTs and LCIs were so numerous that a total count cannot be made. From the engineer point of view this was a period of critical importance as the main bodies of all categories of units were scheduled to land: the engineer combat battalions that were organic to the divisions, those that were attached for the operation, and the battalions which served as shore parties. In addition to human losses the equipment losses had a negative impact on mission performance. The major items of loss were in tank dozers, engineer bulldozers, and in supplies such as explosives. Much engineer effort was devoted to joining of forces with infantry in order to relieve the pinned down condition of much of the landing force.

Positive signs began to appear as this phase of the campaign progressed. The joint infantry-engineer teams made some advances beyond the shingle embankment and up the bluffs. Some of the defensive positions were defeated and enemy personnel were dispatched. Some enemy surrendered. Advances were made over mine-sown ground and in some locations lanes were cleared by engineer details either by detection or by explosive detonation. The other encouraging sign was that the inability to clear and mark lanes through the tidal zone obstacles was mitigated by ramming of the obstacles as the incoming tide brought craft far enough inshore to contact the obstacles.

Previously we noted the role of Col. Benjamin Talley. His assignment at V Corps headquarters had originally been as head of a planning group. During landing operations he had a reporting and liaison assignment in which his team, mounted in two DUKWs, would convey information by a direct channel to the corps commander. Most of his messages are shown verbatim in the accompanying box. A distinct change of tone can be observed in the message marked "1040 hours". The actual messages are underlined for ease in identification.

Messages from Shore to V Corps Headquarters

Extracts from article "The D-Day Connection" published in *National Guard*; June, 1989; author Maj. Gen. Bruce Jacobs.

Their mission was to land behind the assault regiments to keep the Corps Commander informed of the situation as it developed on the beachhead. Talley's detachment was equipped with four radio sets. . . . Talley would take one DUKW and Zwicker the other. They would be launched 12 miles offshore from LSTs. . . . Talley kept a journal as best he could during the hectic hours. . . . A number of the messages reprinted in this article are from this journal . . . the sea was rough; the LST . . . had to do some tricky maneuvering until it was possible to drop the stern anchor and swing precariously with the wind and waves before daring to open her bow door . . . DUKW inched cautiously onto the ramp and then into the inky predawn waters. . . . The amphibious truck jolted, bucked, and rolled in another ground swell and then, miraculously, was seaborn. . . . As the time for the attack finally came, Talley flashed word to the *Ancon*.

0620 hours—At line of departure
0629 hours—Rockets fired.

H-hour was 0630 that fateful morning . . . LCTs passed them, returning empty from the beach. . . . Only later would the sad news come that of the 32 that had been launched only five made it to shore; and of these only two actually survived to see any action. . . . Later, too, Talley's team learned that of all DUKWs ferried to the French shore aboard LST 176, theirs was the only survivor. . . . Time and again Talley's DUKW was driven back from potential landing sites by heavy artillery . . . mission depended upon keeping his commo (Editor: communication) equipment intact, Talley withdrew . . . paralleled beach at a distance of 300 to 500 yards from shore. At 0830 hours there was sudden shifting of positions . . . seemed infantry might be starting to withdraw . . . but grimly they hung on.

0900 hours—From 1,000 yards off Dog Red Beach I see several companies of the 16th Infantry on the Easy Red and Fox Red beaches. Enemy artillery and machine gun fire still effective. LCTs shifting to Dog. About 30 LCTs standing by to land. Obstacles seem thicker than in photos. LCI 85 hit and smoking after unloading. Have seen two LCTs burn—Count 10 tanks on Fox. Landing resuming on Dog.

Talley noted with alarm that landing operations on Easy and Fox beaches had completely halted . . . Naval . . . commander had radioed an order suspending any more landings . . . until traffic . . . sorted out . . . assault troops clung tenaciously to . . . toehold on fire swept beach. Brig. Gen. Norman Cota . . . first general officer to beach, rallied troops bogged down by the enemy's fire. He raced ahead of the men lugging a bangalore torpedo and blew a gaping hole . . . "C'mon" he yelled, "if an old buzzard like me can do that so can you" . . . soldiers venture out to move with him.

1030 hours—On Easy and Fox beaches situation static. On my last approach was driven back by machine gun fire believed to be from house in mouth of Exit D-3. LCT No. 30 . . .

Talley also noted that up to that time, no landing craft had attempted to ram the beach obstacles to see if a passage could be forced . . . the LCT rammed through . . . at full speed, touched down . . . to disgorge its load . . . LCI(L)544 roared through the obstacles too . . . Talley quickly composed a new message.

1035 hours—LCT 30 firing 50-caliber machine guns at enemy positions 100 yards west of house in mouth of Exit E-3. LCI(L)544 firing point blank at same house.

1040 hours—Men advancing up slope behind Easy Red. Men believed ours on skyline . . . House at Exit E-3 silent. Things look better.

. . . Talley's radio DUKW weaved among the submerged and partially submerged obstacles . . . a round hit off the bow and another off the stern . . . bracketed . . .

1055 hours—Enemy artillery registered on Beach Easy Red and fires when craft are there. Believe craft can be seen from church spire at Vierville.

. . . a destroyer started to shell the church spire. Later . . . Army engineers swore to Talley that they saw the church spire sheared at the roofline by one salvo and then struck in mid-air by a second blast!. . . . The 29th Division . . . "a tank's gun brought it down". Before noon, Company C, 116th Infantry had occupied Vierville. . . .

1150 hours—Troops moving up slope. Fox Green and Fox Red. I join you thanking God for our Navy.

. . . Talley's DUKW made it to beach . . . ordered reconnaissance to the top of the cliffs . . . set out to make contact with Brig. Gen. Willard Wyman . . . in command . . . on the beach. . . . Gen. Wyman, who was without any communications . . . relayed message . . .

1347 hours—Wyman to Huebner: Liaison with combat units only. Radio out. Wire going in at present.

. . . heavy artillery bombardment from . . . behind Vierville. A shell struck less than 15 feet . . . near Talley's command vehicle . . . wounded quickly moved to an aid station. Around 1400 hours . . . the beachhead situation was still very much in doubt . . . Talley's journal notes . . . in moving up the beach . . . necessary to step over men without . . . concern over their condition.

1600 hours—(From Rangers to Talley, relayed by a Navy communications station) Located Pointe du Hoc. Mission accomplished. Need ammunition and reinforcement. Many casualties.

A destroyer that intercepted the message sent a small boat loaded with small arms ammunition racing toward the base of the cliff.

1620 hours—Beach is free of small arms fire. Other enemy action against landing on beach is slight. Condition of beach will permit wheeled and tracked vehicular traffic over more of the area before high water line. Cratering due to bombing and shell-fire relatively light. Work on beach is progressing in orderly fashion and beach difficulties should soon be corrected.

Talley's optimism lasted but a moment . . . shattered by . . . heaviest artillery shelling of the day . . . effective, observed fire . . . few misses . . . inflicted casualties . . . Zwicker spotted . . . reinforced artillery battalion . . . not far from Pointe du Hoc . . . had direct observation of Omaha and Utah Beaches . . . word sent to V Corp headquarters . . . destroyer contacted . . . artillery fire stopped abruptly. . . . Every member of detachment was awarded Silver Star for gallantry. . . . Talley was awarded the Distinguished Service Cross.

ENGINEER ACTIVITY ACCELERATES AS INFANTRY FOLLOW-UP LANDS

Up to this point in the evolution of landing operations on Omaha the dominant characteristic was the difficulty in dealing with the determined resistance of the defenders. In the initial infantry-tank assault supporting fire was virtually nil due to the swamping of many of the Sherman DD-tanks and the other tank losses. Most of the infantry was pinned down at the shingle embankment. The joint Army-Navy teams assigned to clear lanes through tidal zone obstacles produced minimum results. The engineer reconnaissance teams and main body groups spent much of their effort joining with infantry detachments attempting to advance up the bluffs. Toward the end of Phase III some progress, however small, was perceptible. A few enemy positions atop the crest were taken and there were some captured enemy troops. An inclination to surrender became evident. Vehicles were then unable to move beyond the beach but some narrow gaps and lanes were cleared of mines making personnel egress a bit safer.

During Phase IV follow-up infantry regiments came ashore marking an acceleration in the build-up. The time interval for this phase was roughly H plus three hours to H plus six hours. The main units involved were the 115th Infantry of the 29th Division landing behind the 116th on the right side beach sectors and the 18th Infantry of the 1st Division landing behind the 16th infantry on the left side beach sectors. An important addition to the forces ashore was the divisional artillery of the assault divisions. Other divisional resources landing in this phase included tanks, anti-aircraft artillery, 4.2-inch mortars, and further engineer increments. A quick scan of the expected landings indicates that a large number of vehicles would be involved.

The physical state of the beach sectors compounded the difficulty of coping with a new batch of arrivals. With high tide at about 1100 hours the tidal obstacles were submerged and the clear beach was minimum. Wreckage of landing craft, tanks, and mobile equipment littered the beach. The pressure on engineer units mounted with each passing hour. From the engineer viewpoint this phase should have been devoted to beach organization. The actual situation was clearly a discrepancy in keeping to schedule—and without heroic effort would become worse. If military traffic could not move quickly off the beach, targets for enemy gun positions would be extremely attractive and the beach clutter problem would be compounded. Even with fire support from the naval fleet which had moved inshore the enemy ability to pick off landing force materiel persisted through most of this phase.

The situation on Dog Green sector on the right flank was a scattered 121st Engineers. No controlling infantry force was operational on this sector. Of the engineers several platoons of Companies A and B had landed early under heavy artillery, mortar, and machine gun fire. The fortunes of the battalion command group were covered previously. A mislanding put the initial contingents well to the east of their correct placement. The first problem was rounding up personnel and in particular the explosives that had been brought ashore. A large group of 121st Engineer troops landing off an LCI suffered heavy casualties. Overall, the estimate of battalion casualties was 62 for D-day. About 1000 hours a patrol reached the crest of the bluffs just east of Vierville and proceeded into the village.

Substantial improvement of the battalion position occurred about 1030 hours with the landing of two platoons of Company C with bulldozers, each loaded with one ton of explosives. However, there was a need to remove sniper fire from the concrete obstacle at the mouth of Exit D-1 before demolition could be started. A patrol located the sniper position and in the process of wiping out the resistance brought in 30 enemy prisoners. By 1300 hours the defensive position guarding the draw was silent. The 1,100 pounds of explosives, as determined by analysis, was positioned against the eight-foot high wall. Then, at about 1400 hours under the watchful eye of Col. Ploger, the wall was demolished and the road from the beach toward Vierville became accessible. The single blast removed all the concrete and steel of the wall from shoulder to shoulder of the roadway. A two-inch depression was left in the roadway. The accompanying photo shows the site after dozing of major chunks of concrete (Fig. 39).

Figure 39—*Upper shot: Explosive Demolition Wrecks Concrete Obstruction at Exit D-1.* *121st Engineer Combat Battalion accumulated adequate explosive munitions after arrival of loaded bulldozers off an* LST. *This action opened access to Vierville.*
Lower shot: Refuse and Flotsam of War Clutter Sectors of Omaha. *This view shows explosives, ammunition containers, reels of signal wire, life preservers and the like impeding traffic over the shingle.*

The contribution of the 147th Engineers to the action at Exit D-1 is clouded in the historical accounts. Earlier the battalion took heavy losses during debarkation from LCIs. Detachments joined with infantrymen in the fight to enter Vierville. The battalion commander pressed the unit in the search for and collection of explosives. There are reports that the role of Master Sgt. M. Arwood was crucial in opening the exit but details of exactly how he fit in are difficult to pin down even among veterans of this particular operation. The 147th continued to provide engineer support on Dog Green throughout this phase. They assisted in clearing mines and debris and in filling tank traps.

Further to the east, the 112th Engineers continued to face problems and frustrations. They joined with infantry in an effort to ease the pressure on the draw at les Moulins. Company C of the battalion helped by breaching wire entanglements and minefields. Despite minor progress the prospect of opening Exit D-3 remained distant. This was the location where the battalion commander, Maj. William Richards, was killed in a burst of artillery fire. He earlier sustained a flesh wound when first landing on the beach and made light of it to a fellow officer. Much of the period under examination was spent pinned down by accurate, observed enemy fire. The absence of substantial progress on opening Exit D-3 must be assessed in connection with other events on Dog Red and Easy Green sectors. The fighting in this area is generally regarded as some of the most intense on Omaha. The surviving tanks of the 743d, which were conventionally waterproofed, saved the day—and also absorbed continual losses.

TENO RONCALIO—2ND LIEUTENANT
18TH INFANTRY REGIMENT
1ST INFANTRY DIVISION
OMAHA BEACH

"I remember extensive relief when I hit the water even though we were being shot at because I had been so sick on board ship. The mortar and artillery fire was really bad but I felt a sense of exultation . . . when I saw a strip of cloth running up through a mine field which meant that some engineer had managed to crawl through [the mine field] earlier and set a line for me to follow. I led my entire platoon through that path on the beach."

On the eastern flank sectors, Easy Red and Fox Green, events were somewhat conformed to the planned schedule. The infantry build-up called for the 18th Infantry to follow the 16th, with landings to commence about 0930 hours. As it happened, landings of the regiment actually began shortly after 1000 hours. The congested state of the eastern sectors can be seen in the accompanying photo taken on Easy Red close to high tide which came about 1100 hours (Fig. 40). Note the PA 26 marking on the LCVP at left which indicates the craft came off the *Samuel Chase*, which transported much of the 1st Division. The status of 1st Engineer landings was also behind schedule. Company A was ashore early in the assault. Company C, less one platoon detailed to the 26th Infantry, was scheduled to land at about 0930 hours but actually reached shore at close to 1100 hours. Company B was assigned to support the 18th Infantry and landed with the regiment, behind schedule.

The first order of importance was the reduction of enemy positions firing at targets in the vicinity of Exit E-1. During this phase naval shore fire control teams brought destroyers in as close as 1,000 yards and produced significant results in lifting hostile fire from the draw. Company A succeeded in collecting equipment and material as the late arriving personnel were still landing. The alternate battalion headquarters team came in by LCI 93 during this period. A reasonable estimate is that work toward clearing the draw and opening the exit commenced between 1000 and 1100 hours. The primary technique for clearing mines was explosive detonation by bangalore torpedoes. Progress accelerated with the continuing arrival of battalion personnel and supplies. By 1400 hours a clear lane reached atop the bluffs and by 1500 hours a vehicle transit area was operational. The accompanying photo shows the use of engineer tape to indicate the limits of cleared lanes. This picture was taken after D-day (Fig. 41 upper) when the ships and craft were closer inshore but the safelane up the draw was not yet widened appreciably.

There is very little to add to the previous description of engineer activity on the Fox Green sector. The vital Exit E-3 was still strongly defended by enemy positions nearby. Following the misfortunes of Company A, the other two companies of the 20th Engineers reached shore but made no progress on engineer tasks during this phase. They continued to join with infantry details attempting to scale the bluffs. The 37th Engineers were widely scattered over both the eastern sectors. They had a bulldozer operating in the vicinity of Exit E-1 which was unquestionably the machine contributing to the progress of the 1st Engineers. After pulling roadblocks from the mouth of the exit, the dozer was used to fill the tanktrap. Personnel of 37th continued to make a strong contribution to infantry efforts to clear enemy positions controlling the draws at the two designated beach exits.

The final phase of the amphibious structure, as reproduced from the paper of Col. Thompson, deals with the continuing power buildup in the period from approximately noon of D-day to the following midnight. Based on the achievements in engineer activity during this period the early glimmerings of optimism were justified. Overall, the planned objectives were not met as scheduled but the recovery from initial catastrophe as the day wore on was a tremendous military achievement. A status review towards the end of the day has numerous highlights.

Figure 40—Upper shot: Stopped Vehicles at Shingle Embankment on Easy Red Sector. *This view at high tide shows stopped vehicles near eastern boundary of Easy Red. Note LCVP of veteran attack transport* Samuel Chase *(APA 26) on the left.*
Lower shot: Engineer Solution to Traction Problem. *Bulldozers with engineer main body troops tow unit supplies and equipment ashore for surfacing beach exits. Wire mesh with fabric backing was uncoiled and staked into shingle to produce a passable surface over the embankment.*

Figure 41—Upper shot: Engineer Effort is Crucial to Exit E-1 Opening. *1st Engineer Combat Battalion cleared mines and obstacles up the draw toward St.-Laurent to open egress off beach by 1400 hours. This was the first safe lane up one of the draws of Omaha. In this post-D-day view note that engineer tape remained in place to indicate limits of cleared lane.*

Lower shot: Easy Red Sector Cluttered with D-day Losses. *As the tide commenced to recede the accumulation of wrecked landing craft, tanks, and other vehicles obstructed movement over the beach. Note that a loss of traction upon reaching the shingle embankment probably made the vehicles easy targets.*

RECAPITULATION OF ENGINEER ACTIONS ON OMAHA

The task of clearing safe lanes through the tidal zone obstacles was not successful despite the heroic efforts of the joint Army-Navy gapping teams. Five gaps were cleared but only one had markers to make it useable at high tide. However, with mines removed from obstacles it became possible, as the tide rose, for landing craft operators to ram their way into beaching positions. Personnel losses reached 52 percent among the Navy contingent and approximately the same level within the Army group. Decorations were numerous and at a high level among both the components of the teams including particularly a DSC to Lt. Col. John O'Neill. At the second low tide of D-day the survivors of the teams returned to work and produced a total of 13 clear lanes, effectively marked.

On Dog Green sector the concrete wall was demolished at about 1400 hours. The 121st Engineers declared the road to Vierville open to traffic by 1800 hours although movement was impeded by damage and debris from interdictory enemy artillery fire. However, the route remained hazardous. Indeed, even after 2000 hours on D plus one, German medium artillery caused major damage to heavy traffic using the route. By dark on D-day remnants of Companies B and C and battalion headquarters of the 121st moved beyond Vierville to their first overnight encampment on the European continent. For its performance on D-day, the 121st Engineers received a Distinguished Unit Citation. Casualties had been heavy within the battalion: 10 officers and 51 enlisted, including all line company commanders. As a short post script to D-day operations the battalion came under heavy attack the following morning and suffered further heavy casualties.

Difficulties at the les Moulins draw containing Exit D-3 cropped up in the descriptions a number of times. Much of the force landing on Easy Green was pinned down. The 112th Engineers spent much of their time joined with infantry in an effort to ease pressure on the exit. With the assistance of the 147th Engineers the beach exit was open by 2000 hours. Both these battalions, along with the 149th Engineers and Headquarters and Headquarters Company of the 6th Engineer Special Brigade were awarded Distinguished Unit Citations.

Engineer work at Exit E-1 commenced before noon and progressed well in the early afternoon period. The technique used for clearing mines was explosive detonation by bangalore torpedo. At 1400 hours the vehicular lane was clear and by one hour later traffic was moving (see Fig. 42) to the vehicle transit area in the vicinity of St.-Laurent for dewaterproofing. The 1st Engineer Combat Battalion had accomplished its D-day mission essentially on schedule in the face of determined opposition. This exit was the main egress off the beach on D-day. Furthermore, whether by good fortune or by experience or expertise, the casualty rate for the battalion was at the comparatively low rate of four killed in action, six missing, and 23 wounded. The battalion earned another citation to go with its awards of previous campaigns.

Contributions to the effectiveness of engineer operations on Easy Red sector were added by the 37th Engineers. In the early efforts to break the impass at the shingle,

Figure 42—*Engineer Bulldozers Assist Grounding and Anchoring of Rhino Ferry.* *Heavy motorized equipment was ferried ashore from LST vessels prior to the time the large beaching ships could be safely brought in. Note the high tide landing with the ferry up to the shingle embankment.*

Lt. Ross took a mixed group of engineers and infantry up the bluffs where they overwhelmed two enemy machine gun positions and killed 40 of the enemy troops. The bulldozer which enabled the opening of Exit E-1 by the 1st Engineers was supplied and operated by the 37th. The operators were Pvts. Vinton Dove and William Shoemaker, whose performance in the face of severe enemy fire was rewarded by DSCs. Lt. Ross was similarly decorated. The battalion received a unit citation. The unit suffered terrible casualties, including 24 killed one of whom was the battalion commander.

Opening of Exit E-3 on Fox Green sector was a very difficult assignment. The 20th Engineers had problems from the outset when their Company A lost its LCTs early in their attempt to land and no troops debarked. An advance party had earlier landed a small detachment which cleared a lane off the beach. Four operational tanks attempted to advance up this path but all were hit and disabled. The other two companies landed at scattered locations both sides of Exit E-3 and spent much of the day fighting enemy control of the draw. It was only at 2100 hours that work commenced to open Exit E-3, and it was not until the following morning that traffic could pass up the draw and reach the vehicle transit area. The battalion was awarded a Distinguished Unit Citation. There were two other battalions of the 5th Engineer Special Brigade with assignments on the far eastern sectors of Omaha.

The 348th Engineers operated in support of the 18th Infantry, a follow-on regiment which landed behind the 16th Infantry shortly after 1000 hours. Companies of the 37th Engineers were off on independent missions, all having landed earlier. The net result was that the accomplishments of the 348th are difficult to separate from those of engineer units in the same general area and which landed earlier. The 336th Engineers were scheduled to land in the afternoon under an assignment to organize Fox Red sector. This beach sector was to the east of Fox Green and was not an assault beach. As it happened the 336th landed on Dog Green, at least two miles west of their destination, about 1500 hours. Their foot march to the east was a harrowing experience, particularly since the column included a tractor towing an explosive-laden trailer which attracted enemy artillery fire. When passing Exit E-1, which was operational at the time, progress was slow due to heavy traffic. At Exit E-3 intense enemy artillery fire forced a halt. The unit reached Exit F-1 at approximately 1700 hours after losing two men killed and 27 injured. Despite all efforts to clear the exit two tanks were disabled by mines in attempting to reach Colleville at about 2000 hours. Several hours later safe passage through the exit was achieved. Both these battalions were awarded unit citations.

KEITH BRYAN—SERGEANT
348TH ENGINEER COMBAT BATTALION
5TH ENGINEER SPECIAL BRIGADE
OMAHA BEACH

"There was Melvin Thompson, the assistant 'cat-skinner' who toiled all of D-day in the surf with the first operator, Albert Martin. Their caterpillar tractor pulled in dozens of foundered vehicles and they saved an untold number of lives. The Captain put them in for the Silver Star, but Brigade kicked it back down, pointing out that the quota was one Silver Star per company. Later in Belgium, when they both got it, Martin was dead."

During mid-afternoon normal command channels were established for the shore engineer battalions. Brig. Gen. William Hoge landed at Exit E-1 just after 1500 hours and the Provisional Engineer Special Brigade Group became operational. At this point the two brigade headquarters assumed control of their subordinate units and the ad hoc command arrangement for landing was set aside.

By the end of D-day, with substantial traffic moving inland through Exit E-1 and increasing traffic thru other exits, there was no prospect that V Corps would surrender any of its hard-won gains. The seaborne build-up was continuing. The battle for the first one thousand yards had been won.

CHAPTER VII

THE BATTLE FOR UTAH BEACH

Utah Beach at base of Cotentin Peninsula—undistinguished terrain

Landing force displaced southward one and one-half miles

Air and sea bombardment of defenders was effective

Broad tidal flat favored engineer work on obstacles

Defenders will to resist ultimately broken by DD-Shermans

Engineer advance parties planned beach egress/breached seawall

Defenders artillery took toll of engineer teams

Mine clearing task formidable . . . various types, some unfamiliar

Beach road net operational on D-day with stabilized surface

4th Division totally ashore in 15 hours . . . credit engineer support

U tah Beach did not appear in the draft outline for Overlord that was delivered by the planners in the early summer of 1943. When the invasion force commanders took charge in late 1943 and early 1944, Utah was added for several purposes. The commanders desired a general strengthening of the assault force, a greater frontage of the landing beaches, and most specifically, a reduction of the distance from the invasion beaches to the port of Cherbourg. Capture of the port at the earliest possible time was among the high priority objectives for Neptune operations, the amphibious phase of Overlord. The 4th Division had the assignment to lead the assault on Utah Beach and put its 8th Infantry Regiment in the vanguard.

The site for Utah Beach was at the base of the Cotentin Peninsula on the eastern shore of the northward projection into the English Channel. This location is just across the Carentan Estuary from Omaha Beach, and separated from Omaha by a distance of approximately 14 miles.

THE TERRAIN AT UTAH BEACH

Topographical features along the lower eastern shore of the Cotentin are fairly typical of coastal sandy beaches. The dunes reach a height of more than 20 feet in some locations, but on the average, are more likely to be somewhere between 12 and 16 feet high. Bluffs, similar to those backing up the beach at Omaha, are not present at Utah. A robust concrete seawall lines the dunes, and varies in height between four and eight feet. The sand of the beach is of medium coarseness, completely free of the shingle and gravel which are found on Omaha Beach.

It must be recognized in any discussion of Utah Beach that the planned target sector was missed by about 2,400 yards. The accompanying map (Fig. 43) shows this displacement in a graphical way. The assault, as planned, was to target two color-coded beach sectors, Uncle Red on the left (southernmost) and Tare Green on the right, each about 1,000 yards in length. These two adjacent beaches were located so that Red beach fell astride Exit No. 3. This road passed through the small village of le Mesnilde, and thence on to Audouville-la-Hubert, several miles behind the beach. With these place names, the beach can be located on the Bigot maps included in the Appendices.

Several factors combined to produce the navigational error which displaced Utah Beach. The intense bombardment, both air and sea, produced a cloud of smoke and dust that prevented the control vessels from accurately picking up the landmarks for the line of departure from which the early wave landing craft were dispatched. Radar intended for control could not aid in distinguishing one beach from another. During the maneuvers, one of the patrol craft serving as a control struck a mine, and very shortly thereafter sank. Compounding the vision problem was the unexpectedly strong tidal current. The line of departure for the early assault waves was thus set about 1,500 yards south of its correct location. On top of this, the landing craft proceeding on a compass course after their dispatch were swept further to the south by the current. As a consequence, assault troops reached shore astride of Exit No. 2, the road to Ste.-Marie-du-Mont, also several miles inland. This location then became Utah Beach, with Uncle Red to the south of Exit No. 2 and Tare Green to the north. As operations evolved, Sugar Red and Roger White were established to the north of the original landings.

A conspicuous feature of the southern area of the Cotentin Penninsula had an impact on invasion planning and conduct of landing operations. The meadow land inland behind the dunes is low-lying and marshy. At high tide the land is below sea level, as are other areas in the drainage system of the Douve and Merderet Rivers. To maintain this land suitable for agriculture, a lock and dam structure installed at la Barquette, just north of Carentan, could be operated to control sea water flow (Fig. 44). With the gates open only at low tide, the area can be drained. The German defenders reversed the flow, and by opening the gates at high tide, created inundated areas at various locations inshore from the beach dunes. Additionally, there were a number of streams running inland from back of the dunes, and these were blocked. The result was a series of flooded meadows behind the beach stretching from Pouppeville in the south to Quinéville in the north, paralleling the shore line. In the east-west direction, the inundations extended a distance of about two miles. The depth of flooding was at most about four feet, but generally much less. The roads crossing through the flooded area, referred to as causeways, were elevated above the water level so that access was available to the defenders to reach their shore line fortifications. Conversely, the causeways became channels of exit from the beaches for the attacking VII Corps.

The bottom slope of the tidal flats on Utah Beach contributed favorably, in one sense at least, to landing operations. Readers will recall that the subject of tides on the channel beaches has come up in several connections in this D-day account. The basic issue is that a landing at low tide leaves the tidal obstacles exposed and there is no hazard to landing craft since they ground out long before reaching the obstacles. The negative aspect about the low tide landing is that troops have a long trek over the tidal flats during which they are vulnerable to defending weapons. The situation at Utah Beach, on the sector actually landed, was that the bottom slope on the left flank was extremely gradual and that the low water line was 1,700 yards out from the high water line. With a dispersed row of ramps approximately 350 yards from the high water line, this is 80 percent of the distance between low tide and high tide. The conclusion to be drawn is that the incoming tide would reach the ramps at about 1000 hours.

In a similar way, it can be found that the incoming tide would reach the ramps in front of Exit No. 2, the junction of Red and Green beaches, at about 0930 hours. These times compare with those at Omaha Beach where the incoming tide reaches to obstacles in the tidal zone at roughly 0800 hours. The Omaha figure is derived from a high water to low water distance, generally at 500 yards and the obstacles extending out to about 250 yards. The farther seaward that the obstacles extend, the earlier they

Figure 43

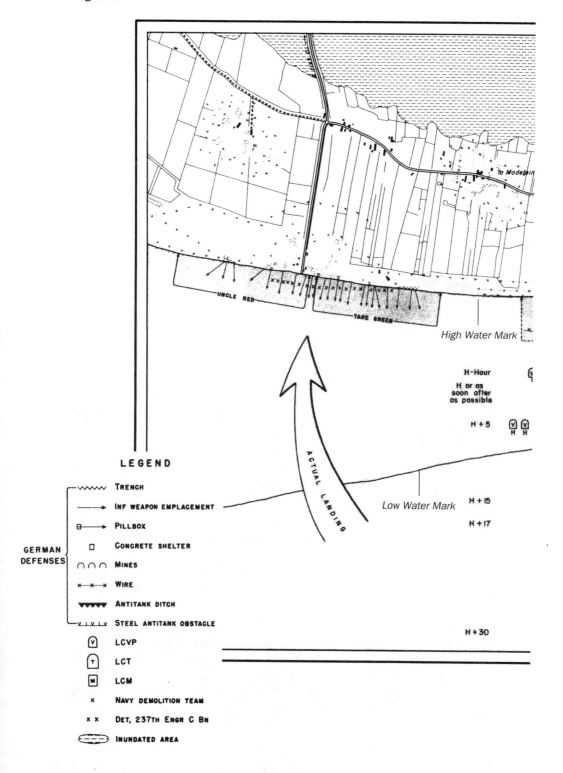

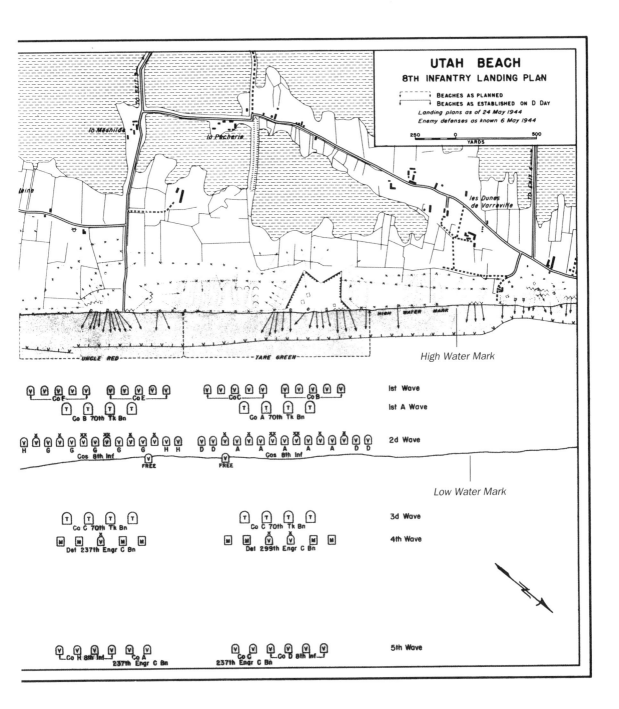

UTAH BEACH
8TH INFANTRY LANDING PLAN

BEACHES AS PLANNED
BEACHES AS ESTABLISHED ON D DAY
Landing plans as of 24 May 1944
Enemy defenses as known 6 May 1944

High Water Mark

Low Water Mark

Figure 44—*Main Control of Inundations Behind Utah Beach.* *This view shows the la Barquette Lock on the Lower Douve. Several engineer units played crucial roles in capturing the controls when infantry units bypassed the resisting enemy positions.*

are reached by the incoming tide. The summary of this examination is that the engineer teams assigned to neutralize the obstacles in the tidal zone at Utah Beach had a reasonable length of time to accomplish the task, especially by comparison with the situation at Omaha Beach where the time allowed appears to have been marginal.

While the beach configuration at Utah has been described as undistinguished, there is one further feature to be noted. About four miles offshore, abreast of the village of Ravenoville, and about three miles north of the planned sector of the landing, there are two small islands, named Iles St.-Marcouf, which are several miles north of Ravenoville. The village of St.-Marcouf is approximately six miles due west of the islands. These low-lying islands were normally unoccupied, but their location was critical to the landing plan. They were just north of the boat lanes leading from the transport area, 12 miles offshore, to the planned landing beaches. The fire support area where the major bombardment force was positioned, including the battleship *Nevada* and three cruisers, was within two miles of the small islands. In short, the Iles St.-Marcouf were in the center of the Utah Beach offshore area, where control would be a vital asset in any plan for the maneuvering of the naval invasion force.

UTAH BEACH DEFENSES

The defense measures at Utah Beach conformed to the broad descriptions of Atlantic Wall installations and their manning, as covered earlier in this account. There was a wide spectrum of fortification types and associated weapons. Similarly, the troops were at various quality levels and degrees of effectiveness. Possibly the tidal zone obstacles were a bit more sparse at Utah than at the other invasion beaches. However, most of the documentary sources on the details of these obstacles were undoubtedly incomplete. It is known that Field Marshal Rommel visited the area on the 11th of May, 1944, to inspect beach defenses, and expressed great dissatisfaction with what had been done. In these circumstances it would be expected that a maximum effort would be made to correct deficiencies. It also happens that Allied intelligence to be disseminated to troops cut off at about the same time. Thus, overprinted maps showing defenses could not include any measures taken in the final weeks before D-day.

Fortifications of heavy concrete construction lined the beaches of the Cotentin Peninsula. In the invasion sectors these positions were spaced about 1,500 yards apart. The accompanying photographs (Fig. 45) show that the weapons casemates were integrated into the seawall structure. It can also be seen that the embrasures were shielded from observation and naval bombardment by wing-walls of heavy concrete. The weapons were, nevertheless, capable of taking large close-in areas of the beach and sea approaches in enfilade fire. Other defensive installations are shown in Fig. 46.

Generous planting of land mines and other obstacles augmented the fixed defensive structures. Land mines in the dune areas included antitank Tellermines and S-type antipersonnel mines, along with numerous non-metallic types. Patterns of mine distribution varied, but a frequently used plan called for six to eight rows in a barrier with a spacing of 10 feet between rows and about 14 feet between mines in a row. Such a barrier might extend between 200 and 800 yards in the direction of the shoreline. The dune area between fortifications also included plain, barbed and concertina wire. Some fortified positions included antitank ditches, but the most elaborate tank traps were located more northerly than the Utah Beach invasion sectors.

Artillery coverage of Utah Beach and its approaches by defending forces was intensive. An apparently reliable estimate puts the number of batteries defending along this coastal sector at 28. The estimate of the number of guns comprising these batteries reaches to 110, of all calibers. The guns included 75-mm and 88-mm rifles and many others of larger caliber. There were six 155-mm, eight 152-mm, eight 122-mm, and sixteen 105-mm guns. The largest guns able to fire on Utah Beach were the 210-mm naval rifles at Crisbecq/St.-Marcouf, housed in extremely heavy-walled casemates described earlier (Fig. 47). These guns were of Czech manufacture by the Skoda works. Note that a number of historians describe the location at one or the other of the two villages. Actually, the fortifications are midway between the two villages which are separated by only one-half mile. Several miles to the southwest another battery of the same coast artillery regiment was sited at Azeville. These guns were of 105-mm caliber, French manufacture, and were also capable of reaching Utah. One final remark

Figure 45—Upper shot: Typical Fortification Along Utah Beach. *Heavy-walled concrete construction dominated the beach. Note the wing-walls which cover the embrasure from seaward bombardment.* **Center shot: Goliath Remote-controlled Weapon.** *These unmanned, miniature versions of a tank-like track vehicle carried a lethal explosive payload. Performance of the device proved to be unreliable.* **Lower shot: An Example of a Fortified Position Integrated with Seawall.** *This design allows gun traverse to about 45 degrees to seaward, a greater arc than most others. This view conveys clear picture of the formidable seawall along Utah Beach. Note the obstacles which had been bulldozed ashore from the tidal zone.*

Figure 46—**Upper shot: Open-type Concrete Gun Emplacement.** *Note that this installation permits wide angle traverse of the gun. Background extends to tidal zone where hedgehogs are visible.*
Lower left shot: Tank Turrets Salvaged from French Materiel. *This type of installation provided a protected machine gun position.*
Lower right shot: A Location in the Tidal Zone Where Poles and Stakes Predominate. *Note that poles are canted to seaward and some are tipped with Tellermines. Density of obstacles in this area at time of photo was light to moderate.*

on the exposure of invading forces to defending artillery is in order. With the displacement of Utah Beach more than a mile to the south due to mislanding, the guns at Pointe du Hoc, on the Omaha Beach side of the Carentan Estuary, improved their reach toward the Utah attackers.

Obstacles in the Utah Beach tidal zone conformed to the general pattern within the Atlantic Wall, but perhaps a bit on the sparse side. Recall that the defenders varied the density of these obstacles according to the probability of invasion on any beach. Undoubtedly, they rated Utah as not attractive to invaders. Tidal flats plans as of the 12th of May 1944 show, on the originally planned Utah Beach, a group of 42 ramps with a spacing of about 50 feet apart. These were backed up by an extensive belt of hedgehogs, four rows deep in some places, with a spacing of about 30 feet between units. On the beach as actually landed, ramps were spaced at about 80 feet apart for a distance of about 1,300 yards, and there were only a few hedgehogs. To the north of the landing beaches, there was extensive use of stakes, many with Tellermine tips, and also a few Element C. Overall, the distribution of obstacle types on the tidal flats appeared decidedly random.

A unique weapon, named Goliath, was available to the German defending forces at Utah Beach. This was a remotely controlled, unmanned, tank-like, but miniaturized vehicle, with an explosive payload. The intended application of the weapon was that it would be set in motion by a controller in a protective bunker, and directed at those landing craft which might have eluded the tidal zone obstacles. Then, with several hundred pounds of explosive, it would be detonated so as to demolish incoming landing craft and cause casualties among the troops about to debark. No further word will be spent here on these devices since they were totally ineffective. Among the explanations offered for their failure is one that says the electronics of the vehicle controls were disabled by the intense pressures created by the preliminary bombardment. The final irony came when demolition men of the 531st Engineers salvaged the explosives for use in breaching the seawall.

The troops manning the defensive installations on the Cotentin were an assorted collection, probably a cross-section of what was available to the German Seventh Army. On the east coast, the main force was the 709th Division, a unit classified by intelligence sources during planning as a *static division*. However, at the time of the invasion, intelligence upgraded the classification to *limited employment*, possibly under the impression that a machine gun battalion had been incorporated into the division. Basically, this was a three-regiment division. The southernmost regiment is shown in some intelligence distributions of troops to be a Georgian Regiment, and certainly had a large percentage of non-Germans. U.S. troops on shore early, at the time the defenders were coming out of the fortified positions, heard a babble of languages. The two regiments to the north of Utah Beach, the 919th Infantry and the 729th Infantry carry conventional numbers, and there is no indication that they contained significant percentages of non-German personnel.

A description of the troops manning Blockhouse W5 further contributes to the picture of defending forces. This fortified position was reputed to be one of the strong-

Figure 47—*Upper shot: The Crisbecq/St.-Marcouf Installation Dominated the Cotentin Peninsula.* *Two positions, each with four massive concrete blockhouses included 210-mm naval rifles and underground ammunition storage. The guns were sited to fire on the beaches and to seaward.* **Lower shot: The Guns Were Not Totally Disabled by Allied Actions.** *Evidence of damage from naval bombardment and engineer demolition are visible to the right and rear of position. On the left are materials in readiness for further construction at site.*

est opposing the Utah Beach invaders. It contained an 88-mm gun, several 75-mm guns supplemented by small caliber antitank guns, mortars, flamethrowers, and machine guns. This position also controlled eight Goliath weapons. This array of ordnance was housed in 20 concrete pillboxes. The troops numbered 75, a mix of infantry and artillery, either very old (over 40) or very young (17 or 18). The commanding officer, a 23-year-old Lieutenant, was also on the young side, but had served on the Russian front where he was seriously wounded. His experience was transmitted to his charges by way of an effective training program.

The other units on the Peninsula were defending the western areas, but were also in position to support the 709th Division. The 243d Division occupied an area behind the 709th, and was rated by intelligence as being capable of reinforcing the 709th commencing at H-hour. An implication has to be drawn that the 243d was not totally devoid of transportation assets. Additionally, the 91st Infantry Division moved into the area shortly before D-day. This unit was rated as a *field division*, which is to say that it was several notches superior to a static division. A consequence of the appearance of the 91st Division was alterations to the plan for drop zones of the U.S. 82d Airborne Division . . . but without any serious impact on the seaborne forces invading at Utah. This reinforcement of defending forces on the Cotentin was clearly confirmation of the wisdom of the airborne operation designed to cover the exposed western flank of the total American invasion force.

THE BOMBARDMENT PHASE AT UTAH BEACH

This account of the Channel crossing has pictured an orderly movement of the huge fleet, despite some miserable weather and rough seas. There was no reason to believe the enemy had detected any of the numerous convoys. In fact E-boats were not out on patrol the night of 5th–6th of June because of foul weather. Field Marshal Rommel had headed the previous morning to his home in Germany for a short period of leave and also to visit the general staff, and if possible, the Fuehrer. He was still concerned about the control of reserve forces. He was convinced that the tides were not suitable for a landing at the time and the foul weather clinched his thinking. Adm. Krancke also felt that the tides were not right for a landing. Moreover, with this spell of bad weather, the Seventh German Army scheduled a command post exercise at Rennes, which took many of the key commanders away from their units.

The major ships began anchoring around 0200 hours in the transport area and the fire support areas. The log of 1st Battalion, 531st Engineer Shore Regiment shows that advance elements on board the *Bayfield* were at boat stations, and troops went over the side, then down rope nets, to landing craft commencing at 0230 hours. The *Barnet* also carried troops assigned to land on Uncle Red beach while the *Dickman* and *Empire Gauntlet* had troops to be landed on Tare Green. For some thoughts of the VII Corps Commander, Maj. Gen. Collins, at this time, see the accompanying box.

A View of Utah Beach from U.S.S. *Bayfield*

Extract from *The War Between The Generals;* David Irving;
Published by Congdon & Lattes, Inc.; 1981.

The rattle of chains through hawsepipes and the splash of anchors plunging into the dark waters of the English Channel were so loud that aboard the U.S.S. *Bayfield*, Rear Adm. Don P. Moon and Maj. Gen. J. Lawton Collins exchanged glances. They were a full twelve miles off the French coast, but it seemed impossible to them, edgy as they were, that the noise would not alert the German defenses on Utah Beach . . . Collins, looking at his friend, again found himself worrying about him. Don Moon was a man of great charm, but he had worked so much overtime on the loading and landing tables, on communications and other details, and delegated so few responsibilities to his staff, that he had become a nervous wreck. (Editor's note: Adm. Moon had been deeply disturbed by the failure of the naval escort to foil the German E-boats during Operation Tiger, and the consequent loss of U.S. servicemen.) . . . Don Moon had already had a tough war. He had served in the escort of the tragic and harrowing convoy to Russia, PQ 17. A few weeks after D-day the accumulated strain would overwhelm him and he would take his own life. Collins forced the concern for Moon from his mind. His troops would hit Utah Beach at H-hour, six-thirty a.m., about one hour after first light—in four hours. The tide would be low by then, enabling combat teams to go in first and demolish Rommel's exposed beach obstacles.

Aboard the *Bayfield,* Collins trained his field glasses on that other American Beach, Utah. . . . Immense convoys stretched across Collins' horizon—visible to him only by their barrage balloons. . . .

Seventeen warships of naval task force began slinging shells into the German gun batteries that had been located in advance by daylight reconnaissance. As the landing craft covered the last few hundred yards to the beaches, this naval bombardment was lifted and moved to targets farther inland. Hundreds of missiles howled towards the beaches from rocket ships—seven hundred from each of them (Editor's note: LCT(R), craft designed primarily for delivering tanks to beach landing sites, but fitted with launchers for 5-inch naval rockets). He (Gen. Collins) gripped the rails of the *Bayfield,* awed by the distant 14-inch naval guns belching yellow flames and by the greasy black gunsmoke rolling across the entire invasion area.

The ships of the Bombardment Group, though primarily American, came from three Navies. The battleship *Nevada* headed the group. There were heavy cruisers *Tuscaloosa*, *Quincy*, and H.M.S. *Hawkins*, the monitor H.M.S. *Erebus*, light cruisers H.M.S. *Enterprise*, and H.M.S. *Black Prince*, and the Netherlands gunboat *Soemba*. The major ships were to deliver their bombardment from a range of about 11,000 yards offshore. Ten destroyers were positioned much closer to shore, and delivered fire on assigned targets from a range of about 5,000 yards. Among the destroyers was the *Corry* which had led the LCT convoy through the difficult turnaround operation on the first sailing, and was about to meet a cruel fate during the bombardment, along with sister ships *Hobson* and *Fitch*. The firing plan called for a high rate of fire to commence at H minus 40 minutes, and to further intensify at H minus 10 minutes when the main batteries of *Nevada* and *Quincy* were brought to bear. Lifting of the naval fire would be signaled by the firing of a black smoke rocket from the first wave command craft. Firing would then be resumed against targets which could be found on the flanks of the landing beaches.

The coup de grace of the naval bombardment was reserved for rocket firing LCT(R)s. With the leading wave about 700 yards from grounding, rocket launching commenced. The total number of 5-inch rockets was about 5,000 distributed among 17 craft. Undoubtedly the accuracy of this weapon left something to be desired. Nevertheless, it could be expected that this quantity of warheads impacting on target beaches of 2,000 yards length, or thereabouts, would produce a frightening effect, and hasten the desire of the defenders to call it quits.

Aerial bombardment made a further contribution to softening the defenders of the Atlantic Wall. Numerous recorded accounts state that four-engined bombers of the R.A.F. ranged over the entire front during the hours of darkness. Moreover, at Blockhouse W5 the defenders were accustomed to periodic night bombing, but thought that the bombing during the night of 5th–6th of June was more intense than usual. It is a difficult question as to whether this night bombing produced any useful effect.

In the period of about 40 minutes before H-hour, practically coinciding with the naval bombardment, the Ninth Air Force was in action at Utah Beach. Most military observers rate the bombing at Utah as much more effective than that at Omaha. In the latter case, four-engined bombers of the Eighth Air Force flew above the cloud cover and in view of safety restrictions hit well inland from their targets. At Utah, the lighter Marauders, numbering about 275 aircraft, dropped a total of 4,400 250-pound bombs on a three-mile length of beach . . . including the beach area where the troops actually landed. This is approximately 400 tons of explosive delivered from a moderately low altitude. Examination of bombardment damage on fortification structures after the campaign leads to the conclusion that many of the hits were due to air attack.

Timewise at least, the problem at Iles St.-Marcouf fits into this phase. This action provided a stark appreciation of mine warfare during the assault of the Atlantic Wall. It was noted in the description of the Utah Beach terrain that the two small islets known as Iles St.-Marcouf were located just offshore in a position to create a hazard to any plan for maneuvering the large naval fleet. As the plan turned out, the islets were adjacent to boat lanes traversed by landing craft of the assault waves. Attention to the problem was required before dawn. At 0430 hours, two hours prior to H-hour, detachments from the 4th and 24th Cavalry Squadrons landed on the islets to reconnoiter and dispose of any observation post or other hostile installation. The site was found to be unoccupied and the mission was completed by 0530 hours. Nevertheless, there was a heavy toll on the raiding party. Of the 132 troops landed, casualties reached 19 dead and wounded. The ground was heavily mined, mainly with the bouncing S-type antipersonnel mines. This experience was a painful lesson in the degree to which mine warfare expertise of the German defending forces could impede assault operations.

The naval bombardment commenced a short while ahead of schedule. Just after 0500 hours shore batteries detected the close-in destroyers and immediately opened fire, particularly at *Fitch* and *Corry*. A short while later, the mine sweepers came under fire, but continued to sweep according to plan. Next, one of the Royal Navy cruisers came under fire. At this point, around 0530 hours, the naval commander ordered the commencement of firing rather than wait for the scheduled time. All ships responded and the assigned targets came under fire. At about this time air cover over the beach put down a smoke screen, as planned, to shield naval activity in the anchorage. Unfortunately, the aircraft assigned to cover the *Corry* was shot down, leaving the destroyer highly visible. The *Corry* had been firing at such a high rate that its gun tubes needed hosing down to maintain a safe temperature. While attempting rapid maneuvers to evade concentrated fire and at the same time to observe the limits of cleared waters, she struck a mine. The mine explosion produced catastrophic damage, including flooding in the engine room and opening of the hull. All power was lost and while the ship was under manual steering control it began settling to the bottom. The sister destroyers lowered boats to recover survivors, while continuing to fire. After the order was given to abandon ship, a lone sailor returned to run an American flag up the main mast. Losses were 13 dead and 33 wounded.

LANDING OF THE EARLY WAVES AT UTAH BEACH

By the way of an overall orientation, the conduct of operations went well at Utah Beach. However some of the historical accounts report that the Utah landings were a walkover, that the resistance was very light or nil, and that casualties were negligible. Such reporting seems to overstate the situation as it actually existed. The weather was supposed to be mild, with the beaches in the lee of the Cotentin Peninsula, but in spite of this, there were a number of LCTs lost due to heavy sea conditions. Losses to sea mines included several ship types, including destroyers and various control ships. Some of the fortified positions held out for more than a week, and placed aimed fire on the beaches throughout this time period. Land mines took a severe toll not only on D-day, but throughout the beachhead establishment phase. Enemy air activity was highly intermittent, but also produced casualties commencing the evening of D-day. As this narrative proceeds through the landings, a reasonably accurate picture should emerge.

The first wave came ashore on schedule. The wave included two battalions of the 8th Infantry Regiment, the first on the right to attack targets on Tare Green, and the second on the left to attack targets on Uncle Red. Each of the LCVP craft brought in a 30-man assault team, as configured by the Assault Training Center, so that with five teams per rifle company, and two companies abreast within each battalion, the wave was comprised of 20 craft. In a loose sense, the DD Shermans (dual-drive tanks) were also within the first wave. The landing plan called for these tanks to land at "H-hour or as soon after as possible." The plan called for four tanks in each of the LCTs, for a total of 32 DD-tanks. In a last minute change, Gen. Collins ordered the launching of the DD-tanks moved from 5,000 to 3,000 yards offshore, a move which certainly improved the chances of their safe arrival ashore.

As events unfolded, the DD-tanks did not quite make the first wave. The LCTs boarding the tanks arrived in the transport area on schedule at 0430 hours. From there on, some serious problems set in. One of the patrol craft escorting the LCTs struck a mine and sank. The rescue activity connected with this loss led to a delay and the tanks eventually arrived ashore, approximately 15 minutes late. Unfortunately, during the launch procedure as one of the LCTs lowered its ramp it struck a mine, and went to the bottom with four out of the total of 32 DDs.

The troops had a difficult time on the final leg of the way in. The rendezvous sequence seemed to be designed to discomfort soldiers. After going round in slow circles, in a dense cloud of diesel exhaust, the waves were completed and dispatched from the line of departure. Sea conditions were indeed rough, and seven of the landing craft in the early waves were lost. After landing craft grounded on the tidal flats of extremely mild gradient, the troops were in arm-pit deep water. Fortuitously, the cold water shock quickly cleared away the lingering seasickness that had plagued nearly all troops. After dragging through the tidal waters for a distance of some 300 yards, or thereabouts, the trek over the open reaches of the low water line to the high water line was next. The distance was more than 1,500 yards on the left and 1,200 yards on the right while the burden carried by each troop was heavy in all cases.

Among the defending troops, the situation was equally grim, or even more so. Using Blockhouse W5 as representative of the fortified positions along Utah Beach, a picture can be sketched. The bombing runs by the Marauders (B-26 two-engined bombers) had been devastating. Each pass over the targets was at progressively lower levels and improved accuracy. The concrete casemates had been hit, but they withstood the impact reasonably well. The 88-mm gun had been damaged. In the open shelters and trenches, the 75-mm cannon were destroyed. Some of the ammunition reserves in the open positions had been hit, initiating a series of explosions. Casualties, both dead and wounded, were mounting. Destroyers of the naval bombardment force moved in closer. By this time, the only remaining German weapon with a useful range was a small bore mortar, and this was directed at the destroyers. No damage was done by the mortar, and in the process, its position was revealed to the naval gunners who promptly zeroed in on the firing position. Thus, the last weapon at Blockhouse W5, other than small arms, was eliminated . . . except for the Goliaths.

As the assault waves closed in to the shore line, the defenders' capability to put up a fight was ebbing. The trenches were buried. The concrete casemates and shelters had been damaged. Crucial weapons were out of action, and ammunition reserves had been exploded during the preparatory bombardment. The final thrust of the softening process consisted of 5-inch naval rockets, launched off LCTs, and these had rained over the total extent of Utah Beach. Telephone communications were a shambles, preventing a situation report from reaching higher headquarters. A messenger sent off with a desperate plea for support was hit during the air bombardment, and never reached his destination. The will to fight held up reasonably well as the naval fire intensified, but as the defensive weapons went out one by one, the end was becoming evident. The blockhouse commander, a veteran of the Russian front, had never experienced such violence.

Resistance persisted as the local defenders used their rifles and machine guns. Moreover, artillery weapons of various calibers, from 88-mm and up, were capable of reaching the landing beaches of Utah from remote positions. The long range weapons in the Crisbecq fortifications were especially lethal. In this period, the first wave of attacking troops reached as far as seawall positions and had a moment of respite. Their next move was to go over the seawall (Fig. 48). The assault teams set about to attack defending troops in trenches and shelters, and place prepared charges against pill boxes.

The second wave, scheduled to arrive at H plus five minutes, brought additional infantry of the two assault battalions including, particularly, their weapons companies, and the first of the engineers to reach shore. This latter group, in 12 LCVPs, included both the naval underwater demolition units (NUDUs, augmented with Army demolition personnel) and the Beach Obstacle Demolition Party, analogous to the Special Engineer Task Force units of Omaha Beach. The mission of these teams was to neutralize the obstacles in the tidal zone while low tide conditions prevailed. Personnel and commanders of the Demolition Party were drawn from the 237th Engineer Combat Battalion, of the 1106th Engineer Combat Group, and one company of the 299th Engineers, which was attached to the Group while its main force was at Omaha. The records of the 1106th Group indicate that the beach obstacle teams landed approximately 12 minutes late. The mission of the teams called for clearing of 50-yard wide lanes, four on each of the two beaches. Obstacles were divided between Army and Navy teams with the offshore rows to be handled by the Navy teams and the inshore rows to be an Army responsibility. Assistance would be available from tank dozers attached to the teams from the 70th Tank Battalion and the 612th Light Equipment Company, two dozers from each of the two organizations.

Figure 48—*Upper shot: Engineer Troops Move onto Dunes to Reconnoiter and Clear Mines.* *Heavy loads burdened troops reaching shore early and with no support vehicles. The seawall offered a brief respite prior to a resumption of the advance.*
Lower shot: Continual Pounding of Utah Beach by Enemy Artillery. *As resistance in the beach area was overwhelmed, artillery in remote locations took up the fire missions.*

Misfortune hit the Beach Obstacle Demolition Party at the outset of its mission. As the ramp of one of the landing craft was being lowered, an artillery shell exploded against the craft causing six deaths. Additionally, there were 39 wounded. The Navy teams suffered four killed and 11 wounded. Problems surrounded Maj. Herschel Linn, commanding officer of the 237th Engineers and the ostensible commander of the Demolition Party teams. Several historical accounts state that his landing craft was sunk, but there is no explanation of when, or how this happened. The *Group History* of the 1106th, for June of 1944, says merely, "Major Linn became separated from the Demolition Party and did not land until several days after the main force."

Despite the difficulties, obstacles in the tidal zone were cleared in a workman-like manner. The types and dispositions of obstacles conformed closely to the intelligence information provided in briefing sessions. Stakes, ramps, tetrahedra, and hedgehogs were all encountered, roughly ranked in frequency of appearance. Many of the stakes were tipped with Tellermines, contrary to descriptions provided by some historical works. Numerous photographs show the mounting of the mines on obstacles. The main discrepancy between what was expected and what was found was in the density of obstacle distribution, primarily due to the mislanding and to the lesser strength of defenses toward the Carentan Estuary. The first attack on the obstacles was by means of hand-placed charges several of which were connected by primacord. There was no problem in coordinating the efforts of Army and Navy teams and continuous clear lanes were produced. With the availability of tank dozers, they were put to work using brute mechanical force to dislodge the obstacles after removal of all mines. This was found to be an expeditious technique and shortly became the preferred means of clearance. Several photographs in the standard historical accounts, including those contained herein, show piles of the obstacles accumulated up against the seawall. In some cases, the foundation concrete came along with the main structure of the obstacle.

During this period the DD-tanks reached shore, roughly 15 minutes behind their scheduled landing with the first wave of infantry assault teams, and more or less concurrently with the Demolition Party teams. The DDs deflated their floatation gear to reveal a full tank company ready to commence firing. The shock effect was profound—the defending troops were absolutely amazed to see the tanks arrive so mysteriously. The 88-mm gun would have been the primary weapon for use against invading tanks, but it was no longer operative, nor were the 75-mm guns. The last resort would be the Goliaths. While the match-up would seem to be ludicrous, with miniaturized unmanned tanks of the defenders versus main battle tanks of the invaders, actually the Goliaths carried enough of an explosive payload to be a serious weapon. The problem facing the defenders was to get the Goliaths into operation.

All attempts to get the miniature tanks started were unsuccessful. The malfunction was believed to be in the control units. Resistance at the shoreline fortifications of Utah Beach was in its final stages. Nevertheless, medium and large caliber guns, putting aimed fire from various remote locations on all elements of the landing force, continued to make life precarious for the invaders.

Before the first half hour of the assault was reached, the initial landing teams were making significant progress in dealing with the defending forces and were being augmented by further arrivals. This applied to infantry, armor, and engineers alike. The two leading battalions of the 8th Infantry Regiment were essentially complete, at least to the extent of their tactical elements. The 70th Tank Battalion had its third company ashore, these tanks being conventionally waterproofed. The Beach Obstacle Demolition Party of the 237th Engineers contained support teams to back up the early landing teams with additional explosives, equipment, and manpower; and these additional teams reached shore at this time. However, the most significant turn of events was that defending troops began to come out of their positions to surrender.

ENGINEER RECONNAISSANCE OPERATIONS

From about H plus 30 to H plus 60 minutes there was good progress on engineer assignments. Obstacles in the tidal zone were well above the incoming sea and hostile fire on the working parties was diminishing as defending troops were giving up their shoreline positions. Artillery fire from supporting positions continued to take a toll as it continued to be accurate and selective as to worthwhile targets. Tank dozers were speeding the removal of the obstacles, as compared to the tedious process of fixing explosives by hand. In fact, the obstacle removal was going so well that a decision was made to drop the plan for 50-yard wide clear lanes and to get the entire tidal zone clear. Meanwhile the advancing infantry were moving across the dunes and heading inland, notwithstanding the heavily mine-laced conditions encountered.

Reconnaissance teams of the 531st Engineer Shore Regiment, the primary engineer unit of the 1st Engineer Special Brigade, came ashore reasonably close to their scheduled landing time of H plus 60 minutes. There is no way to establish the exact time of landing, but it may very well have been earlier rather than the usual case of being later. The basis for this supposition is that participants have a recollection of the distance from touchdown of landing craft to the high water mark and the distance values tend to exceed a value which would prevail at two hours past low tide, i.e., 0730 hours. The 1st Battalion landed on Uncle Red and the 2d Battalion on Tare Green. Command groups of each battalion landed with each of the battalions, headed by the respective commanders, Lt. Col. Robert May, of the 1st; and Lt. Col. Stephen Force, of the 2d. The 3d Battalion was due ashore later in the day with an assignment to a more northerly beach. The mislanding and its explanation have been covered previously. Suffice it to say that map coordinates for the planned exit and the actual exit were 442982 and 452968 respectively (see Bigot maps of the Appendices). These two exits fall quite close to the boundary between the two color-coded beaches. It may be helpful to have alternate identification of these beach exits which appear on certain maps in wide use. The planned primary exit may appear as Exit No. 3, or Road T-7, while the actual exit may appear as Exit No. 2, or Road U-5.

A mission statement for the two leading battalions of the 531st Engineers can be put briefly: to support the 4th Infantry Division in its assault landing on Utah Beach by beach development, with primary emphasis on exploitation of existing beach exits; to reconnoiter beach areas; to clear obstacles and mines; to establish assembly areas for vehicles and personnel; to operate beachhead facilities; and to provide local security. The 2d Battalion had an additional responsibility, generally within its mission, of reconnoitering Sugar Red beach, lying to the north of its own beach, Tare Green, prior to the arrival of the 3d Battalion, which would operate the additional beach area.

It must be assumed that the reconnaissance parties were not aware of the mislanding as they came ashore and found their way around the area. There are very few structures or landmarks which would distinguish the two exits from each other. Fortunately, Brig. Gen. Theodore Roosevelt, assistant division commander of the 4th Division, had insisted on landing with the early waves and was the ideal individual to deal with such a crisis. He had been in the 1st Division through its most difficult times, and if a plan had to be revised, it would not be a new experience; and this general would not shrink from taking responsibility. Just as soon as Gen. Roosevelt became aware of the mislanding, he reached the decision that any attempt to relocate the forces ashore would be chaotic, and that the best solution was to push forward immediately. He shouted the order, "We jump off from here." Col. Caffey, of the 1st Engineer Special Brigade had also managed to get ashore very early, and was with Gen. Roosevelt at the time. Gen. Roosevelt directed Col. Caffey to spread the word, and to be certain that the Navy continue with landings on the new beach location.

The make-up of the reconnaissance parties was a conventional engineer platoon of three squads, plus reinforcements in the range of 10 to 20 percent, for a total strength of 44 to 48 troops. The initial allotment of shore party engineers was two companies on each of the two beaches, and each of these companies supplied one platoon. Thus, there were, altogether, four of the reconnaissance platoons in operation. The usual practice in the regiment was to select platoons for this duty on the basis of their proficiency in mine detection, and in particular, in the tuning and use of the SCR-625 mine detector. Expertise in handling explosives was a further criterion for selection.

The reconnaissance teams on Utah Beach were evenly distributed across the front. On the left half of Uncle Red beach, the team from Company A concentrated on a route to tie into Exit 2 at a location beyond the dunes. Such a route entailed a breach of the sea wall on the left front of the Battalion sector. An adequate supply of explosives had been brought ashore. The issue material for the mission was Composition C, probably from British sources, and reputed to be about 30 percent more effective than TNT, the long-standing preference of U.S. engineers mainly on the basis of its safe handling characteristics. About 40 men of the team were designated to carry 40 pounds each, packaged in carrying cases with shoulder straps, 20 pounds in each case. The men not carrying cases brought in the mine detectors in their standard carrying cases, which were sealed for watertightness. The result was a bulky, difficult package, but it produced the desired results: a set of mine detectors in operating condition, despite their reputation as prone to malfunction when wet. Early in the conduct of its scouting, the party encountered the inoperative Goliath weapons and unloaded the explosive payloads, which turned out to be an excellent substitute for what had been so laboriously carried ashore. The German material was used on the seawall job, and the Composition C stock was preserved for future use. Working conditions were extremely hazardous, regardless of the widespread reports to the contrary. Enemy artillery in unknown locations, but probably north of the beach, pounded away incessantly, and the dense distribution of mines in the dune area also caused casualties. Despite the difficulties, and the time lost to care for casualties, the reconnaissance on the left of Uncle Red went well. The quantity of explosives proved to be just about right to remove the amount of seawall for the passage. The clearance of the connecting lane showed reasonable progress, mines were found and lifted. An ability of the mine detector operators to find the Schumine, small wooden box mines, was gratifying.

On the right half of Uncle Red beach, a platoon of Company C was active, but with a slightly different orientation. Road U-5 (Exit 2) terminated at the seawall. Even with a gap in the sea wall, the junction was blocked, and needed some demolition attention. The emphasis of this platoon was to reconnoiter along Road U-5, and to assure that the mines were completely removed from the exit. After reaching the lateral road running parallel to the shoreline, mine clearing was performed from Road U-5 over to T-7. During the time of this work, an artillery battery came ashore and required a cleared area behind the dunes in order to set up for firing. Their request was handled so expeditiously, despite the intensity of hostile fire, that the 4th Division Artillery Commander commended their performance.

On Tare Green beach, the situation was analogous to that which prevailed on Uncle Red. The 2d Battalion of the 531st Engineers had its two reconnaissance platoons, plus a command group ashore, approximately on schedule at about H plus 60 minutes. The defenders were still feeling the effects of the preliminary bombardment, but nevertheless, invader targets on the beach were under concentrated small arms, machine gun, mortar, and artillery fire. Personnel and equipment came through with only minor harm. The two teams set about their mission, concentrating initially on gapping the seawall. Next, lanes were cleared, extending through the dunes, and reaching to the lateral road parallel to the shoreline.

Additional reconnaissance actions were performed by the 1106th Engineer Combat Group. The principal components of the Group were the 49th Engineer Combat Battalion, the 237th Engineer Combat Battalion, Company B of the 299th Engineers attached (the main body of this outfit was at Omaha, where it provided troops for the Special Engineer Task Force), two detachments of tank dozers, an engineer dump truck company, and an engineer treadway bridge company. It is difficult to fathom the attachment status of the 1106th Group, even though a few clues are provided by the unit history for the month of June, 1944. It appears that Companies A and C of the 237th Engineers were attached to the 4th Division where they completed an assignment connected with the seawall, and then proceeded to move forward in contact with infantry. The two companies reverted to Group control by dark of D-day. The 238th Engineers do not appear in the troop list of the Group, but do show up in descriptions of tasks accomplished by the Group.

The reconnaissance team of the 1106th Group could be described as an ad hoc organization to focus on the problems presented by the causeways. Their assigned mission included coverage of Roads V-1, U-5, and T-7. The team numbered 16, including several key officers of the group staff and representatives from most all the engineer units of the Group. Landing occurred about 0730 hours, in the vicinity of Road U-5. The team moved forward on Road U-5, and reached the farthest advance of the infantry. On Road T-7, the team went even beyond the advance of the infantry. Due to the intensity of fire on Road V-1, it was found best to delay examination of this avenue of advance off the beach. The findings of the team were reported to 4th Division headquarters at about H plus 180 minutes. Continuing assignments to the elements of the Group were determined by the recommendations derived from the reconnaissance effort.

ENGINEER MAIN BODY LANDINGS—
THE BUILD-UP PHASE

Progress on Utah Beach conformed reasonably closely to the phase diagram superimposed on the terrain map presented earlier in this account. The assault teams of the 8th Infantry, following closely behind the air and sea bombardment, made good progress in clearing the fortified positions on the shore line and on the dunes, and began to move inland. Support from Sherman DD-tanks and conventionally waterproofed tanks contributed to the final breakdown in the beach defenders' will to resist. The Beach Obstacle Demolition Party made excellent progress in clearing the tidal zone in advance of the incoming sea. Reconnaissance parties of the shore engineers scouted favorable routes off the beach to tie into the existing hard surface network. The seawall was gapped, and mines were lifted to clear lanes. Initially engineer tasks were performed under small arms fire, in addition to artillery. But, as the beach areas were cleared, the primary hazards reduced to artillery from adjacent weapons covering the limits of Utah Beach, and land mines planted in dense patterns. Sea mines also took a substantial toll on the Utah invaders, not only during the assault phase, but continuing on through the early days of the operation.

In the period up to about H plus three hours, the dominant characteristic of the landings was the build-up to a fairly complete infantry regimental combat team. Within the engineer units, the landing rate intensified. The main bodies of the shore companies were aboard LCTs capable of handling bulldozers with their sled loads in tow (Fig. 49). The accompanying photographs convey a clear impression of the size of this equipment and the difficulties of safely reaching shore. The large rolls are Sommerfeld matting material, which when staked to the sandy surface of dunes greatly aid in stabilizing and improving traction on what would shortly afterwards become beach roads. These mats are prepared by starting with wire mesh where the grid is formed by wire on about four-inch centers. Then, burlap or similar coarse and sturdy fabric is attached to the wire mesh with stout cord. This composite structure proved serviceable for the purpose in prior campaigns, and repeated its satisfactory performance at Utah Beach. Various other pioneer equipment was included in the sled loads such as sledgehammers, axes, stakes, a reserve supply of engineer marking tape, and additional explosives.

The results of the effort to get these vital loads of equipment and supplies ashore were decidedly mixed. One platoon of Company A, of the 531st Engineers, was scheduled to land at H plus 105 minutes off an LCT, only to have its craft strike a sea mine. The craft sank and carried all equipment on board to the bottom including bulldozers and sled loads. Fortunately, other vessels came to the rescue and all personnel were safely recovered. They reached shore at various times on the following day. The company was able to borrow sufficiently from Company C to fulfill its mission. At the same time, Company C itself experienced misfortune. Its LCT loaded with bulldozers, equipment, and supplies was shelled while attempting to land at H plus 120 minutes. One man was lost, and two bulldozers were disabled. Sometime afterward, three men were killed while working on the lateral road beyond the dunes. While the loss of these bulldozers was a severe handicap, the presence of the tank dozers partially made up for the losses. These machines lacked the versatility of the standard engineer dozers, but were entirely capable of finishing off the demolition gaps in the sea wall, and leveling off a cut through the dunes.

The photographs convey some noteworthy information regarding progress in getting the major elements of the 531st Engineers on shore. These same photographs appear in many of the standard works on Utah Beach landing operations, including, among others, the official histories. The captions with the illustrations usually state the time to be "shortly after the initial landings". First, the house shown in Fig. 49 prominently situated on the dunes places the location as Tare Green beach. The water line is approximately 75 yards short of the seawall. Reference to the data provided with the map *Utah Beach—South (la Madeleine)* (Appendix C) shows that this waterline is quite close to high tide, from which the time can be estimated at about 1030 hours, or just short one half hour of the time of high tide. Since the dozer operator has left his perch, one can speculate that he is off attempting to locate his contact for directions about the destination of the sled load of road materials.

Since the landing schedule calls for the arrival ashore of these LCTs at about two hours after H-hour, it appears that engineer activity is close to being on plan. Several other noteworthy points can be gleaned from the photographs. It appears that the

Figure 49—Upper shot: Engineer Main Bodies Reach Shore with Bulldozers and Sled Loads. *Towards high tide LCT craft land main bodies of engineers. Note dozer just arrived but materials not yet positioned; operator off perch probably to seek further direction. Activity in dunes area visible in background.*
Lower shot: A Platoon of DD-Tanks Awaits Engineer Progress to Move Over the Dunes. *Note that buoyancy gear has been lowered after clearing tidal zone. Engineer support in breaching the seawall and in clearing a safe lane through mined areas was required for continuation of advance.*

losses of bulldozers on Tare Green beach were not nearly so severe as on Uncle Red. This conclusion can be confirmed by the remarks in the After Action Report of the 2d Battalion of the 531st Engineers, the unit assigned responsibility on Tare Green beach. There is no record in the report of any major losses during the run into shore, nor upon reaching shore. The report does state that: "Organization of the beach progressed slowly throughout the first part of the day, largely due to persistent enemy artillery fire. Little damage was done to equipment or personnel. The Battalion proceeded to accomplish its initial mission. . . ."

A comparison of the situation on the two beach sectors comprising the initial targets at Utah Beach highlights the difficulty of sorting out generalizations in landing force progress. Prevailing opinion has it that the mislandings in the southerly direction proved to be a stroke of good fortune because of weaker defenses on the southern sectors of Utah Beach. However, the situation described above shows that losses among the early landings of critical engineer equipment, particularly bulldozers with their sled loads, were most severe on Uncle Red sector, lying to the south of Tare Green. The losses can be attributed to several sources: sea mines, land mines, and artillery, both from close-in and long-range weapon installations.

There is a further anomaly to be observed in the photographs. The DD-Sherman tanks are aligned along the advancing tide while the infantry progress has clearly carried beyond the dunes (see also Fig. 50). No gaps are visible in the seawall. A plausible explanation would be that the reconnaissance teams on Tare Green beach did not "hand-carry" explosives ashore, but rather included their explosives within the sled loads arriving by way of LCTs. If this were the case, the seawall gapping could not have occurred until approximately three hours after H-hour, or somewhere on the order of 0930 hours. If this speculation is correct, it provides an explanation for the presence of these tanks in their static positions. The 2d Battalion After Action

Figure 50—*Build-up of Engineer Main Bodies Continues Near High Tide.* *The DD-tanks visible to the left were still unable to advance at this point. Note that craft beach in shallow water as the bottom slope increases inshore. Note also that troops moved ashore with ease even though still heavily loaded. This picture is a stark comparison with the situation during earlier landings when troops were landed in deep water due to the flat bottom farther offshore. A mine detector is visible in the foreground.*

Report contains no indication of how its explosives were brought ashore, nor at what time their seawall gapping occurred.

Otherwise, engineer operations on Tare Green beach closely paralleled what was happening on Uncle Red. Multiple gaps were blown through the seawall, and obstacles and mines were cleared from the beach areas. Lanes for roads were cleared back to the lateral road in the rear of the beach. Assembly areas were cleared of mines. In due time, the mats were in place to stabilize road surfaces (see both views of Fig. 51). A primary defense line was set up on the right flank of the beach to protect against a possible enemy counter-attack.

The admixture of misfortune continued to hit the landing force at Utah Beach as the main body of the 1106th Engineer Combat Group came ashore. The missions of the battalions of the Group were oriented to assignments at locations more inland than the units which landed earlier. The main body of the 1106th Group landed in two waves, with the first beaching at 0930 hours, and the second just 15 minutes behind. Five LCTs were found to be missing, having turned back, or foundered in the heavy seas during the Channel crossing. All personnel were recovered. Despite the losses, all battalions of the group set out on their assignments expeditiously. The first problem was assembly of the troops following the arrival of landing craft, with an officer posted on the beach to direct units to the designated area. The officer was wounded by enemy artillery fire and evacuated off the beach.

The battalions of the 1106th Group proceeded to extend the distances at which the beach exits were passable. The 49th Engineers moved out on Road V-1, the southernmost of the exits. The Group reconnaissance team had earlier attempted to scout in this direction, but after encountering intense artillery fire, had chosen to delay and exploit its success on the other beach exits. In the meantime the 2d Battalion of the 8th Infantry had made progress in the southerly direction with one company moving along the inundated area and another moving along the seawall. This force moved against heavy artillery fire and found its way through minefields in their haste to make contact with airborne elements in the vicinity of Pouppeville. In the process, a number of enemy positions were bypassed, including the lock just north of Grand Vey, which was an important part of the system controlling the inundations. Facing this situation, the 49th Engineers inherited the mission of controlling the locks and initiating drainage. The resisting enemy force was attacked, 28 prisoners were taken and the major part of the force was contained while work on Road V-1 continued. Large numbers of Tellermines and S-mines were removed during the course of this task. The capture of the locks was completed early in the morning of D-day plus one. By this time a total of 126 prisoners and two usable artillery pieces were in the hands of Company B of the 49th Engineers. In addition to the actions of the 49th Engineers, the 1st Battalion of the 531st Engineers dispatched patrols to move into this same area, and also had a hand in restoring the normal operation of the flood control gates and draining the inundated area.

The other battalions of the 1106th Engineer Combat Group were active in the

Figure 51—*Upper shot: Engineer Progress Continued as Aid Station Prepared Wounded for Evacuation.* *The passage of time is indicated by the disassembly of sled loads seen in the background. The rolls of surfacing material would be staked into place for traction improvement.* ***Lower shot: A Beach Exit was Ready for Traffic as Tide Receded.*** *Note that the crest of the dunes was reduced to improve trafficability and Sommerfeld mats were staked into place. The pool of water indicates that the tide is receding and the low spot had not yet drained. This exit was on Tare Green Beach.*

center and northerly sectors of Utah Beach. The 238th Engineers headed for Roadway U-5, marked as Exit 2 on some maps, shortly after landing with the main body of the Group. The condition of the causeway portion of the exit presented several problems. A bridge spanning a deep culvert, at about the midpoint of the causeway, was demolished by retreating enemy units. Effectiveness of this demolition was enhanced by siting an antitank gun and placing antitank mines in crucial positions. Two of our tanks were lost before the resistance was eliminated. Following tanks were able to ford the stream, but the process was tedious, and a column of vehicles backed up to the beach. The 991st Engineer Treadway Bridge Company promptly responded, and upon reaching the point of the demolition, deployed the necessary bridging equipment. The work of restoring this bridge was accomplished under hostile artillery fire. After the pace of friendly advance was restored, the 238th Engineers moved to Roadway T-7 (Exit 3) to survey needs for engineer support. The 237th Engineers did not operate as an integrated unit, having detached one company, along with key battalion personnel, to the Beach Obstacle Demolition Party, and assigned the other two companies to support assault infantry battalions of the 8th Infantry on usual engineer tasks.

The 4th Engineer Combat Battalion had a variety of assignments throughout the division operations. The main body of the engineer battalion was embarked on LSTs, and was not ashore until after 1400 hours on D-day. Most of these elements were headed to inland positions to join the advance of the infantry units of the division, and played little, or no role in the early phases on the beach as described here. However, Company C was an exception, having been attached to the 22d Infantry Regiment. The 3d Battalion of the 22d Infantry landed on Tare Green beach at about H plus 75 minutes, and moved to the north to attack fortified positions along the shoreline. The commendation awarded to Company C of the 4th Engineers includes these words, "From initial landings . . . attached to 22d Infantry . . . magnificent contribution to the success of Team 22 . . . ." A Presidential Unit Citation was awarded to a platoon of Company C and includes the words, ". . . In the face of heavy enemy fire cleared area of mines, wire entanglements, and obstacles, and assisted in the reduction of the numerous reinforced casemates within this sector."

ENGINEERS ORGANIZE BEACHES AS INFANTRY FOLLOW-UP LANDS

A brief recapitulation may be helpful to the reader in understanding a new phase of the landing operations covering the period from approximately H plus three hours to H plus six hours. The bombardment by air and sea, prior to initial landings, was reasonably effective in damaging fortifications and devastating open positions, along with a psychological demoralization of the defenders. The landing waves held close to schedule, although the entire operation was displaced more than 2,000 yards in a southerly direction due to a combination of circumstances. The assault troops of the 8th Infantry Regiment quickly closed in on defensive positions, and took prisoners while suffering light losses. The Beach Obstacle Demolition Party, after losing one landing craft and its personnel, were successful in clearing the tidal flats, and in fact, had time to alter its plan to create safe lanes in favor of clearing large areas. The extent of the tidal zone allowed adequate time in advance of the incoming tide. Throughout this early period, supporting fire was available from DD-Sherman tanks, which had lost only four of 32 tanks during the launching process and the run into shore; this success being due in large part to the VII Corps decision to limit the launch line to only 3,000 yards offshore. Enemy resistance in the early period included small arms, mortars, and artillery direct-fire from close-in positions. As local resistance was overcome at shoreline positions, there was intensification of enemy artillery fire of various calibers from supporting positions.

Following the initial assault, the leading infantry battalions were reinforced, and advance parties of engineer units arrived on shore. This could be considered a second phase. The infantry heavy weapons companies brought in larger mortars, water-cooled machine guns, and a stronger antitank capability. The engineer parties reconnoitered for the best means of egress off the beaches, and to tie into existing hard surface roadways. While plans were crude at the time, a basis was established for breaching the seawall, and commencing obstacle clearance and mine removal through the dunes. The reconnaissance parties of the 531st Engineers were self-contained, having hand-carried 40 pounds of explosives per man, along with mine detectors, beach markers, and pioneer tools. The reconnaissance activity of the 1106th Group was oriented more towards the causeways passing through the inundations. Meanwhile, the infantry elements advanced through the low-lying meadows, up to the inundations, and along the causeways.

In the period of approximately H plus one hour, to H plus three hours, the tempo of landings accelerated. The reserve battalion of the 8th Infantry came ashore along with supporting components of the division, which rounded out the Regimental Combat Team. A battalion of the 22d Infantry landed. Infantry advances included actions northward along the shoreline and southward in the direction of Pouppeville. The main bodies of the principal engineer units reached shore by LCT, which provided lift for bulldozers with sled-loads of vital materials in tow. Losses of craft were significant. An LCT with a platoon of Company A of the 531st Engineers struck a sea mine and went down with bulldozer; personnel were recovered. The 1106th Engineer Combat Group reported the loss of five LCTs. The effect of the losses was moderated by redistribution of remaining assets. The main accomplishment of this phase was the preparation of clear lanes through the dunes and initiation of work on the causeways. Materials were towed into position by the bulldozers. Dozers then proceeded to clean up the seawall demolitions and to prepare the grade through the dunes for the anticipated flow of vehicles. Tank dozers were useful in compensating for the loss of bulldozers.

As the next phase took form, several high priority tasks became evident. Mine removal required acceleration so that clear lanes could be extended, and a network could become operational. Grading and surfacing had to be expedited to keep pace with mine and obstacle clearing. Areas had to be provided where unit vehicles could be assembled and dewaterproofed. Sites were required for various other essential functions, such as antiaircraft weapons, prisoner of war holding space, and dumps for the receipt of supplies due ashore imminently. Wounded troops had to be evacuated in a timely, orderly way. And certainly not the least, was the task of maintaining the flow of traffic, especially in the tidal zone where vehicles were drowning out in high water, but also ashore through the dunes. Some descriptions will be sketched out to cover these engineer tasks.

Mine removal at Utah Beach was a task of the first magnitude. Much of what followed was contingent upon establishment of clear lanes and areas. Antipersonnel and antitank mines of various types were found throughout the area. Infantry leading elements had passed through largely unscathed, but engineer troops working here and criss-crossing the ground, began to take casualties until the cleared areas were well marked. The S-type mines, which bounced up from the ground upon detonation and then burst their main charge when about waist high, were particularly deadly. These were readily found by engineer troops using detectors. The Schumine 42 presented a much more difficult problem by virtue of its small wooden box and minimum content of metal parts. It had been in service for more than a year, but not in large numbers, up to the time when they were distributed through the Atlantic Wall. These antipersonnel mines could be found only by mine detectors which were tuned to a high degree of sensitivity. As a result, a number of the Schumines remained undetected, and produced casualties, not only on D-day, but also for weeks thereafter as engineer work in the dune areas continued. Those units which brought their mine detectors ashore in standard carrying cases, and there were some, paid the penalty of extra weight to be hand-carried but benefited by the more exacting performance of their detectors. It was known that moisture had an adverse effect on the detectors.

One of the battalions of the 531st Engineers accumulated data which helped in visualization of the mine clearing scope. The unit reports, in a ten-day review after the action, that 131 acres were cleared. On a reasonable estimate, the D-day activity could easily have reached the extent of 18 to 20 acres for the one battalion, or twice that for the Regiment. This estimate omits any effort by the 3d Battalion which commenced landing later in the day and immediately set about preparation of Sugar Red beach, just north of the assault beaches. The 3d Battalion reported that mines were found as far inland as 600 yards beyond the seawall and that types were included which had not been found before. One of the battalion reports compiles the types of mines found as follows:

- Concrete Stock mines
- S-mines
- Schumines
- Mortar AP mines
- Hawkins mines

- Tellermines
- Wooden box mines (AT)
- British MK IV AT mines
- French AT mines

It can be readily appreciated that the mine clearing task would proceed tediously when this diverse collection of types was encountered, some of which were unfamiliar.

An incident on Uncle Red beach illustrates the difficulties that were encountered in organizing beaches. During this period, towed weapons were arriving ashore. An antiaircraft unit reconnoitered and selected positions for digging emplacements.

The shore party engineers responded by clearing the areas requested. One of the gun crews then proceeded with their digging and reached a depth of more than six feet in some places, at which point an unexploded nose-up naval rocket became exposed. The gun was moved into the emplacement. In the process, the fuse of the rocket was unintentionally struck, the rocket exploded, and the gun crew was a total loss. The particular team involved in this mine clearing assignment was thoroughly competent and had made a number of difficult detections of mines. Obviously, the SCR-625 mine detector was not capable of probing to such depths, even to find a mass of metallic material as in the rocket casing.

As clear lanes were marked with engineer tape the bulldozers, which arrived by LCT with shore party main body units, dropped their sled loads and commenced some leveling of the lanes through the dunes. The area through the breached sea wall needed to be cleared. Earlier, the tank dozers made a useful contribution toward getting some of the congestion on the beach moving forward. But, it remained for the engineer dozers to move the large quantity of sandy soil through the dunes, and to prepare the ground for an efficient egress off the beach. Side by side lanes were prepared for track and wheeled vehicles, so as to spare the Sommerfeld mat surfaces from excessive wear by tanks and half-track vehicles.

The evolution of the beach exit can be seen graphically in the accompanying photos. Earlier there were several views of engineer dozers arriving on shore with sled loads still in tow, obviously searching for their exact destination. The picture which focuses on the aid station on the beach is relevant, with its background showing the breakout of road surfacing material, the rolls of mat (Fig. 51). The lower photo shows a beach exit completed and ready for a stream of traffic. Note that the crest of the dunes has been cut back drastically, and made accessible for wheeled vehicles, both as to grade and traction. A boat load of personnel has just reached shore and dropped off their partially inflated life preservers. The time can be estimated at about noon, or shortly afterward since the tide is receding after reaching maximum height and filling the small depressions, about 150 yards seaward from the seawall.

Another high priority task required the attention of engineer bulldozers. The problem of vehicles drowning out in the surf, upon exiting from landing craft, reached an unexpected magnitude (see comments of Col. Caffey in the following box). All vehicles were required to be waterproofed. Standard operating procedures were available for waterproofing vehicles at embarkation camps. The approved technique was intended to enable submergence to a depth of seven feet. Nevertheless, at various stages of the tide the landed vehicles encountered water depth they could not cope with. In some cases, low spots in the bottom produced very deep water which magnified the problem and increased the number of vehicles stalled. In other cases, landing craft grounded on high spots in fairly deep water. A problem also became evident that naval crews dropped their ramps before a hard grounding occurred. Additionally, the crews were often not adequately experienced to cope with the speed of the incoming tide, this being a rate of about one foot of water depth every 15 minutes. Where a vehicle drowned immediately off the ramp of an LCT there was an inevitable

Extract from files of Cornelius Ryan
Author of *The Longest Day,* published
by Simon and Shuster; New York, NY; 1959

From an interview with Col. Eugene M. Caffey:

One thing that particularly had my attention all of D-day, while Utah
was under double enfilade fire, was the way in which the bulldozer
drivers went about their work with such complete nonchalance. Of
course, the bulldozers make so much noise that they could not hear
the shells burst, but they certainly could see the water and sand
churned up by the fragments. All during that long day, they drove
back and forth along the beach assisting in dragging out drowned
artillery and vehicles, in shoving off landing craft, and in grading out
rough roads and trails. They were remarkable people.

delay in getting the other vehicles off, with the water depth increasing all the while. The means of recovering these stranded vehicles, all of which were urgently required ashore, was towing and winching by the engineer bulldozers. Primarily due to the experience within the 1st Engineer Special Brigade, this task was performed with high efficiency, and often under incoming artillery fire. The remarks of Col. Caffey contained in the accompanying inset are a fitting tribute to this performance.

The development plan of the total beach area became apparent as the phase covering H plus three hours to H plus six hours wore on. Beach organization prepared for a heavier stream of vehicle traffic and the initiation of supplies coming ashore. Clear space on the dunes and behind required that there be no let-up in mine lifting. The task of mine work was a contest against time and space. All the while the enemy shelling of all beach areas persisted. When large attractive targets appeared on the beach the rate of incoming fire obviously picked up. But all tasks were carried on. Sharing of bulldozers and road materials throughout the 1st Battalion of the 531st Engineers was a continuing process. The 2d Battalion dispatched a reconnaissance team to the north in anticipation of the arrival of the 3d Battalion and the opening of Sugar Red beach. The battalion medical detachments were operating on the open beaches, but preparing to move to structures behind the dunes. The personnel of the detachments performed in a praiseworthy fashion, frequently leaving positions of comparative safety to treat casualties and to remove casualties from unsheltered positions. The security function of the battalions was carried on as advance detachments reconnoitered the beach area and selected positions for antitank weapons arriving later in the afternoon.

The line of demarkation between organizing a beach and operating a beach is not clear-cut, but certainly much of the transition took place on the afternoon of D-day. The evolution could be regarded as a distinct phase taking up the period from H plus six hours to H plus 12 hours. During this span of six hours all the activities of the preceding phase continued. The combatant nature of the environment also persisted, as incoming artillery fire picked up whenever attractive targets appeared on shore. At about 1400 hours and later in the afternoon the shelling on the left flank of Uncle Red beach was especially heavy.

The primary new element which added to the capability of the Utah Beach facilities was the arrival of additional equipment, thereby enabling the operation of dumps. Each of the shore party companies brought in six cargo trucks (two and one-half ton GMC models) and one truck-mounted crane. This level of equipment was not adequate to meet planned cargo transfer rates, but any level of mechanization was an improvement over an all-manual effort. Furthermore, the troops were more than able to keep up with incoming supply deliveries off landing craft. There were times when craft were performing erratically as they headed for a touchdown, but then abruptly changed course and headed for a different destination. The naval beachmaster on shore had great difficulty in enforcing discipline over the individual coxswains resulting in wasteful divergence from plans. Nevertheless, even if stock levels on shore were building at a somewhat tardy rate, there was no evidence of shortages. Dumps were operating for Classes I, III, IV, and V supplies, i.e., water and rations, motor fuel, fortification materials, and ammunition. In short, all that was needed at an early stage of the campaign was on hand.

The role of the 2d Naval Beach Battalion, which was assigned to the 1st ESB, was of great benefit in helping organize the beach under extremely difficult conditions as described in the following box. Also, Naval Construction Battalions performed extremely important duties on both Omaha and Utah. These units are identified in the List of Engineer Units at the back of the book.

Progressively, the exits were improved and extended. The surfaced lanes in parallel with lanes for track vehicles were continuously maintained. A lateral road was in place behind the dunes. Work progressed on finger roads to provide additional connections between the beach and the lateral road. The accompanying quote is an example of the difficulties encountered during this period.

The 3d Battalion of the 531st Engineers commenced landing with advance elements of two companies via Tare Green beach, shortly after 1200 hours. They headed for Sugar Red and commenced mine removal. Progress was labored as the mines encountered were of unfamiliar type. Additionally, casualties were taken at an unexpectedly high rate during mine removal. Also landing around midday were two bulldozers with sled loads in tow, and these headed north to the new beach. The main body of the battalion commenced landing about 1600 hours when battalion headquarters transferred to an LCM from their LST. Other elements landed about 1830 hours off an LCT and an LCI. Sometime later the balance of the main body transferred to a rhino ferry after having crossed the channel in an LST. Misfortune struck the 531st again when the ferry was bombed and strafed at about 2300 hours, resulting in 21 wounded of which some were serious cases. The tug was destroyed, leaving the ferry

Extracts from a narrative report by Commander John F. Curtin, USNR, given 25 July 1944, concerning his experiences as Commanding officer of the 2d Naval Beach Battalion on Utah Beach on 6 June 1944.

The beach area itself or, rather, the area behind the stone wall which ran along the beaches (just above the high-water line) was heavily mined. Losses were sustained, in clearing the area and in clearing paths through it for men and equipment, for many days after the landing.

There was a certain amount of aimed (manual and automatic) small-arms fire on the beaches at the time of the landing and the beach defenses, which included guns up to 88-mm, were also active. Those on the assault beaches were put out-of-action quite early and without too many casualties.

The beaches, however, were under fire from enemy batteries, located north and south of them, for many days after the landing—the batteries consisting of 155's (so nearly as we could judge) and of 88's.

stranded and the wounded to await evacuation the next morning. Meanwhile on shore, the mine removal task continued into darkness and through the night. In due course, Sugar Red took its place beside the two assault beaches as a productive facility in the Utah Beach composite.

Returning to the fortunes of the 4th Engineer Combat Battalion of the 4th Division, recall that elements of one company were attached to the 22d Infantry. The main body of the battalion commenced landings off an LST at 1600 hours. The mission of the unit centered on conventional engineer support to the three regimental combat teams of the division which were advancing in three directions from the assault beaches. The problems of the beaches—mines, obstacles, and defensive positions—were encountered to some degree at inland locations. One particularly troublesome matter found during the advance inland was the cratering of road junctions. To quickly overcome the impediment to vital military traffic, bypasses were prepared around the road junctions. This approach minimized losses to artillery fire which was targeted on the obvious choke points. The battalion was prepared for, and called upon for, support of assault on numerous fortified positions. The commendation to Company C of the 4th Engineers by the commanding officer of the 22d Infantry was cited earlier.

HERBERT AFTON TAYLOR—2ND LIEUTENANT
1ST ENGINEER SPECIAL BRIGADE
UTAH BEACH

"My first assignment was to straighten out a traffic jam caused by heavy vehicles moving on inadequate roads . . . we were under definite orders to tip over any vehicles found blocking the road. They were to be tipped over not rolled off the shoulder in an upright position in order to minimize the danger from mines. All along the roads and the edges of the fields . . . were German signs indicating the presence of mines. Engineers were immediately put to work de-mining the roads and fields."

UTAH BEACH D-DAY HIGHLIGHTS

An accurate statistical summary of the engineer achievements on D-day at Utah Beach is virtually impossible to compile. Unit histories and after action reports contain only a few random items. Nevertheless, some salient data can be presented. The most compelling achievement of the reinforced 4th Infantry Division was the landing of approximately 20,000 troops and 1,700 vehicles in the space of 15 hours. A reasonable estimate of the proportion of engineer troops is approximately 25 percent, based on the number of battalions in the force at seven. This is nearly the same as the number of infantry battalions. However, the total force ashore comprising the VII Corps landing force included numerous battalions of field artillery, antiaircraft artillery, armor, naval beach party, transportation elements and the like. An even more stunning comparison occurs in the matter of casualties. The most reliable figure covering only D-day for the Brigade is 21 killed in action and 96 wounded. For the infantry regiments, the comparable figures are 12 killed and 106 wounded. For the 4th Division as a whole, the total number of casualties is 197 including 12 fatalities listed above plus 60 missing when part of a field artillery battery was lost at sea. A substantial portion of the credit for the expedited progress of the landing forces should certainly be attributed to the engineer contributions. Obstacles and mines were neutralized in a thoroughly workmanlike manner. Engineer tasks were generally pursued regardless of hostile fire. Interruptions caused by enemy action were only short-lived as the engineer leadership urged subordinate troops to persist in their duties regardless of danger and difficulty. The presence and the example of Col. Caffey reflected through the echelons of command. Despite the change in assignments following the catastrophe of Exercise Tiger, continuity of tradition and policy were maintained throughout units of the Brigade.

The records of the 1st Engineer Special Brigade units contain mention of personnel who performed in an exemplary manner. Archival records are deteriorating so that a comprehensive search for names is growing more difficult with each passing year. Nevertheless, the case of the 1st Battalion of the 531st Engineers will be used as a representative example of what can be found in unit histories. Three names are present in the Battalion history. The mine clearing platoon of 1st Lt. Sidney Berger was working on lanes over the dunes under artillery fire when one of his squads took a direct hit. He directed his men to continue work while obtaining aid for the injured. Another shell landed in the immediate area and resulted in more injuries. Lt. Berger, while refusing to take cover himself, restored order, and continued to direct both the evacuation of the wounded and the clearing of mines. He helped save the lives of several men and inspired those around him to continue to work. For his actions, he was awarded the Silver Star. Pvt. Everett Brumley received the Silver Star for rescuing a wounded soldier who was staggering along the beach. The man's eyes were covered with a bandage and he could not find an aid station. Pvt. Brumley immediately left the security of his foxhole during an artillery bombardment and carried the wounded soldier to a first aid station 100 yards down the beach. Sgt. James McGrath was awarded the Bronze Star for his actions while sweeping for mines. Despite enemy artillery fire, Sgt. McGrath and his squad continued their assigned task with no regard for cover. When a mine detonated, seriously wounding a member of his squad, Sgt. McGrath ordered the rest of the squad to take cover, but remained exposed while he rendered first aid to the wounded.

In final summary of actions on Utah Beach on D-day, the words of Navy Commander Curtin, Commanding officer of the 2d Naval Beach Battalion, are particularly appropriate:

"The operation of the Utah Beaches brought much commendation from military and naval authorities—who had inspected all of the beaches in the Neptune Operation. The efficiency and smoothness with which the landing was made and the operation of the beaches carried on were stated not to have been surpassed anywhere.

"Much of the credit for the success of the operation is due the 1st Engineer Special Brigade and the 531st Engineer Shore Regiment which was a component of it. (The Brigade had worked with the Navy in Mediterranean operations; the Regiment had been in all of our landing operations.)

"Brigade and Regimental Commands not only had the knowledge, skill and experience necessary to successfully carry-on the operation but, as well, consistently were motivated by a spirit of cooperation and help, which did much to facilitate the performance of duty by the Navy. The thanks of the 2d Beach Battalion are extended for that cooperation."

EPILOGUE

A retrospective view of the events of D-day shows that both American beachheads were securely in the hands of First Army landing forces before the day ended. Thus, by the most crucial overall measure the invasion has to be rated a success. On Omaha the line of advance extended inland to one and one-half miles and by dark was nearly continuous at that penetration. The bulk of the 1st Division was ashore and except for one regiment in reserve the same applied to the 29th Division. On Utah the progress was rather close to plan and the 4th Division was totally ashore, as were numerous units of corps troops, before the end of the day. The division had advanced five miles at several points and had fought through to linkup with the airborne forces. The two airborne divisions had taken several important D-day objectives following scattered drops. The rate of buildup, which was so vital in the face of a potential counterattack in force, was at a satisfactory level.

The achievements were in great part attributable to the efforts of engineer troops. They contributed to the victory in their dual roles as both engineers and infantry. Particularly on Omaha a prompt start on engineer tasks ashore was not possible due to the accuracy and intensity of enemy fire. During this period sparks of inspiration and leadership were frequently provided by engineers as movement up the bluffs commenced. In the tidal zone the demolition teams were manned, in the majority, by engineer troops who went about their assignments with little regard for personal safety. In the clearing of safe lanes across the beach and up the draws engineers remained in exposed positions to open egress and clear the blockages from the beaches. On Utah, as on Omaha, there were significant losses during debarkation but engineer units went about reconnaissance, obstacle and mine clearing, and beach exit preparation with little regard to continuing hostile artillery. Without this kind of performance the achievement on Utah Beach of movement of 20,000 troops and 1,700 vehicles across the beach in 15 hours would not have been possible. Some sources estimate the strength ashore on Utah on D-day as high as 30,000 troops.

The toll for achievements of the invading forces was severe. In most after-action reports there is no segregation of D-day casualties from those over longer periods of time. Most military historians consider various published data to be estimates at best. Nevertheless, some perspective can be gained from the figures which are available.

For example, both Cornelius Ryan in *The Longest Day* and Hanson Baldwin in *Battles Won and Lost* quote First Army reports as follows: 1,465 killed, 3,184 wounded, 1,928 missing, and 26 captured, for a total of 6,603. Approximately one-third of these losses were suffered by the two airborne divisions. To emphasize that these are clearly approximate numbers Gordon Harrison in *Cross-Channel Attack* notes that after initial reports to V Corps both 1st and 29th Divisions submitted revised casualties that were somewhat lower than the first report. Additionally, Harrison estimates that engineer casualties were about 40 percent of the total engineer component of D-day forces. This figure obviously reflects the heavy losses during the early period ashore when the demolition teams on Omaha were having such a difficult time with the obstacles in the tidal zone.

A top level issue that cropped up during the early strategic phase of planning for an attack on the Atlantic Wall may have been settled with finality by the performance of Allied forces on D-day. In Chapter I this account covered early planning where it was noted that there was opposition to an amphibious operation across the Channel. Primarily, the British high command had a segment which favored an expedition into the Balkans, and/or elsewhere around the periphery of the European continent, as preferable to facing the hazards and inevitable losses associated with a frontal attack on well-defended shores along the Channel. The strength of the argument was based on the terrible loss rate during the Dieppe raid and other more ancient experiences in British military history. The opposite point of view held that the seas provided a favorable avenue of approach and that the northwest shore of the continent was the direct route to the enemy heartland. This kind of view dominated among American planners. As it turned out the more pessimistic forebodings of 25,000 casualties within the landing forces crossing the Channel were far in excess of the actual toll of about 10,000 for the combined Allied forces. The pro-Channel crossing arguments appear to be supported by the successes of the invasion.

The amphibious option of itself, and without reasonably well developed tactics and technical resources, would not necessarily have produced results as actually occurred. Several examples can be cited in a brief way. The Allied fleet of landing craft was a tremendous asset to the invaders. The several distinct designs provided a mix of capabilities from transport of small troop units to landing of the heavy equipment items of engineers and armor. The craft were capable of beaching on the tidal flats of Normandy where an exceptionally mild gradient is the general rule. An important attribute of all designs was their rapid offloading provisions. The production capability delivered quantities as required for the invasion. Recall also that the lack of resources in the matter of landing craft was a factor in the German decision to abandon a northward crossing of the Channel at a time when British strength was at a low ebb following the evacuation from the Continent. Joint Army-Navy capabilities were also evident in the area of fire support on shore targets by vessels standing offshore.

Another area of technical expertise was air support. While the results of aerial bombardment of Omaha Beach defenses were ineffective the results on Utah Beach were favorable to the seaborne attack forces. Indeed, the latter case demonstrated the potential to soften the will to resist among the defenders. An unsung aspect of air support was the collection of intelligence data by aerial reconnaissance. The information gleaned from the photographs was essential to plans for neutralizing the obstacles in the tidal zone and for attacking fortified positions. Also, training was conducted under realistic conditions on the basis of data from photographs brought back from these air missions.

A tradition did clearly exist upon which the amphibious capability was amplified and honed. The joint Marine Corps-Army maneuvers have been noted, along with Corps of Engineers activity at Fort Belvoir and Camp Edwards. Development and training were continuously pursued as the war progressed. The main examples were the Fifth Army Invasion training Center in North Africa, the Assault Training Center at Woolacombe, and the exercise area at Slapton Sands. To some degree there was a transfer of lessons learned between the Pacific and Mediterranean/European Theaters.

We come now to consider some of the planning decisions which impacted the events of D-day. The obvious starting point is the matter of selection of a landing area. Factors bearing on the decision have been repeatedly thrashed over. It is axiomatic that defenses will be concentrated on the most attractive landing areas. As compared to Normandy, at Pas-de-Calais the density of tidal obstacles was greater and their construction was stouter. The fortification concrete was thicker and the caliber of guns was greater. It may be noted that the installation at Crisbecq/St. Marcouf containing naval rifles with long range capability was not taken for more than one week and during that period fire was effectively delivered on Utah Beach. To sum up, the mission of attacking at Pas-de-Calais would have been more time consuming, might have produced an effective counterattack, and most certainly would have inflicted more casualties on Allied troops. The advantages of facilitating fighter air cover and a shorter route to the German heartland would not have been much compensation for the inevitable pain of the more difficult landing. It should be noted that had the more difficult target been selected the burden on engineer troops would have been greater and undoubtedly their casualty rate would have been higher. All investigations incident to this account find that the tradeoffs by which Normandy was selected have been sound and valid.

In a similar way the case for the frontage and size of the attack can be supported. The original plan produced by the COSSAC organization was generally criticized as being inadequate in both these regards. Gens. Montgomery and Bradley were among the more vocal antagonists of the original plan and insisted on two additional seaborne divisions and one more airborne division. Gen. Montgomery was also firm about the need for larger space to accommodate the rapid buildup as planned. He also insisted on a landing on the Cotentin Peninsula as a means of reducing the distance to the nearest port. Events proved the critics of the original plan had a superior estimate of the situation. There is no question but that the incorporation of Utah Beach into the plan was an auspicious move. And, the general increase in space to accommodate the increasing arrivals on shore was visibly necessary. As to whether five seaborne divisions was the optimum size for the combined Allied force the answer has to be affirmative. All sources of additional ships and craft had been exploited. The landing date had been set back one month to gain additional production time—at the risk of upsetting coordination of offensive actions with the Soviet forces. The southern France landings were set back to allow transfer of sea lift and double useage—when Gen. Eisenhower was a strong advocate of a pincer action on the western Continent. There was no possibility to further increase the landing force without a significant setback in the schedule, and this would have meant a loss of summer weather for campaigning. Any setback would also have been an opportunity for Field Marshall Rommel to continue strengthening his defensive preparations.

Among the contentious questions the matter of tides is of particular interest to engineer troops with assignments during the assault phase. The demolition teams could work on the tidal obstacles only at low tide. However, Gen. Bradley was concerned that troops arriving at extreme low tide had a long trek through the tidal zone in a fully exposed condition before reaching relatively covered positions at the seawall or at the shingle embankment. A compromise was formulated whereby landing craft of the early waves would arrive just before the rising tide reached the obstacles. Then there would be a period of about 30 minutes before the depth of water reached two feet at the most seaward of the obstacles. Tests were conducted to assure that the demolition teams could complete the assignment in 30 minutes and that two feet of water did not preclude demolition at the obstacles. This plan did not contain any allowance for mishaps, of which there were several types. First, the demolition teams did not reach shore exactly on schedule thus subtracting valuable time from the allotted work period. Next, the troops coming ashore during the demolition period, which should have been a clear period, took cover behind the obstacles thereby preventing firing of explosives. Additionally, the defenders delivered accurate fire against the demolition teams. The plan failed and, despite valiant effort by the demolition teams, clear lanes for following waves to beach at high tide were not established. Whether a more conservative approach on this problem would have succeeded shall remain an unknown.

The situation described above pertains only to Omaha Beach where the distance from the low water mark to high water is approximately 500 yards along the beach. On Utah Beach the distance is more than double that value. As a consequence the incoming tide did not reach the obstacles nearly as early so there was a longer period available for the demolition task. Furthermore, *local* resistance at Utah was in the process of crumbling at the time of work to neutralize the tidal obstacles. Extensive use was made of tankdozers to speed the removal of the tidal obstacles to onshore locations.

A brief review of the results of the duplex-drive tanks is warranted. The intention of the plan to use the DD tanks was to fill the gap in fire support after air bombardment and after naval gun fire lifted. The tanks were American Shermans modified according to a British development to become amphibian vehicles. On Omaha the losses of these tanks were startling when they were launched at the planned offshore distance of 6,000 yards. They could not cope with sea conditions. The survival rate of conventionally waterproofed Sherman tanks was better. However, losses of both tank types on shore due to hostile fire were also severe. The situation on Utah Beach went much more nearly according to plan. Gen. Collins issued clear orders that launching of DD-tanks be only 3,000 yards offshore and from this distance the transit to shore was a much safer venture. These tanks, along with their conventional counterparts, proved effective in supporting the dismounted infantry and engineers. But the question remains as to whether the risks of using the unproven DD tanks were warranted when conventionally waterproofed Shermans could have been landed directly off LCT craft. Otherwise stated the question might be whether the plan sacrificed a conservative margin of safety for some nebulous performance advantage.

Probably the source of most controversy of all the issues emanating from study of the attack on the Atlantic Wall is the degree of difficulty experienced on Omaha Beach. The most usual explanation is that the quality of the defending troops encountered at Omaha was superior to that of the neighboring divisions. It is, of course, a fact that the 352d Division defending on Omaha was rated as a field division while the others were rated as static. On the other hand, when the 352d Division moved into defensive positions several months before the landings it lost its capability to counterattack and for all practical purposes became a static division. It most certainly did contain personnel who were a notch above those in the static divisions. However, the static divisions contained substantial seasoned leadership and were trained to levels prevailing in German units generally. It is not an absolute certainty that the personnel difference accounts for the observed difference in the outcomes on the several beaches. There are other possible explanations, particularly the air bombardment preparatory to landing. The defenders at Utah Beach, even those who had seen action on the eastern front were a shaken and unnerved group as a result of the pounding administered by the Ninth Air Force, in combination with the naval bombardment. By contrast the Eighth Air Force dropped its bombs far inland—as a consequence of safety precautions due to the prevailing cloud cover. But, there are still puzzling aspects to the question even after the main factors are studied. For example, the 1st Engineers had a very light casualty level while the 121st Engineers suffered heavily, both units landing on Omaha at about same scheduled times. The casualty level of the 1st Engineers was nearly identical to that of the 1st Battalion of the 531st Engineers at Utah, both these units being about the same size and both having the benefit of prior campaigns.

Closely related to the matter of preparatory bombardment were the plans for security and deception. There was complete success in concealing all invasion plans. Even when Field Marshal von Rundstedt got word that an Allied landing was underway in Normandy he remained convinced that only a feint was in progress and that the principal attack was yet to come and that it would be directed at Pas-de-Calais. No significant repositioning of forces was made. As to security, the vast invasion fleet was totally undetected until it arrived just offshore of the coast. No German naval patrols were out since the bad weather gave reassurance that no invasion activity could be conducted under such conditions. One of the key measures that guarded the location of the Allied destination was a limitation on preliminary bombardment. Air activity was maintained at a uniform level over numerous candidate areas so as not to disclose the selected target. It was only for the brief period between dawn and H-hour that intensive preparatory fire was conducted and no opportunity was given the defenders to reinforce positions along the Normandy coast. This is just one more instance where the planning inputs to the tradeoff may have been somewhat off the optimum.

During amphibious operations the conduct of engineer tasks is acutely affected by equipment and supplies reaching shore. Obviously all required items should be available on a sound schedule. Unfortunately a frequent occurrence was an excess or an early arrival of materiel which had an adverse result. Several senior engineer commanders, when discussing the lessons coming out of the landing operations, put emphasis on this problem area. Individual loads in some cases included satchel charges, flamethrowers, fortification materials, and the like, in excess of mission requirements. These encumbrances slowed troops as they hurried ashore under fire. Bulk materials arrived in advance of the needs on shore. This applied to both unit property and stocks for dump accumulation. Early arrival of supplies added to the clutter which impeded movement across the beach and consumed manpower which might have been better applied to high priority tasks. This was a case where logisticians applied conservative estimates in their planning and produced negative results.

Finally, a brief consideration of the plans of the defenders shows that their problems were even greater than those of the invading Allies. By disposing forces almost totally along the main line of resistance, in accordance with the Rommel approach, the ability to counterattack was lost. The intent to achieve victory by stopping the Allies on the beaches proved to be impossible and in the process the defending units were broken. Also the reserves were trimmed to an unsafe level.

In final summary, the story of engineer accomplishments on D-day in Normandy is an exciting account of their substantial contribution to the successful invasion. This achievement of a secure beachhead put the Allies in advantageous position when the contest to match build-up rates commenced, and led ultimately to the liberation of Western Europe.

_____

NOTE: Appendices A-D are contained in the maps which are folded in the back of the book.

APPENDIX E

EMC/lt
201-Caffey, Eugene M. (O)   19 July 1951

SUBJECT: Clarification of Record

TO: The Adjutant General
           Department of the Army
           Washington 25, D.C.

1. This letter is inspired by some statements which I saw a few days ago in "A Soldier's Story" by General of the Army Omar N. Bradley.

2. As it appears in my 201 file, my record in World War II is good. However, there was an occurrence which I am sure has caused a lot of uncharitable talk and has placed a question mark by my name: Shortly before the invasion of Normandy I was relieved from command of the 1st Engineer Special Brigade which was to land and support the VII Corps and the follow-up troops coming to Utah Beach. My relief took place a few days after a full dress amphibious rehearsal on the south coast of England at Slapton Sands. The exercise was participated in by the 4th Infantry Division, elements of the 1st Engineer Special Brigade, the Navy, and the Air Corps. The exercise, held about 28 April 1944, did not come off at all well. I supposed that those in authority knew the major reason for the disappointing showing and that they knew that it had nothing to do with me. Therefore it was a crushing surprise when my Corps Commander, Major General J. Lawton Collins, informed me a few days later that I was relieved from command of my brigade. He did not say why. I did not ask why. He permitted me to continue on with the brigade as deputy commander. The new brigade commander empowered me to run the brigade as I had been doing so I continued to attend to its operations just as I always had.

3. I went on to Utah Beach with the brigade on 6 June 1944. The record shows that then and thereafter I did well. However, I have always felt shamed and discredited because it is a fact that at a crucial time I was relieved from command of an organization destined to play an important part in one of the great undertakings of all warfare. To make the disgrace more unbearable, if such a thing could be, there was a complete unawareness on my part of anything I had done or failed to do to deserve it.

4. Concerning the exercise at Slapton Sands, the book referred to in Paragraph 1, above, has this to say toward the bottom of page 248:

"While motoring back to Dartmouth following the rehearsal I checked my findings with ___, ___, ___, and ___. Like me, they were disturbed on two counts. The beach engineer organization had broken down....

". . . I suggested to Collins that he assign a new commander to the Utah Beach engineer brigade.

"Not until four years after the war did I learn that these engineer troubles during the Utah rehearsal had not been caused by a breakdown in command but rather by the S-boat (sic) attack. For what I had been led to believe was a minor brush with the enemy was revealed to have been one of the major tragedies of the European War. Two LST's were sunk in that attack with a loss of more than 700 men. Yet for some unexplained reason the report had been withheld from me . . ."

5. Thus, after seven years, the blot on my good name seems to have been erased. I understand now why I was relieved. It is ironic that I was relieved for a reason which it is stated did not exist. I would have been spared seven miserable years had the facts been known and evaluated then instead of later. However, in the hurry and pressures of a big war odd things happen and I have no complaint.

6. I request that this letter be placed with my 201 file so that it may be considered should there be occasion in the future to review my record. I further request that I be advised that the letter has been so filed.

EUGENE M. CAFFEY
Colonel, J.A.G.C.

APPENDIX F

PRINCIPAL TYPES OF GERMAN TIDAL FLAT DEFENSES

Stakes were heavy logs driven into the ground at an angle pointing towards the sea. Some of the stakes were mined.

Hedgehogs consisted of three or more seven-foot steel angles crossed at their center and reinforced so that the ends would stave in the bottoms of landing crafts. An enterprising U.S. Army tank sergeant later devised a means of ripping through the Normandy hedgerows by cutting up the obstacles that the engineers had dismantled and welding blades to the front of tanks and tank destroyers.

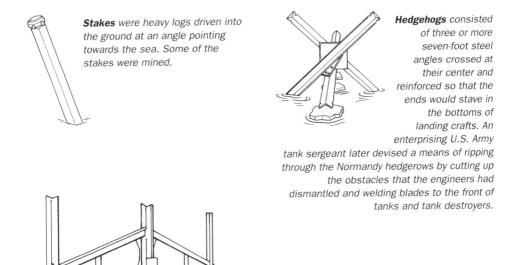

Element C, also known as Belgian gates, were built of reinforced iron frames, measuring ten feet high and nine feet across. Tellermines, tarred to render them waterproof, were lashed to the forward face of the gate.

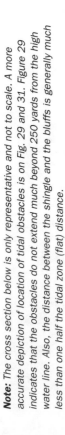

Note: *The cross section below is only representative and not to scale. A more accurate depiction of location of tidal obstacles is on Fig. 29 and 31. Figure 29 indicates that the obstacles do not extend much beyond 250 yards from the high water line. Also, the distance between the shingle and the bluffs is generally much less than one half the tidal zone (flat) distance.*

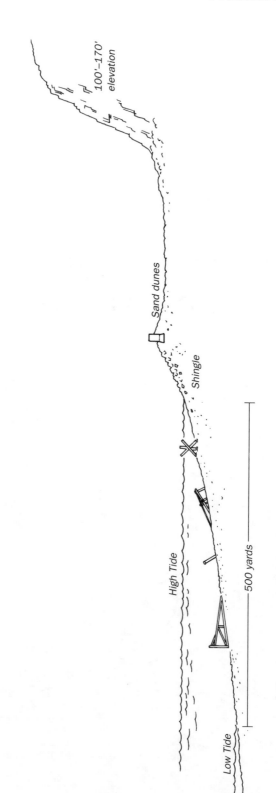

Systematic Cross Section of Omaha Beach

Appendix G

Additional Details on Beach Obstacles

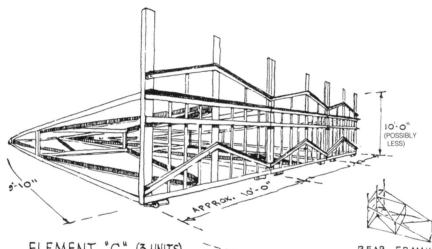

10'-0"
(POSSIBLY LESS)

9'-0"

APPROX. 10'-0"

REAR FRAMING
OF ELEMENT "C"
(ONE UNIT)

ELEMENT "C" (3 UNITS)
CONSTRUCTED OF STEEL
ANGLES AND PLATES.

TETRAHEDRON
USUALLY CONSTRUCTED OF
STEEL RAILS — CHANNELS
AND ANGLES MAY BE USED.

2'-6" OR 4'-0"

HEDGEHOG
CONSTRUCTED OF
STEEL ANGLES OR
RAILS.

5'-7"

NOTE:
THESE OBSTACLES MAY HAVE WELDED,
BOLTED, OR RIVETED JOINTS, AND/OR
CONCRETE ANCHORS.

APPENDIX H

Items below were among many vital elements used by engineers to clear the tidal obstacles and prepare exit routes off the beaches.

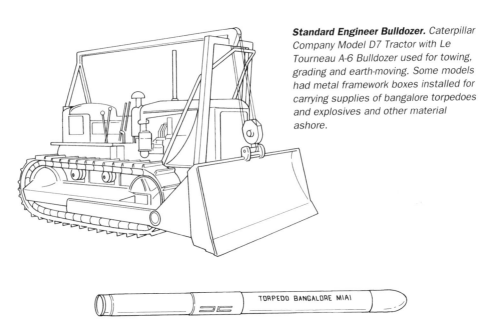

Standard Engineer Bulldozer. *Caterpillar Company Model D7 Tractor with Le Tourneau A-6 Bulldozer used for towing, grading and earth-moving. Some models had metal framework boxes installed for carrying supplies of bangalore torpedoes and explosives and other material ashore.*

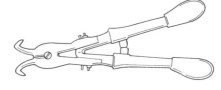

Torpedo Bangalore, M1A1. *A five foot steel tube filled with TNT and amatol, the bangalore torpedo was used primarily for blasting openings through wire entanglements and clearing mine fields. A connecting sleeve was provided to allow assembling of up to three torpedoes.*

"Searchnose" Wire Cutters. *They were specifically designed for cutting barbed wire. The bent hooks were used to pull the wire towards the operator. The rubber-covered handles insulated against live wire.*

Engineer Units at Normandy

The following is a listing of Engineer units, battalion or higher, officially credited in War Department general orders with participation in the Normandy amphibious or airborne assaults (some of the units did not land on D-day):

OMAHA BEACH

Army Engineer Units
H & H Co., Provisional Engineer Special Brigade Group
H & H Co., 5th Engineer Special Brigade
H & H Co., 6th Engineer Special Brigade
H & H Co., 1121st Engineer Combat Group
1st Engineer Combat Battalion
20th Engineer Combat Battalion
37th Engineer Combat Battalion
112th Engineer Combat Battalion
121st Engineer Combat Battalion
146th Engineer Combat Battalion
147th Engineer Combat Battalion
149th Engineer Combat Battalion
203d Engineer Combat Battalion
234th Engineer Combat Battalion
254th Engineer Combat Battalion
299th Engineer Combat Battalion (less Company B at Utah)
336th Engineer Combat Battalion
348th Engineer Combat Battalion
1340th Engineer Combat Battalion

Naval Engineer Units

6th U.S. Naval Beach Battalion

7th U.S. Naval Beach Battalion

Naval Construction Battalion 108

Naval Construction Battalion 111

Naval Construction Battalion 146

Construction Battalion Detachment 1006 (also at Utah)

UTAH BEACH

Army Engineer Units

H & H Co., 1st Engineer Special Brigade

H & H Co., 1106th Engineer Combat Group

H & H Co., 1110th Engineer Combat Group

38th Engineer General Service Regiment

531st Engineer Shore Regiment

4th Engineer Combat Battalion

49th Engineer Combat Battalion

237th Engineer Combat Battalion

238th Engineer Combat Battalion

307th Airborne Engineers Battalion

315th Engineer Combat Battalion

326th Airborne Engineer Battalion

602nd Engineer Camouflage Battalion

819th Engineer Aviation Battalion

Naval Engineer Units

2d Naval Beach Battalion

Naval Construction Battalion 81

Construction Battalion Detachment 1006

A number of other engineer units participated in Normandy landings. These included light equipment, dump truck, light ponton, and treadway bridge companies as well as detachments of other engineer organizations, among these were the following Naval Engineer Units:

Naval Construction Battalion 28

Naval Construction Battalion 69

Naval Construction Battalion 114

Naval Construction Battalion (Special) 30

Note: All of the Naval Construction Battalions listed above were assigned to the 25th Naval Construction Regiment.

GLOSSARY

AAF Army Air Forces

AAR After action report

AFHQ Allied Force Headquarters, Mediterranean Theater

Anvil Allied landing operations against Southern France, 1944

AP Antipersonnel mine

APA U.S.N. amphibious troop transport

Assault Force "O" Naval attack force with embarked Army landing force destined for Omaha Beach

Assault Force "U" Naval attack force with embarked Army landing force destined for Utah Beach

AT Antitank mine

Avalanche Allied invasion of Italy at Salerno, September 1943

Bangalore torpedo Metal tube containing explosives and a firing mechanism used to counter minefields and obstacles, usually of sectionalized design.

BAR Browning automatic rifle

Bazooka Rocket launcher, hand-carried, individually fired

Beachhead Position ashore organized in depth with a view to further offensive or defensive operations

Beach party Navy task organization for control from high-water mark seaward

Belgian gate Frequent name for tidal zone obstacle also known as Element C

Bigot Highest security classification of Neptune, especially applied to target area and date

Bolero Build-up of U.S. forces and supplies in U.K. for cross-Channel attack in 1942, reactivated in 1943

Bouncing Betty Frequent name for German antipersonnel S-mine

Bn Battalion

Casemate Fortified position or armored structure from which guns are fired through embrasures

Chocolate bars Precast concrete units with checkerboard surface used in hardstanding construction

Co Company

CO Commanding Officer

Composition C Explosive, relative strength—1.35 (see TNT)

COSSAC Chief of Staff to The Supreme Allied Commander (Designate)

Dragoon Final name for Anvil operations, southern France

DD Duplex-drive amphibious tank; a modified Sherman tank.

D-day The first day of an operation, applied most often to Overlord

DSC Distinguished Service Cross

DUKW A 2½-ton, 6-by-6 amphibian truck with sea speed about five knots and land speed of 50 mph

EAB Engineer Amphibian Brigade

EAC Engineer Amphibian Command

E-boat German torpedo boat, also referred to as S-boat (German)

ECB Engineer Combat Battalion

ECG Engineer Combat Group

Embarkation Preparatory measures to assemble troops and equipment and the actual loading of transports or landing craft

Embrasure An outwardly flared opening in a wall of a casemate or similar fortification to allow the firing of a cannon

Enfilade Gunfire delivered in a lengthwise direction at an objective

ESB Engineer Special Brigade

ESR Engineer Shore Regiment

ETOUSA European Theater of Operations, U.S. Army

Exit D-1 Draw at Vierville, Omaha Beach

Exit D-3 Draw at Les Moulins, Omaha Beach

Exit E-1 Draw on Easy Red sector, Omaha Beach leading to St. Laurent

Exit E-3 Draw on Fox Green sector, Omaha Beach leading to Colleville

Exit F-1 Draw on Fox Red sector, Omaha Beach

Fabius I Exercise conducted in early May 1944 at Slapton Sands by units destined for Omaha Beach

Fortitude Deception operations intended to direct attention of defenders to Pas-de-Calais and other potential landing areas

FUSA First U.S. Army

FUSAG First U.S. Army Group

GHQ General Headquarters

HE High explosive

Hedgehog Portable obstacles emplaced in the tidal zone—constructed of three pieces of angle iron

Husky Allied landings on Sicily in 1943

Inf Infantry

Landing craft Various capacity, flat-bottom vessels capable of landing on and retracting from beaches of gradual gradients, usually with hinged bow ramps

Landing force Army units which execute landing operations on hostile shores

LCA Landing Craft, Assault—British equivalent to U.S. LCVP

LCI Landing Craft, Infantry

LCM Landing Craft, Mechanized

LCT Landing Craft, Tank

LCVP Landing Craft, Vehicle and Personnel

LST Landing Ship, Tank

Luftwaffe German Air Force

MG Machine gun

Mine Encased explosive with a detonating device designed to destroy enemy targets

MLR Main Line of Resistance

Mulberries Portable harbor structures designed for towing across the Channel

NATO North African Theater of Operations

Naval attack force Naval component in landing operations including transports, bombardment group, minesweepers, and support

NCDU Naval combat demolition unit

NDRC National Defense Research Committee

Neptune Code name initially applied to all Overlord plans containing highest classification of security data; subsequently applied to amphibious phase of Overlord

OPD Operations Division, War Department General Staff

Overlord Code name for plans and operations comprising the invasion of northwest Europe in the spring of 1944

Panther German Mark V tank

Plat Platoon

R.A.F. Royal Air Force

Rankin Plan for cross-Channel operation in the event of German decline

Regt Regiment

Rhino ferry Raft constructed of naval pontoon units

RN Royal Navy

Roundup Plan for major Allied attack across the Channel in 1943

SCR-**625** U.S. mine detector

SHAEF Supreme Headquarters Allied Expeditionary Force

Sherman U.S. main battle tank

Shingle Code name for Allied landings on Italy at Anzio, January 1944

Shingle Coarse, rounded stone material of larger size than gravel found on a seashore, especially Omaha Beach

Sledgehammer Plan for limited objective attack across the Channel in 1942 to hold position in Normandy until relieved by Roundup

SS German Elite Guard (Schutzstaffel)

Tellermines German antitank mines

Tetrahedron Pyramidal-shaped steel obstacle used in tidal zone as anti-invasion measure

Tiger Exercise conducted in late April 1944 at Slapton Sands by units destined for Utah Beach—follow-on serial hit by E-boats

Tiger German Mark VI tank

TNT Trinitrotoluene, relative explosive strength—1.00 (U.S. standard)

T/O Table of Organization

Torch Code name for Allied landings in northwest Africa, 1942

Transport area Offshore area assigned for transferring troops from transports to landing craft during ship-to-shore operations

Underwater obstacles Frequently used term for obstacles deployed in tidal zone

Wave All boats which carry troops that are to land approximately simultaneously

WPB War Production Board

PHOTO/ILLUSTRATION CREDITS

COVER ART

Battle of Normandy Foundation; Artist—John Krott (painting commissioned by
   Cornelius Ryan)

CHAPTER I

Figure 1a   *Victory in the West*—The Battle of Normandy; Her Brittanic Majesty's
   Stationary Office, Norwich, U.K.
Figure 1b   *West Point Atlas;* USMA, West Point, NY
Figure 2   US Army/War Department
Figure 3   Ibid
Figure 4   Ibid
Figure 5   *The Corps of Engineers: Troops and Equipment;* OCMH, US Army

CHAPTER II

Figure 6   *The Marshall Story;* Robert Payne/US Army

CHAPTER III

Figure 7   *The Second Front;* Time-Life/Bundesarchiv, Koblenz
Figure 8   *Victory in the West* (see Figure 1a above)
Figure 9   *The Second Front;* Ullstein Bilderdienst, Berlin, courtesy Manfred
   Rommel, Stuttgart
Figure 10   U.S. Army
Figure 11   *The Invasion of France and Germany;* Samuel Morison/US Naval
   Archives
Figure 12   *Omaha Beachhead;* US Government Printing Office (GPO)
Figures 13, 14, 15, and 16   *The Second Front* (see Figure 7 above)

CHAPTER IV

Figure 17   *D-Day;* Warren Tute et al, Sidgewick & Jackson, London/SHAEF
Figure 18   Bigot Maps; SHAEF
Figure 19   *The Second Front;* Time-Life/Imperial War Museum, London, art by
    John Batchelor
Figure 20   *Omaha Beachhead;* US GPO
Figure 21   *The Corps of Engineers;* (see Figure 5)
Figure 22   William J. Hennessy, Jr.; Theodore Hamady
Figure 23   Ibid

CHAPTER V

Figure 24   *The Second Front;* Time-Life; Yanks in Britain/US Army
Figure 25   William J. Hennessy, Jr.; Theodore Hamady
Figure 26   *The Second Front;* Time-Life; Imperial War Museum, London/National
    Archives
Figure 27   *The Second Front;* Time-Life; Imperial War Museum/Royal
    Canadian Navy

CHAPTER VI

Figures 28, 29, 30, 31 and 32   *Omaha Beachhead,* US GPO
Figure 33   SHAEF/US Army Center of Military History
Figure 34   *Omaha Beachhead;* US GPO
Figure 35   Robert Capa, *Life Magazine*/US National Archives
Figure 36   Ibid
Figure 37   *Omaha Beachhead;* US GPO
Figure 38   US National Archives
Figure 39   Ibid
Figure 40—Upper   *Omaha Beachhead;* US GPO
Figure 40—Lower   *The Corps of Engineers* (see Figure 5)
Figure 41   *Omaha Beachhead,* US GPO
Figure 42   US National Archives

Chapter VII

Figures 43 through 51   *Utah Beach to Cherbourg;* US GPO

Appendix A–D

Bigot Maps   Battle of Normandy Foundation/SHAEF

Appendix F and H

Line Drawings   William J. Hennessy, Jr., and Theodore Hamady

Appendix G

SHAEF

Engineer Monuments

1st ESB—Top   French Air Force
1st ESB—Bottom   American Battle Monuments Commission—Paris
5th ESB   American Battle Monuments Commission—Paris
Provisional ESB Group   Ibid
6th ESB   Maj. Gen. C.L. Wilson, USAF (ret.)
147th ECB   Lt. Col. George Itzel, USA (ret.)
Pritchett Road Marker   Sid Berger/531st Shore Regiment Assoc.

BIBLIOGRAPHY

Baldwin, Hanson; *Battles Won and Lost;* New York; Harper and Row, 1966

Baldwin, William C. and Barry W. Fowle. "WWII: Engineers in the European Theater", *Engineer* 14, no. 4 (Winter 1984–1985): 10–19

Bass, Richard; *Spirits of The Sands;* Lee Publishers; 1992

Beck, Alfred, et al; *The Corps of Engineers: The War Against Germany;* Washington; OCMH-US Army; 1957

Botting, Douglas; *The Second Front;* Alexandria; Time-Life Books; 1978

Bradley, Gen. Omar; *A Soldier's Story;* New York; Holt; 1951

Churchill, Winston; *The Hinge of Fate;* Boston; Houghton Mifflin; 1950

Churchill, Winston; *Closing The Ring;* Boston; Houghton Mifflin; 1951

Coll, Blanche, et al; *The Corps of Engineers: Troops and Equipment;* Washington; OCMH-US Army; 1957

Collins, Maj-Gen J. Lawton; *Lightning Joe, An Autobiography;* New Orleans; Louisiana State University Press; 1979

Crowley, T.T. and G.C. Burch; "Eight Stars to Victory". Unpublished Unit History, 1st Engineer Battalion, 1945

Eisenhower, Gen. Dwight; *Crusade In Europe;* New York; Doubleday; 1948

Eisenhower Foundation; *D-Day, The Normandy Invasion in Retrospect;* University Press of Kansas; 1971

Ellis, Lionel; *History of the Second World War, Victory in the West: Vol. 1, The Battle of Normandy.* London: Her Majesty's Stationery Office, 1962

Fane, Cmdr. Francis; *The Naked Warriors;* New York; Appleton-Century-Crofts; 1956

Greene, Ralph and Oliver, Allen; "What Happened Off Devon"; *American Heritage;* New York; February/March 1985

Harrison, Gordon; *Cross-Channel Attack;* Washington; OCMH-US Army; 1951

Hastings, Max; *Overlord;* New York; Simon and Schuster; 1984

Heavy, William F.; *Down Ramp: The Story of the Army Amphibian Engineers.* Washington, D.C.: Infantry Journal Press, 1947

Howarth, David; *D-Day;* New York; McGraw-Hill; 1959

Hoyt, Edwin; *The Invasion Before Normandy;* New York; Military Heritage Press; 1985

Ingersoll, Ralph; *Top Secret;* New York; Harcourt Brace; 1946

Irving, David; *The War Between The Generals;* New York; Congden & Lattes; 1981

Jacobs, Maj-Gen. Bruce; "The D-Day Connection"; *National Guard;* Washington; June 1989

Lewis, Nigel; *Exercise Tiger;* London; Viking; 1990

MacDonald, Charles; "Slapton Sands—The Cover-up That Never Was"; Arlington; *ARMY;* June 1988

Majdalany, Fred; *The Fall of Fortress Europe;* New York; Doubleday; 1968

Marshall, Brig.-Gen. Samuel; "First Wave at Omaha Beach"; *Atlantic Monthly;* Boston; November 1960

Mayer, Ernest and Wilson, Oliver; "German Mines and Booby Traps" *The Military Engineer;* Washington; March 1945

Ministry of Information; *Combined Operations, 1940–1942;* London; His Majesty's Stationery Office, 1943

Montgomery, Field-Marshal Bernard; *The Memoirs of Field-Marshal Montgomery;* Cleveland; World Publishing; 1958

Morison, Samuel; *The Invasion of France and Germany 1944–1945;* Boston; Little, Brown; 1968

Payne, Robert; *The Marshall Story;* New York; Prentice-Hall; 1951

Perret, Geoffrey; *There's A War To Be Won;* New York; Random House; 1991

Ramsay, Winston; "The Other D-Days"; *After The Battle;* No. 44; London; 1984

Ruppenthal, Maj. Roland; *Utah Beach to Cherbourg;* Washington; Historical Division, Dept. of The Army; 1947

Ryan, Cornelius; *The Longest Day—June 6, 1944;* New York; Simon and Schuster; 1959

Small, Ken; *The Forgotten Dead;* London; Bloomsbury; 1988

Smith, Sherwood; "Defenses of The Normandy Peninsula", *The Military Engineer;*
    Washington; February 1945

Taylor, Col. Charles; *Omaha Beachhead;* Washington; Historical Division, Dept.
    of The Army; 1947

Thompson, Col. Paul; "D-Day on Omaha Beach"; *Infantry Journal;* Washington;
    June 1945

Trudeau, Lt.-Gen. Arthur; *Engineer Memoirs;* Washington; OCE-US Army; 1986

Tute, Warren, et al; *D-Day;* London; Sidgewick and Jackson; 1974

War Department; *Landing Operations on Hostile Shores;* Basic Field Manual FM
    31-5; Washington; 1941

War Department; *Engineer Troops;* Engineer Field Manual FM 5-5;
    Washington; 1943

War Department; Corps of Engineers Reference Data; War Department Field
    Manual FM 5-35; Washington; 1944

Weigley, Russell; *Eisenhower's Lieutenants;* Indiana University Press; 1981

ENGINEER MONUMENTS IN NORMANDY

BACKGROUND

A desire to create an appropriate memorial to those who died in the Normandy landings began to take form in the fall of 1944. Motivation to construct monuments on or near the beaches originated mainly at the level of Brigade Hq. Additional motivation for monument construction was the pride of unit which prevailed in the engineer organizations. As a result of much deliberation and planning, decisions were taken by individual units to construct five monuments: one on Utah Beach—the 1st Engineer Special Brigade (ESB)—and four on or near Omaha Beach: the 5th and 6th ESB's; the Provisional Special Engineer Brigade Group; and the 147th Engineer Combat Battalion. Engineer units which were organic to divisions are recognized by their respective division monuments which are at various locations throughout the invasion beach areas.

Detailed planning and initiation of construction of the engineer monuments became possible as the level of activity on the beaches decreased with the onset of foul weather in the fall. Winter weather was worse and over-the-shore operations were further reduced as the ports were concurrently being restored to productive levels of cargo transfers. Also, the engineer battalions of the Normandy landing forces, primarily those in the Engineer Special Brigades, were preparing to rejoin the field armies which by then were crossing the Seine River and heading for the German border. In the late Spring of 1945, as the war in Europe was approaching a successful conclusion, the monument construction projects were resumed and completed.

Passage of time and the harsh environment along the shores of the Channel have produced some deterioration of the monuments. The American Battle Monuments Commission (ABMC) can not correct this increasing deterioration because it is forbidden by law to expend appropriated funds for maintenance of monuments which were built with private—i.e., non-appropriated—funds. Since the engineer monuments described here, and many other military monuments, were constructed with hastily collected private funds the costs of their maintenance must come from sources other than the ABMC.

The problem of upkeep for the monuments has been recognized for many years by the European Region of the Society of American Military Engineers (SAME), which has periodically received urgent requests from the ABMC's Paris office to provide funds for monument maintenance. A particularly urgent request for funds to repair the 1st ESB monument was received a few months before the 40th Anniversary of D-day. There exists only a very small number of functioning associations of veterans of Normandy engineer units. These have contributed to monument maintenance funds but their numbers are decreasing with the passage of time. In 1984 the European Region of SAME did react promptly and successfully to the plea for funds—and subsequently decided that before the 50th Anniversary of D-day there should be created a trust fund which would generate sufficient revenue to maintain all of the engineer monuments in Normandy. The publication of this book is the key element in achieving this objective because all revenue from its sale will go into a trust fund for monument maintenance.

A brief description and pictures of each of the monuments on Utah Beach and on or near Omaha Beach follows. Also, a map showing locations of the monuments is provided after the photos.

UTAH BEACH

1st Engineer Special Brigade (ESB)

The monument of the 1st Engineer Special Brigade is on top of a former German fortified structure in a dominating position on Utah Beach. The location is seaward of the town of Ste-Marie-du-Mont. This structure was captured early on D-day and was subsequently used as a site for Brigade Headquarters. The notion of a monument at this location began to form in November of 1944 when there were frequent shutdowns of beach operations due to foul weather and functions on the beach were being steadily transferred to the port of Cherbourg, where the Brigade also had operating responsibility. Since many of the integral and attached units were being stripped from the Brigade it was apparent that fund raising had to start from unit personnel promptly. Collection of voluntary contributions was a success and the necessary materials were thereby accumulated. The Brigade Commander, Colonel Caffey proposed a design for the monument. It evolved as a concrete stela with polished plaques on each of the four faces. The main face on the inland side carries the Engineer Amphib-

*1st Engineer Special Brigade
Monument on Utah Beach*

ian Command shoulder patch design plus the seahorse badge, with a simple inscription dedicating the monument to proud memory of the lost men. All subordinate units are listed on the other faces. The interior of the blockhouse beneath the monument forms a crypt with inscription on the walls of all Brigade men lost in the battle.

Access to the 1st ESB monument is by Highway No. D 913, through Ste.-Marie-du-Monte to la Madeleine. The final leg of this route retraces Exit No. 2 as designated during the landings. The monument is just north of the point where the route reaches the shore. In the vicinity of the 1st ESB monument, and on lower ground, are three additional monuments: those of the 4th and 90th Infantry Divisions and the Federal Monument, erected and dedicated in 1984, which memorializes losses among U.S. Forces. As a group these U.S. monuments demand a very high

1st Engineer Special Brigade

standard of maintenance. Also, 59 members of the 1st
ESB who were killed on D-day have been recognized by
giving their names to 59 different roads in the Utah Beach
area and erecting prominent sign posts, bearing their
names on each of these roads. This idea for memorializ-
ing those individual personnel who made the ultimate
sacrifice was first proposed by Col. Caffey.

Maintenance of the 1st Brigade monument has been
intermittent over the years since the end of the war. The
veterans of the Brigade, through their association, have
accumulated a modest fund and have provided monies
from time to time to the municipality of Ste.-Marie-du-
Mont to cover costs of repairs to the monument. The
association has also provided funds for audio-visual
equipment at the Utah Beach museum. Jointly with the
Brigade veterans association a local group, the Comité
des Plages du Debarquement d'Arromaches, has provided
for some repair work. The European Region of the So-
ciety of American Military Engineers has also responded to several requests for funds
to provide for maintenance of this monument. The most recent and urgent request
was in 1984, just prior to the 40th anniversary ceremonies which were held very near
this monument and attended by heads of State, including the President of the U.S.

FOUR ENGINEER MONUMENTS ON AND NEAR OMAHA BEACH

5th ESB

On the eastern sector of the beach one finds the monument of the 5th Engineer Special Brigade. The location is between Colleville-sur-Mer and St.-Laurent-sur-Mer and
generally on an extension of the boundary between Easy Red and Fox Green beaches.
In this area the memorial of the 1st Infantry Division is at the top of a steep hill and
the 5th ESB site is just lower, and atop an unfinished pillbox. This location is 400
meters east of the American Cemetery on Omaha Beach. The monument is a stoutly
formed stela of concrete, 10 feet high with a six-foot square base tapering to a five-
foot square section at the top. Four stone benches surround the main structure. The
original temporary facings were replaced with bronze plaques. The seaward face is
the honor roll of Brigade members who made the supreme sacrifice, the inland face
contains a roster of units comprising the Brigade and the other two faces carry the
Amphibian Command insignia. An impressive ceremony on June 6, 1945 marked the
dedication of the monument. The principal speaker was the Brigade Commander,
Colonel William Bridges, whose remarks obviously stirred the assembled group of

299th Engineer Combat Batallion

20th Engineer Combat Batallion

5th Engineer Special Brigade Monument with plaques from 299th Engineer Combat Batallion and 20th Engineer Combat Batallion

6th Engineer Special Brigade Monument

returning members of the Brigade and key civilians of the French communities. Recently two plaques have been affixed to the monument, as shown in the photo. They are, respectively, the 20th Engineer Combat Battalion and the 299th Engineer Combat Battalion.

6th ESB

On the western sector of Omaha Beach, just west of les-Moulins, and inland from what had been Dog Red beach, the 6th Engineer Special Brigade placed its monument. The site is high on the bluff with a commanding view of the western end of Omaha Beach. Construction took place in November of 1944, coincident with other monument activity. The design was pro-

duced by Captain Samuel Dunbar, S-2 of the 147th Engineer Combat Battalion, who had also done the design for his unit monument. Masonry work was performed under the direction of Staff Sgt. Louis Mierose, also of the 147th Engineers. The design incorporates tiles for each of the subordinate units of the Brigade into a stone structure, along with a replica of the Engineer Amphibian Command insignia in the center of the monument face and a bronze engineer castle on the top. When deterioration of the base was found repair work was funded by the European Region of SAME at the time of the 40th anniversary ceremonies at Normandy. More recently a survey by the Paris Bureau of the American Battle Monument Commission indicates that additional repairs are needed to assure preservation of this monument for the years to come. The 6th ESB does not have a well-organized veterans association so the current attempt to solicit funds from former members is not proceeding well.

Provisional Engineer Special Brigade Group

The overall command authority over engineer operations on Omaha Beach, the Provisional Engineer Special Brigade Group, Commanded by B/General W.M. Hoge, located its monument just west of the Ameri-

Provisional Engineer Special Brigade Group Monument

can Cemetery (about 600 meters) and at the foot of high ground. This is also the site of the 2d Infantry Division memorial. The engineer monument consists of a polished black granite plaque attached to the side of a blockhouse inscribed with a troop list along with a marble base unit. Design and construction was provided by Brigade units before leaving the beach area. It needs but has not had any maintenance support.

147th Engineer Combat Battalion

The 147th Engineer Combat Battalion placed a monument in the western sector of Omaha Beach in the area of its operations. This is the only monument among engineer units at the battalion level. The site is in the courtyard of the Château Englesqueville-la-Percee, approximately seven kilometers west of Vierville-sur-Mer. This château is a typical Normandy farm commune dating from the early 14th century. The proprietor, M. Robert LeBrec warmly welcomes visitors seeking access to

147th Engineer Combat Battalion Monument

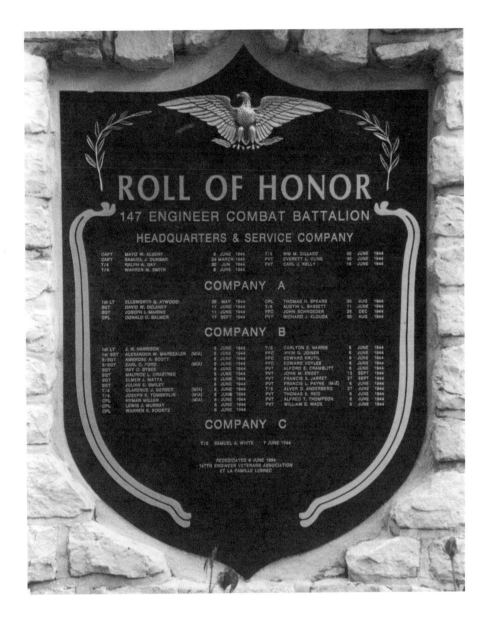

the monument. The Battalion was billeted at the château toward the close of beach operations in October 1944, when Lt. Col. Arthur Tooze, the Battalion Commander, initiated the monument project. Monument design was executed by Capt. Samuel Dunbar, S-2 Officer of the Battalion. Local stone is incorporated in the structure which includes a Roll of Honor plaque listing the names of the individuals lost in battle. The original plaque was not of a durable material and was replaced by the LeBrec family. Subsequently in 1979, the veterans association of the 147th Engineers installed a bronze plaque. Other features of the monument include four original 88-mm shells. Recently flagstaffs have been added.

266

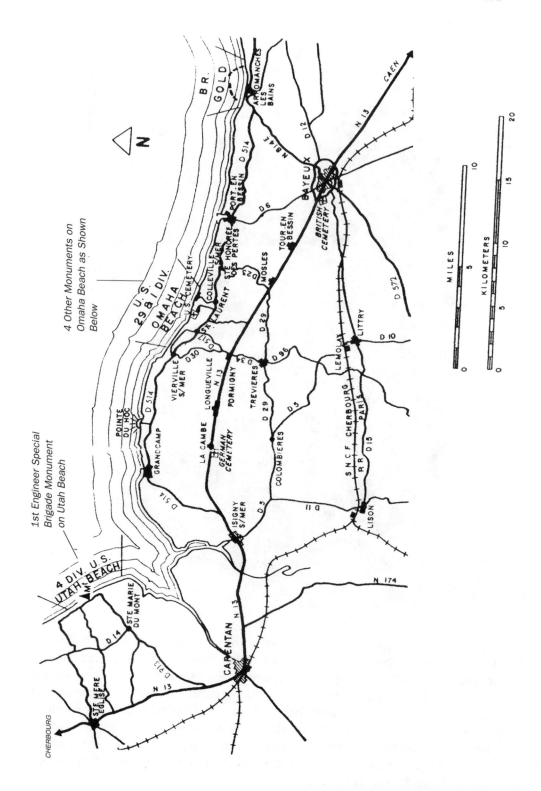

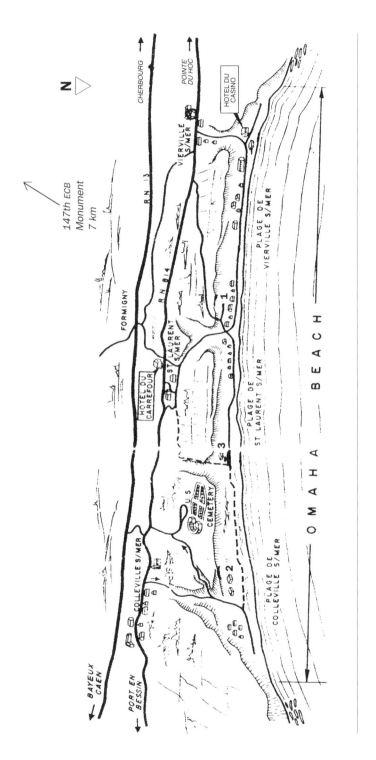

Legend: 1—6th Engineer Special Brigade Monument, 2—5th Engineer Special Brigade Monument, 3—Provisional Engineer Special Brigade Group Monument

DIRECT DONATIONS SOUGHT TO PRESERVE US ENGINEER MONUMENTS ON NORMANDY BEACHES

As noted elsewhere in this book, revenue from its sale will be used by the American Battle Monument Commission to repair and maintain Engineer monuments on and near Omaha and Utah Beaches.

Readers who can make a direct contribution to the Monument Fund will receive a parchment quality, full color certificate, signed by the President of SAME and suitable for framing. A black and white representation of this certificate is on the adjoining page.

Contributions will be distinguished according to the following donor categories:

Distinguished Benefactors	$1,000 or more
Benefactors	$500–$999
Distinguished Patrons	$100–$499
Patrons	$50–$99
Distinguished Patriots	$20–$49
Patriots	$10–$19

Please send tax deductible contributions to:

SAME Engineer Monument Fund
P.O. Box 19523
Alexandria, VA 22320-0523

Please allow 2–4 weeks for preparation and mailing of certificate.

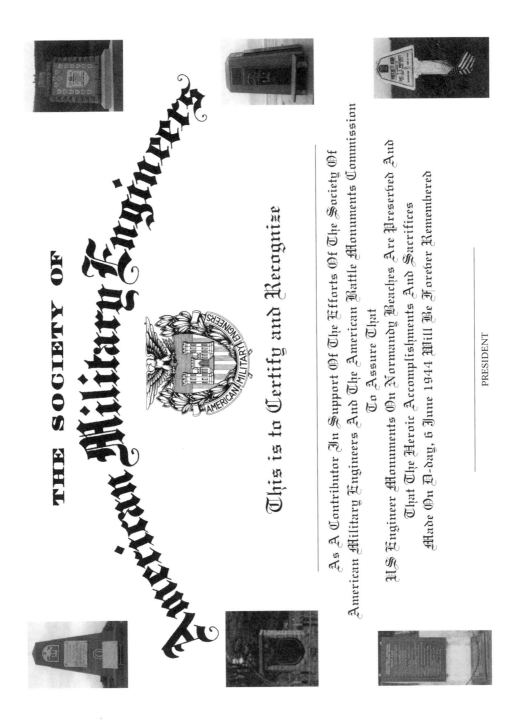

THE SOCIETY OF
American Military Engineers

AMERICAN MILITARY ENGINEERS

This is to Certify and Recognize

As A Contributor In Support Of The Efforts Of The Society Of
American Military Engineers And The American Battle Monuments Commission
To Assure That

U.S. Engineer Monuments On Normandy Beaches Are Preserved And
That The Heroic Accomplishments And Sacrifices
Made On D-Day, 6 June 1944 Will Be Forever Remembered

_____
PRESIDENT

BREACHING FORTRESS EUROPE

The Story of U.S. Engineers in Europe on D-day

Order form for additional copies (for making tax deductible contribution to the Monument Maintenance Fund, please see preceeding pages.)

To order additional copies and for information on multiple order discounts call **1-800-228-0810**

BREACHING FORTRESS EUROPE ISBN 0-8403-9516-7

☐ Check Enclosed ☐ Charge My Account (see below)

Quantity	Price	SubTotal	Total Amount of Order*
	$19.95	$	

*Add $3 shipping for the first book, $.50 each additional, also KY, IA, CA, LA and NY residents add sales tax.

Make check payable to:
Kendall/Hunt Publishing
4050 Westmark Drive, P.O. Box 1840
Dubuque, Iowa 52004-1840

Call **1-800-228-0810** to order by phone.

Call **1-800-346-2377** to order by fax.

Please charge my credit account:

☐ American Express ☐ MasterCard ☐ VISA

Account #_____

Expiration Date _____

Signature _____

Send book to:

Name _____

Affiliation _____

Address _____

City_____ State _____ Zip _____

Phone _____

Special discounts available to SAME *members and for orders of 5 or more books (put additional addresses on reverse).*

Send book to:

Name _____

Affiliation _____

Address _____

City_____ State _____ Zip _____

Phone _____

Send book to:

Name _____

Affiliation _____

Address _____

City_____ State _____ Zip _____

Phone _____

Send book to:

Name _____

Affiliation _____

Address _____

City_____ State _____ Zip _____

Phone _____

Send book to:

Name _____

Affiliation _____

Address _____

City_____ State _____ Zip _____

Phone _____

NOTE: *The BIGOT map Utah Beach (south) is not the same color or condition as the other three maps. The reason for this is that this is the map that the author used in his planning and actual landing at Utah Beach. His platoon landed on the extreme left of the assault forces, where the distance from the low water mark to the beach is approximately 1 mile—almost double the distance to be covered if the landing had occured where planned.*